EQUATIONAL LOGIC

as a

PROGRAMMING LANGUAGE

MIT Press Series in the Foundations of Computing

Michael Garey, editor

Complexity Issues in VLSI: Optimal Layouts for the Shuffle-Exchange Graph and Other Networks, by Frank Thomson Leighton, 1983.

Equational Logic as a Programming Language, by Michael J. O'Donnell, 1985.

EQUATIONAL LOGIC

as a

PROGRAMMING LANGUAGE

Michael J. O'Donnell

The MIT Press

Cambridge, Massachusetts

London, England

This book was composed using the UNIX tools *eqn, troff,* and *ms,* set on the APS-5 phototypesetter, and printed and bound in the United States of America.

Library of Congress Cataloging in Publication Data

O'Donnell, Michael J., 1952-

    Equational logic as a programming language.

    (MIT Press series in the foundations of computing)
    Bibliography: p.
    Includes index.
    1. Programming languages (Electronic computers)
2. Logic, Symbolic and mathematical. 3. Equations, Theory of. I. Title. II. Series.
QA76.7.036 1985   001.64'24   84-29507
ISBN 0-262-15028-X

To Julie and Benjamin

Table of Contents

10. Errors, Failures, and Diagnostic Aids   68

11. History of the Equation Interpreter Project   75

12. Low-Level Programming Techniques   78

Series Foreword

Theoretical computer science has now undergone several decades of development. The "classical" topics of automata theory, formal languages, and computational complexity have become firmly established, and their importance to other theoretical work and to practice is widely recognized. Stimulated by technological advances, theoreticians have been rapidly expanding the areas under study, and the time delay between theoretical progress and its practical impact has been decreasing dramatically. Much publicity has been given recently to breakthroughs in cryptography and linear programming, and steady progress is being made on programming language semantics, computational geometry, and efficient data structures. Newer, more speculative, areas of study include relational databases, VLSI theory, and parallel and distributed computation. As this list of topics continues expanding, it is becoming more and more difficult to stay abreast of the progress that is being made and increasingly important that the most significant work be distilled and communicated in a manner that will facilitate further research and application of this work.

By publishing comprehensive books and specialized monographs on the theoretical aspects of computer science, the series on *Foundations of Computing* provides a forum in which important research topics can be presented in their entirety and placed in perspective for researchers, students, and practitioners alike. This volume, by Michael J. O'Donnell, presents an elegant and powerful interpretive system for programming in terms of abstract logical equations. The language is similar to Prolog, in that it is descriptive rather than procedural, but unlike Prolog its semantic description allows an efficient implementation that strictly adheres to the given semantics. The presentation provides the definition of the language, many examples of its use, and discussion of the relevant underlying theory. It is essential reading for anyone interested in the latest ideas about nonprocedural programming and practical programming language semantics.

Michael R. Garey

Preface

This book describes an ongoing equational programming project that started in 1975. Principal investigators on the project are Christoph Hoffmann and Michael O'Donnell. Paul Chew, Paul Golick, Giovanni Sacco, and Robert Strandh participated as graduate students. I am responsible for the presentation at hand, and the opinions expressed in it, but different portions of the work described involve each of the people listed above. I use the pronoun "we" throughout the remainder, to indicate unspecified subsets of that group. Specific contributions that can be attributed to one individual are acknowledged by name, but much of the quality of the work is due to untraceable interactions between several people, and should be credited to the group.

The equational programming project never had a definite pseudocommercial goal, although we always hoped to find genuinely useful applications. Rather than seeking a style of computing to support a particular application, we took a clean, simple, and elegant style of computing, with particularly elementary semantics, and asked what it is good for. As a result, we adhered very strictly to the original concept of computing with equations, even when certain extensions had obvious pragmatic value. On the other hand, we were quite willing to change the application. Originally, we envisioned equations as formal descriptions of interpreters for other programming languages. When we discovered that such applications led to outrageous overhead, but that programs defined directly by equations ran quite competitively with LISP, we switched application from interpreter generation to programming with equations.

We do not apologize for our fanaticism about the foundations of equational programming, and our cavalier attitude toward applications. We believe that good mathematics is useful, but not always for the reasons that motivated its creation (non-Euclidean geometry is a positive example, the calculus a negative one). Also, while recognizing the need for programming languages that support important applications immediately, we believe that scientific progress in the principles of programming and programming languages is impeded by too quick a reach for applications. The utility of LISP, for example, is unquestionable, but the very adjustments to LISP that give it success in many applications make it a very imprecise vehicle for understanding the utility of declarative programming. We would rather discover that pure equational programming, as we envision it, is *unsuitable* for a particular application, than to expand the concept in a way that makes it harder to trace the conceptual underpinnings of its success or failure.

Without committing to any particular type of application, we must experiment with a variety of applications, else our approach to programming is pure speculation. For this purpose, we need an implementation. The implementation must perform well enough that some people can be persuaded to use it. We interpret this constraint to mean that it must compete in speed with LISP. Parsers, programming support, and the other baggage possessed by all programming languages, must be good enough not to get in the way, but the main effort should go toward demonstrating the feasibility of the novel aspects, rather than solving well understood problems once again.

The equational programming project has achieved an implementation of an interpreter for equational programs. The implementation runs under Berkeley UNIX* 4.1 and 4.2, and is available from the author for experimental use. The current distribution is not well enough supported to qualify as a reliable tool for

---

*UNIX is a trademark of AT&T.

important applications, but we have hopes of producing such a stronger implementation in the next few years. Sections 1 through 10 constitute a user's manual for the current implementation. The remainder of the text covers a variety of topics relating to the theory supporting equational programming, the algorithmic and organizational problems solved in its implementation, and the special characteristics of equational programming that qualify it for particular applications. Some sections discuss work in progress. The intent is to give a solid intuition for all the identifiable aspects of the project, from its esoteric theoretical foundations in logic to its concrete implementation as a system of programs, and its potential applications.

Various portions of the work were supported by a Purdue University XL grant, by the National Science Foundation under grants MCS-7801812 and MCS-8217996, and by the National Security Agency under grant 84H0006. The Purdue University Department of Computer Sciences provided essential computing resources for most of the implementation effort. I am grateful to Robert Strandh and Christoph Hoffmann for critical readings of the manuscript, and to AT&T Bell Laboratories for providing phototypesetting facilities. Typesetting was accomplished using the *troff* program under UNIX.

EQUATIONAL LOGIC

as a

PROGRAMMING LANGUAGE

1. Introduction (adapted from HO82b)

Computer scientists have spent a large amount of research effort developing the semantics of programming languages. Although we understand how to implement Algol-style procedural programming languages efficiently, it seems to be very difficult to say what the programs mean. The problem may come from choosing an implementation of a language before giving the semantics that define correctness of the implementation. In the development of the equation interpreter, we reversed the process by taking clean, simple, intuitive semantics, and then looking for correct, efficient implementations.

We suggest the following scenario as a good setting for the intuitive semantics of computation. Our scenario covers many, but not all, applications of computing (e.g., real-time applications are not included).

A person is communicating with a machine. The person gives a sequence of assertions followed by a question. The machine responds with an answer or by never answering.

The problem of semantics is to define, in a rigorous and understandable way, what it means for the machine's response to be correct. A natural informal definition of correctness is that any answer that the machine gives must be a logical consequence of the person's assertions, and that failure to give an answer must mean that there is no answer that follows logically from the assertions. If the language for giving assertions is capable of describing all the computable functions, the undecidability of the halting problem prevents the machine from always detecting those cases where there is no answer. In such cases, the machine never halts. The style of semantics based on logical consequence leads most naturally to a style of programming similar to that in the descriptive or applicative languages such as

LISP, Lucid, Prolog, Hope, OBJ, SASL and Functional Programming languages, although Algol-style programming may also be supported in such a way. Computations under logical-consequence semantics roughly correspond to "lazy evaluation" of LISP [HM76, FW76].

Semantics based on logical consequence is much simpler than many other styles of programming language semantics. In particular, the understanding of logical-consequence semantics does *not* require construction of particular models through lattice theory or category theory, as do the semantic treatments based on the work of Scott and Strachey or those in the abstract-data-types literature using initial or final algebras. If a program is given as a set of assertions, then the logical consequences of the program are merely all those additional assertions that *must* be true whenever the assertions of the program are true. More precisely, an equation A=B is a logical consequence of a set E of equations if and only if, in *every* algebraic interpretation for which every equation in E is true, A=B is also true (see [O'D77] Chapter 2 and Section 14 of this text for a more technical treatment). There is no way to determine which one of the many models of the program assertions was really intended by the programmer: we simply compute for him all the information we possibly can from what we are given. For those who prefer to think of a single model, term algebras or initial algebras may be used to construct one model for which the true equations are precisely the logical consequences of a given set of equations.

We use the language of equational logic to write the assertions of a program. Other logical languages are available, such as the first-order predicate calculus, used in Prolog [Ko79a]. We have chosen to emphasize the reconciliation of strict adherence to logical consequences with good run-time performance, at the expense of generality of the language. Current implementations of Prolog do not always discover all of the logical consequences of a program, and may waste much time searching through irrelevant derivations. With our language of equations, we lose some of the expressive power of Prolog, but we always discover all of the logical consequences of a program, and avoid searching irrelevant ones except in cases that inherently require parallel computation. Hoffmann and O'Donnell survey the issues involved in computing with equations in [HO82b]. Section 17 discusses the question of relevant vs. irrelevant consequences of equations more specifically.

Specializing our computing scenario to equational languages:

The person gives a sequence of equations followed by a question, "What is E?" for some expression E. The machine responds with an equation "E=F," where F is a simple expression.

For our equation interpreter, the "simple expressions" above must be the *normal forms*: expressions containing no instance of a left-hand side of an equation. This assumption allows the equations to be used as rewriting rules, directing the replacement of instances of left-hand sides by the corresponding right-hand sides. Sections 2 and 3 explain how to use the equation interpreter to act out the scenario above. Our equational computing scenario is a special case of a similar scenario developed independently by the philosophers Belnap and Steel for a logic of questions and answers [BS76].

The equation interpreter accepts equations as input, and automatically produces a program to perform the computations described by the equations. In order to achieve reasonable efficiency, we impose some fairly liberal restrictions on the form of equations given. Section 5 describes these restrictions, and Sections 6-8 and 10 present features of the interpreter. Section 15 describes the computational power of the interpreter in terms of the procedural concepts of parallelism, non-determinism, and pipelining.

Typical applications for which the equation interpreter should be useful are:

1. We may write quick and easy programs for the sorts of arithmetic and list-manipulating functions that are commonly programmed in languages such as LISP. The "lazy evaluation" implied by logical-consequence semantics allows us to describe infinite objects in such a program, as long as only finite portions are actually used in the output. The advantages of this capability, discussed in [FW76, HM76], are similar to the advantages of pipelining between coroutines in a procedural language. Definitions of large or infinite objects may also be used to implement a kind of automatic dynamic programming (see Section 15.4).

2. We may define programming languages by equations, and the equation processor will produce interpreters. Thus, we may experiment with the design of a programming language before investing the substantial effort required to produce a compiler or even a hand-coded interpreter.

3. Equations describing abstract data types may be used to produce correct implementations automatically, as suggested by [GS78, Wa76], and implemented independently in the OBJ language [FGJM85].

4. Theorems of the form A=B may sometimes be proved by receiving the same answer to the questions "What is A?" and "What is B?" [KB70, HO88] discuss such theorem provers. REVE [Le83, FG84] is a system for developing theorem-proving applications of equations.

5. Non-context-free syntactic checking, and semantics, such as compiler code-generation, may be described formally by equations and used, along with the conventional formal parsers, to automatically produce compilers (see Section 13).

The equation interpreter is intended for use by two different classes of user, in somewhat different styles. The first sort of user is interested in computing results for direct human consumption, using well-established facilities. This sort of user should stay fairly close to the paradigm presented in Section 2, should take the syntactic descriptions as fixed descriptions of a programming language, and should skip Section 20, as well as other sections that do not relate to the problem at hand. The second sort of user is building a new computing product, that will itself be used directly or indirectly to produce humanly readable results. This sort of user will almost certainly need to modify or redesign some of the syntactic processors, and will need to read Sections 13 and 20 rather closely in order to understand how to combine equationally-produced interpreters with other sorts of programs. The second sort of user is encouraged to think of the equation interpreter as a tool, analogous to a formal parser constructor, for building whichever parts of his product are conveniently described by equations. These equational programs may then be combined with programs produced by other language processors to perform those tasks not conveniently implemented by equations. The aim in using equations should be to achieve the same sort of self-documentation and ease of modification that may be achieved by formal grammars, in solving problems where context-free manipulations are not sufficiently powerful.

2. Using the Equation Interpreter Under UNIX (*ep* and *ei*)

Use of the equation interpreter involves two separate steps: preprocessing and interpreting. The preprocessing step, like a programming language compiler, analyzes the given equations and produces machine code. The interpreting step, which may be run any number of times once preprocessing is done, reduces a given term to normal form.

Normal use of the equation interpreter requires the user to create a directory containing 4 files used by the interpreter. The 4 files to be created are:

1. *definitions* - containing the equations;

2. *pre.in* - an input parser for the preprocessor;

3. *int.in* - an input parser for the interpreter;

4. *int.out* - an output pretty-printer for the interpreter.

The file *definitions*, discussed in Section 3, is usually typed in literally by the user. The files *pre.in*, *int.in* and *int.out*, which must be executable, are usually produced automatically by the command *loadsyntax*, as discussed in Section 4.

To invoke the preprocessor, type the following command to the shell

   ep Equnsdir

where *Equnsdir* is the directory in which you have created the 4 files above. If no directory is given, the current directory is used. *Ep* will use *Equnsdir* as the home for several temporary files, and produce in *Equnsdir* an executable file named interpreter. Because of the creation and removal of temporary files, the user should avoid placing any extraneous files in *Equnsdir*. Two of the files produced by *ep* are not removed: *def.deep* and *def.in*. These files are not strictly necessary for operation of the interpreter, and may be removed in the interest of space conservation, but they are useful in building up complex definitions from simpler ones (Section 14) and in producing certain diagnostic output (Section 10). To invoke the interpreter, type the command:

> *ei Equnsdir*

A term found on standard input will be reduced, and its normal form placed on the standard output.

A paradigmatic session with the equation interpreter has the following form:

> *mkdir Equnsdir*
> *loadsyntax Equnsdir*
> edit *Equnsdir/definitions* using your favorite editor
> *ep Equnsdir*
> edit *input* using your favorite editor
> *ei Equnsdir* <*input*

The sophisticated user of UNIX may invoke *ei* from his favorite interactive editor, such as *ned* or *emacs*, in order to be able to simultaneously manipulate the input and output.

In more advanced applications, if several equation interpreters are run in a pipeline, repeated invocation of the syntactic processors may be avoided by invoking the interpreters directly, instead of using *ei*. For example, if *Equ.*1, *Equ.*2, *Equ.*3 are all directories in which equational interpreters have been compiled, the following command pipes standard input through all three interpreters:

> *Equ.1/int.in* | *Equ.1/interpreter* | *Equ.2/interpreter* |
> *Equ.3/interpreter* | *Equ.3/int.out;*

Use of *ei* for the same purpose would involve 4 extra invocations of syntactic processors, introducing wasted computation and, worse, the possibility that superficial aspects of the syntax, such as quoting conventions, may affect the results. If

Equ. 1, *Equ.* 2, and *Equ.* 3 are not all produced using the same syntax, careful consideration of the relationship between the different syntaxes will be needed to make sense of such a pipe.

After specifying the directory containing definitions, the user may give the size of the workspace to be used in the interpreter. This size defaults to $2^{15}-1=32767$: the largest that can be addressed in one 16-bit word with a sign bit. The workspace size limits the size of the largest expression occurring as an intermediate step in any reduction of an input to normal form. The effect of the limit is blurred somewhat by sharing of equivalent subexpressions, and by allocation of space for declared symbols even when they do not actually take part in a particular computation. For example, to reduce the interpreter workspace to half of the default, type

   ep Equnsdir 16384

The largest workspace usable in the current implementation is $2^{31}-2=2147483646$. The limiting factor is the Berkeley Pascal compiler, which will not process a constant bigger than $2^{31}-1=2147483647$, and which produces mysteriously incorrect assembly code for an allocation of exactly that much. On current VAX Unix implementations, the shell may often refuse to run sizes much larger than the default because of insufficient main memory. In such a case, the user will see a message from the shell saying *"not enough core"* or *"too big"*.

3. Presenting Equations to the Equation Interpreter

Input to the equation interpreter, stored in the file *definitions*, must be of the following form:

> *Symbols*
>   *symbol_descriptor$_1$;*
>   *symbol_descriptor$_2$;*
>
>   .
>   .
>   .
>
>   *symbol_descriptor$_m$.*
>
> *For all variable$_1$, variable$_2$, $\cdots$ variable$_n$:*
>   *equation$_1$;*
>   *equation$_2$;*
>
>   .
>   .
>   .
>
>   *equation$_p$.*

The principal keywords recognized by the preprocessor are *Symbols*, *For all*, and *Equations*, appearing at the beginning of a line. *Equations* is an alternative to *For all* used in the unusual case that there are no variables in the equations. Capitalization of these keywords is optional, and any number of blanks greater than 0 may appear between *For* and *all*. The only other standard keywords are *include*, *where*, *end where*, *is*, *are*, *in*, *either*, *or*, and *end or*. The special symbols used by the preprocessor are ":", ";", ".", ",", """, and "". Particular term syntaxes (see Section 4) may entail other keywords and special symbols. Blanks are required only where necessary to separate alphanumeric strings. Any line beginning with ":" is a comment, with no impact on the meaning of a specification.

*symbol_descriptor*s indicate one or more symbols in the language to be defined, and give their arities. Intuitively, symbols of arity 0 are the constants of the language, and symbols of higher arity are the operators. A *symbol_descriptor* is either of the form

$$symbol_1, \; symbol_2, \; ... \; symbol_m: arity \qquad m \geqslant 1$$

or of the form

$$include \; symbol\_class_1, \; ... \; symbol\_class_n \quad n \geqslant 1$$

Syntactically, *symbol*s and *symbol_class*es are identifiers: strings other than keywords beginning with an alphabetic symbol followed by any combination of alphabetic symbols, base-ten digits, "_", and "-". Identifiers are currently limited to 20 characters, a restriction which will be removed in future versions. A *symbol_class* indicates the inclusion of a large predefined class of symbols. These classes are discussed in Section 6. Symbols that have been explicitly declared in the *Symbols* section are called literal symbols, to distinguish them from members of the predefined classes.

*variable*s are identifiers, of the same sort as symbols. An *equation* is either of the form

$$term_1 = term_2$$

of the form

$$term_1 = term_2 \; where \; qualification$$

or of the form

$$include \; equation\_class_1, \; \cdots \; ,equation\_class_m$$

The syntax of terms is somewhat flexible, and is discussed in Section 4. *qualifications* are syntactic constraints on substitutions for variables, and are discussed in Section 8. *equation_class*es are identifiers indicating the inclusion of a large number of predefined equations. These classes are discussed in Section 7.

For larger problems, the notation presented in this section will surely not be satisfactory, because it provides no formal mechanism for giving structure to a large definition. Section 14 describes a set of operators that may be applied to one or more equational definitions to produce useful extensions, modifications, and combinations of the definitions. The idea for these definition-constructing operators comes from work on abstract data types by Burstall and Goguen, implemented in the language OBJ [BG77]. Users are strongly encouraged to start using these operators as soon as a definition begins to be annoyingly large. The current version does not implement operators on definitions, so most users will not want to attack large problems until a more advanced version is released.

The syntax presented in this section is collected in the BNF below.

<program> ::= **Symbols** *<symbol descriptor list>*.

             For all *<variable list>*:*<equation list>*.

<symbol descriptor list> ::= *<symbol descriptor>*; ... ; *<symbol descriptor>*

<symbol descriptor> ::= *<symbol list>*:*<arity>* |

             include *<symbol class list>*

<symbol class list> ::= *<symbol class>*, ... , *<symbol class>*

<symbol class> ::= **atomic_symbols** | **integer_numerals** | **truth_values**

<symbol list> ::= *<symbol>*, . . . , *<symbol>*

<symbol> ::= *<identifier>*

<arity> ::= *<number>*

<variable list> ::= *<variable>*, . . . , *<variable>*

<variable> ::= *<identifier>*

<equation list> ::= *<equation>*; . . . ; *<equation>*

<equation> ::= *<term>* = *<term>* |

      <term> = *<term>* **where** *<qualification>* **end where** |

      include *<equation class list>*

<qualification> ::= *<qualification item list>*

<qualification item list> ::= *<qualification item>*, . . . ,*<qualification item>*

<qualification item> ::= *<variable>* **is** *<qualified term>* |

      <variable list> **are** *<qualified term>*

<qualified term> ::= **in***<symbol class>* |

      <term> |

      <qualified term> **where** *<qualification>* **end where** |

      either *<qualified term list>* **end or**

<qualified term list> ::= *<qualified term>* **or** . . . **or** *<qualified term>*

4. The Syntax of Terms (*loadsyntax*)

Since no single syntax for terms is acceptable for all applications of the equation interpreter, we provide a library of syntaxes from which the user may choose the one best suited to his application. The more sophisticated user, who wishes to custom-build his own syntax, should see Section 20 on implementation to learn the requirements for parsers and pretty-printers.

To choose a syntax from the current library, type the command

loadsyntax Equnsdir Syntax

where *Equnsdir* is the directory containing the preprocessor input, and *Syntax* is the name of the syntax to be seen by the user. *Loadsyntax* will create the appropriate *pre.in*, *int.in*, and *int.out* files in *Equnsdir* to process the selected syntax. If *syntax* is omitted, *LISP.M* is used by default. If *Equnsdir* is also omitted, the current directory is used.

In order to distinguish atomic symbols from nullary literal symbols in input to the interpreter, the literal symbols must be written with an empty argument list. Thus, in *Standmath* notation, $a()$ is a literal symbol, and a is an atomic symbol. In *LISP.M*, the corresponding notations are $a[]$ and a. This regrettable notational clumsiness should disappear in later versions.

4.1 *Standmath*: Standard Mathematical Notation

The *Standmath* syntax is standard mathematical functional prefix notation, with arguments surrounded by parentheses and separated by commas, such as $f(g(a,b),c,h(e))$. Empty argument lists are allowed, as in $f()$. This syntax is used as the standard of reference (but is not the default choice), all others are described as special notations for *Standmath* terms.

4.2 *LISP.M*: **Extended LISP Notation**

LISP.M is a liberal LISP notation, which mixes M-expression notation freely with S-expressions [McC60]. Invocation of *LISP.M* requires declaration of the nullary symbol *nil* and the binary symbol *cons*. An M-expression accepted by *LISP.M* may be in any of the following forms:

$$atomic\_symbol$$

$$nil()$$

$$(M{-}expr_1 \; M{-}expr_2 \cdots M{-}expr_m) \qquad\qquad m \geqslant 0$$

$$(M{-}expr_1 \; M{-}expr_2 \cdots M{-}expr_{n-1} \,.\, M{-}expr_n) \quad n \geqslant 1$$

$$function[M{-}expr_1; \; M{-}expr_2 \,; \cdots M{-}expr_p] \qquad p \geqslant 0$$

$$(M{-}expr_1 \; \cdots \; M{-}expr_{n-1} \,.\, M{-}expr_n)$$

is a notation for

$$cons\,(M{-}expr_1, \; \cdots \; cons\,(M{-}expr_{n-1}, M{-}expr_n) \; \cdots \;)$$

$$(M{-}expr_1 \; \cdots \; M{-}expr_m)$$

is a notation for

$$cons\,(M{-}expr_1, cons\,(M{-}expr_2, \; \cdots \; cons\,(M{-}expr_m, nil()) \; \cdots \;))$$

$$function[M{-}expr_1; \; \cdots \; M{-}expr_p]$$

is a notation for

$$function\,(M{-}expr_1, \; \cdots \; M{-}expr_p)$$

4.3 *Lambda*: A Lambda Calculus Notation

Lambda notation is intended for use in experiments with evaluation strategies for the lambda calculus. This notation supports the most common abbreviations conveniently, while allowing unusual sorts of expressions to be described at the cost of less convenient notation. Because of the highly experimental nature of this syntax, less attention has been given to providing useful error messages. Since this lambda notation was developed to support one particular series of experiments with reduction strategies, it will probably not be suitable for all uses of the lambda calculus.

$\backslash x.E$

is a notation for

Lambda(cons(x, nil()), E)

where x must be an atomic symbol representing a variable.

(E F)

is a notation for

AP(E, F)

In principle, the notations above are sufficient for describing arbitrary lambda terms, but for convenience, multiple left-associated applications may be given with only one parenthesis pair. Thus,

$(E_1 \, E_2 \, E_3 \, \cdots \, E_n)$ · $n \geqslant 2$

is a notation for

$$AP(\ \cdots \ AP(AP(E_1, E_2), E_3), \ \cdots \ E_n)$$

Similarly, many variables may be lambda bound by a single use of "\". Thus,

$$\backslash x_1 \ x_2 \ \cdots \ x_n.E \qquad n \geqslant 1$$

is a notation for

$$Lambda\,(cons\,(x_1, \ cons\,(x_2, \ \cdots \ nil\,()) \ \cdots \ ),E)$$

Notice that the list of variables is given as a LISP list, rather than the more conventional representation as

$$Lambda\,(x_1, \ Lambda\,(x_2, \ \cdots \ Lambda\,(x_n, E) \ \cdots \ ))$$

It is easy to write equations to translate the listed-variable form into the more conventional representation, but the listed form allows reduction strategies to take advantage of nested Lambdas. In order to write equations manipulating lists of variables, it is necessary to refer to a list of unknown length. So,

$$\backslash x_1 \ x_2 \ \cdots \ x_n{:}rem.E \qquad n \geqslant 0$$

is a notation for

$$Lambda\,(cons\,(x_1, \ cons\,(x_2, \ \cdots \ rem) \ \cdots \ ), E)$$

That is, *rem* above represents the remainder of the list beyond $x_1 \cdots x_n$. In the special case where $n=0$,

\:*list.E*

is a notation for

Lambda(list, E)

In order to deal with special internal forms, such as de Bruijn notation [deB72], the form

\:*i.E*

is allowed as a notation for

Lambda(i, E)

where i is an integer numeral. If function symbols other than Lambda and AP must be introduced, a bracketed style of function application may be used, in which

$$f[E_1, \cdots E_n] \qquad\qquad n \geqslant 0$$

is a notation for

$$f(E_1, \cdots E_n)$$

4.4 Inner Syntaxes (for the advanced user with a large problem)

Independently of the surface syntax in which terms are written, it may be helpful to use different internal representations of terms for different purposes. For example, instead of having a number of function symbols of different arities, it is sometimes convenient to use only one binary symbol, *AP*, representing function application, and to represent all other functions by nullary symbols. Application of a function to multiple arguments is represented by a sequence of separate applications, one for each argument. The translation from standard notation to this applicative notation is often called *Currying*. For example, the term

f(g(a, b), h(c))

is Curried to

AP(AP(f, AP(AP(g, a), b), AP(h, c))).

Since the performance of the pattern-matching techniques used by the equation interpreter is affected by the internal representation of the patterns, it may be important to choose the best such representation in order to solve large problems. The current version of the system is not particularly sensitive to such choices, but earlier versions were, and later versions may again be so. In order to use an alternate internal representation, type

    loadsyntax Equnsdir Outersynt Innersynt

where *Outersynt* is one of the syntaxes described in Sections 4.1-4.3, and *Innersynt* is the name of the chosen internal representation. Currently, only two internal representations are available. *Standmath* is the standard mathematical notation, so

    loadsyntax Equnsdir Outersynt Standmath

is equivalent to

loadsyntax Equnsdir Outersynt

The other internal representation is *Curry*, described above.

5. Restrictions on Equations

In order for the reduction strategies used by the equation interpreter to be correct according to the logical-consequence semantics, some restrictions must be placed on the equations. The user may learn these restrictions by study, or by trial and error, since the preprocessor gives messages about each violation. Presently, 5 restrictions are enforced:

1. No variable may be repeated on the left side of an equation. For instance,

    $$if(x, y, y) = y$$

    is prohibited, because of the 2 instances of y on the left side.

2. Every variable appearing on the right side of an equation must also appear on the left. For instance, $f(x)=y$ is prohibited.

3. Two different left sides may not match the same expression. So the pair of equations

    $$g(0,x) = 0; \quad g(x,1) = 0$$

    is prohibited, because both of them apply to $g(0,1)$.

4. When two (not necessarily different) left-hand sides match two different parts of the same expression, the two parts must not overlap. E.g., the pair of equations

    $$first(pred(x)) = predfunc; \quad pred(succ(x)) = x$$

    is prohibited, since the left-hand sides overlap in $first\,(pred\,(succ\,(0)))$.

5. It must be possible, in a left-to-right preorder traversal of any term, to identify an instance of a left-hand side without traversing any part of the term below that instance. This property is called left-sequentiality. For example,

the pair of equations

$$f(g(x, a), y) = 0; \quad g(b, c) = 1$$

is prohibited, since after scanning $f(g$ it is impossible to decide whether to look at the first argument to g in hopes of matching the b in the second equation, or to skip it and try to match the first equation.

Violations of left-sequentiality may often be avoided by reordering the arguments to a function. For example, the disallowed equations above could be replaced by $f(g(a,x),y) = 0$ and $g(c,b) = 1$. Left-sequentiality does not necessarily imply that leftmost-outermost evaluation will work. Rather, it means that in attempting to create a redex at some point in a term, the evaluator can determine whether or not to perform reductions within a leftward portion of the term without looking at anything to the right. Left-sequentiality is discussed in more detail in Sections 17 and 18.3.

All five of these restrictions are enforced by the preprocessor. Violations produce diagnostic messages and prevent compiling of an interpreter. The left-sequentiality restriction (5) subsumes the nonoverlapping restriction (4), but later versions of the system will remove the sequentiality constraint. Later versions will also relax restriction (3) to allow compatible left-hand sides when the right-hand sides agree.

6. Predefined Classes of Symbols

It is sometimes impossible to list in advance all of the symbols to be processed by a particular set of equations. Therefore, we allow 4 predefined classes of symbols to be invoked by name. These classes consist entirely of constants, that is, nullary symbols.

6.1. *integer_numerals*

The *integer_numerals* include all of the sequences of base-10 digits, optionally preceded by "-". Numerals are limited to fit in a single machine word: the range -2147483647 to +2147483647 on the current VAX implementation. Later versions will use the operators of Section 14 to provide arbitrary precision integer arithmetic.

6.2. *truth_values*

The *truth_values* are the symbols *true* and *false*. They are included as a predefined class for standardization.

6.3. *characters*

The *characters* are ASCII characters, presented in single or double quotes. The only operations available are conversions between *characters* and *integer_numerals*. Later versions will use the operators of Section 14 to provide arbitrarily long character strings, and some useful string-manipulating operations.

6.4. *atomic_symbols*

The *atomic_symbols* are structureless symbols whose only detectable relations are equality and inequality. Every identifier different from *true* and *false*, and not having any arguments, is taken to be an atomic symbol. In order to distinguish nullary literal symbols from atomic symbols, the literal symbols are given null strings of arguments, such as *lit* () (in *Standmath* notation) and *lit* [] (in *LISP.M* notation). Currently, *atomic_symbols* are limited to lengths from 0 to 20. Later versions will use the operators of Section 14 to provide arbitrarily long *atomic_symbols*.

Section 7 describes predefined functions which operate on these classes of symbols.

7. Predefined Classes of Equations

The predefined classes of equations described in this section were introduced to provide access to selected machine instructions, particularly those for arithmetic operations, without sacrificing the semantic simplicity of the equation interpreter, and without introducing any new types of failure, such as arithmetic overflow. Only those operations that are extremely common and whose implementations in machine instructions bring substantial performance benefits are included. The intent is to provide a minimal set of predefined operations from which more powerful operations may be defined by explicitly-given equations. So, every predefined operation described below has the same effect as a certain impractically large set of equations, and the very desirable extensions of these sets of equations to handle multiple-word objects are left to be done by explicitly-given equations in later versions.

For each predefined class of symbols, there are predefined classes of equations defining standard functions for those symbols. Some of the functions produce values in another class than the the class of the arguments. Predefined classes of equations allow a user to specify a prohibitively large set of equations concisely, and allow the implementation to use special, more efficient techniques to process those equations than are used in general. When a predefined class of functions is invoked, all of the relevant function symbols and classes of symbols must be declared as well. We will describe the functions defined for each class of symbols. The associated class of equations is the complete graph of the function. For example, the integer function add has the class of equations containing $add(0,0)=0$, $add(0,1)=1$, ... $add(1,0)=1$, $add(1,1)=2$, ...

7.1. Functions on *atomic_symbols*

equatom $equ(x,y) = true \ if \ x = y,$

$false \ otherwise$

7.2. Integer Functions

multint $multiply(x,y) = x * y$

divint $divide(x,y) = the \ greatest \ integer \leqslant x/y \ if \ y \neq 0$

modint $modulo(x,y) = x - (y*divide(x,y)) \ if \ y \neq 0,$

$x \ otherwise$

addint $add(x,y) = x + y$

subint $subtract(x,y) = x - y$

equint $equ(x,y) = true \ if \ x = y,$

$false \ otherwise$

lessint $less(x,y) = true \ if \ x < y,$

$false \ otherwise$

An expression starting with the function *divide* will not be reduced at all if the second argument is 0.   Thus, the output will give full information about the erroneous use of this function. Similarly, additions and multiplications leading to overflow will simply not be performed. Later versions will perform arbitrary precision arithmetic (see Section 9.6), removing this restriction.

7.3. Character Functions

equchar $equ(x,y) = true \ if \ x = y,$

$false \ otherwise$

intchar   *char(i)* $=$ *the ith character in a standard ordering*

charint   *seqno(x)* $=$ *the position of x in a standard ordering*

An application of *char* to an integer outside of the range 0 to $2^7 - 1 = 127$, or an application of *seqno* to a string of length other than 1 will not be reduced. Later versions will use the operations of Section 14 to provide useful string-manipulating operations for arbitrarily long character strings.

8. Syntactic Qualifications on Variables

Even with a liberal set of predefined functions, there will arise cases where the set of equations that a user wants to include in his definition is much too large to ever type by hand. For example, in defining a LISP interpreter, it is important to define the function atom, which tests for atomic symbols. The natural set of equations to define this function includes $atom(cons(x,y))=false$, $atom(a)=true$, $atom(b)=true$, ... $atom(aa)=true$, $atom(ab)=true$, ... We would like to abbreviate this large set of equations with the following two:

> $atom(cons(x,y))$ = *false;*

> $atom(x)$ = *true where x is either*
> > *in atomic_symbols*
> > *or in integer_numerals*
> > *end or*
> *end where*

Notice that the qualification placed on the variable x is essentially a syntactic, rather than a semantic, one. In general, we allow equations of the form:

> *term* = *term where qualification end where*

A *qualification* is of the form

> *qualification_item*$_1$, $\cdots$ *qualification_item*$_m$ $m \geqslant 1$

and *qualification_item*s are of the forms

> *variable is qualification_term*

> *variable*$_1$, $\cdots$ *variable*$_p$ *are qualification_term*

and *qualification_term*s are of the forms

> *in predefined_symbol_class*

term

qualification_term where qualification end where

either qualification_term₁ or · · · qualification_termᵣ end or

Examples illustrating the forms above:

> *atompair_or_atom(x) = true*
>   *where x is either*
>   *cons(y,z) where y,z are in atomic_symbols end where*
>   *or in atomic_symbols*
>   *end where;*

> *atom_int_pair(x) = true*
>   *where x is cons(y,z)*
>   *where y is in atomic_symbols,*
>   *x is in integer_numerals*
>   *end where*
>   *end where*

If the same variable is mentioned in two different nested qualifications, the innermost qualification applies.

The interpretation of the restrictions on equations in Section 5 is not obvious in the presence of qualified equations. Restrictions 1 and 2, regarding the appearance of variables on left and right sides of equations, are applied to the unqualified equations, ignoring the qualifying clauses. Restrictions 4 and 5, regarding possible interactions between left sides, are applied to the results of substituting variable qualifications for the instances of variables that they qualify. For example, the equation

f(x) = y where x is g(y) end where

is prohibited, because the variable *y* is not present on the unqualified left side, and the pair of equations

$f(x) = 0$ *where* x *is* $g(y)$ *end where;* $g(x) = 1;$

is prohibited because of the overlap in $f(g(a))$. In general, a variable occurring in a *where* clause is local to that clause, so $g(x,y) = z$ *where* x *is* y is equivalent to $g(x,y) = z$, rather than $g(x,x) = z$. The details of interactions between variable bindings and *where* clauses certainly need more thought, but fortunately the subtle cases do not occur very often.

9. Miscellaneous Examples

This section contains examples of complete equational programs that do not fit any specific topic, but help give a general feeling for the capabilities of the interpreter. The first ones are primitive, and should be accessible to every reader, but later ones, such as the *lambda−calculus* example, are intended only for the reader whose specialized interests agree with the topic.

9.1. List Reversal

The following example, using the *LISP.M* syntax, is chosen for its triviality. The operation of reversal (*rev*) is defined using the operation of adding an element to the end of a list (*addend*). A trace of this example shows that the number of steps to reverse a list of length n is proportional to n^2. Notice that the usual LISP operators *car* and *cdr* (first element, remaining elements of a list) are not needed, because of the ability to nest operation symbols on the left-hand sides of equations. This example has no advantage over the corresponding LISP program, other than transparency of notation. It is easy to imagine a compiler that would translate equational programs of this sort into LISP in a very straightforward way.

Symbols

: List constructors
    cons: 2;
    nil: 0;

: Operators for list manipulation
    rev: 1;
    addend: 2;

  include atomic_symbols.

For all x,y,z:

    rev[()] = ();
    rev[(x . y)] = addend[rev[y]; x];

addend[(); *x] = (x);*
addend[(x . y); *z] = (x . addend[y*; *z]).*

The following equations redefine list reversal in such a way that the equation interpreter will perform a linear-time algorithm. Just like the naive quadratic time version above, these equations may be compiled into a LISP program in a very straightforward way.

Symbols
  cons: 2;
  nil: 0;
  rev: 1;
  apprev: 2;
  include atomic_symbols.

For all x,y,z:

  rev[x] = apprev[x; ()];

: apprev[x; z] is the result of appending z to the reversal of x.

  apprev[(); *z] = z;*

  apprev[(x . y); *z] = apprev[y*; *(x . z)].*

9.2. Huffman Codes

The following definition of an operator producing Huffman codes [Hu52, AHU83] as binary trees is a little bit clumsier than the list reversals above to translate into LISP, since the operator *Huff*, a new constructor combining a partially-constructed Huffman tree with its weight, would either be omitted in a representing S-expression, or encoded as an atomic symbol. Either way, the list constructing operator is overloaded with two different intuitive meanings, and the expressions become a bit harder to read.

The following equations produce Huffman codes in the form of binary trees constructed with cons. To produce the Huffman tree for the keys $K_1, K_2, \cdots K_n$ with weights $w_1, w_2, \cdots w_n$ in decreasing numerical order, evaluate the term $BuildHuff[(Huff[w_1;K_1] \cdots Huff[w_n;K_n])]$.

Symbols

: List construction operators
  cons: 2;
  nil: 0;

: Huff[w; t] represents the tree t (built from cons) having weight w.
  Huff: 2;

: Tree building operators
  BuildHuff: 1;
  Insert: 2;
  Combine: 2;

: Arithmetic and logical symbols and operators
  if: 3;
  add: 2;
  less: 2;
  include truth_values;
  include integer_numerals;
  include atomic_symbols.

For all weight1, weight2, tree1, tree2, x, y, remainder, item:

: if is the standard conditional function, and add, less
: are the standard arithmetic operation and test.
  if[true; x; y] = x;   if[false; x; y] = y;

  include addint, lessint;

: BuildHuff[list] assumes that its argument is a list of weighted trees, in
: decreasing order by weight, and combines the trees into a single tree
: representing the Huffman code for the given weights.

  BuildHuff[(Huff[weight1; tree1])] = tree1;

  BuildHuff[(x y . remainder)] =
    BuildHuff[Insert[remainder; Combine[x; y]]]
    where x, y are Huff[weight1; tree1] end where;

: *Insert[list; tree] inserts the given weighted tree into the given list of weighted*
:   *trees according to its weight. Insert assumes that the list is in decreasing*
:   *order by weight.*

   Insert[(); item] = (item);

   Insert[(Huff[weight2; tree2] . remainder); Huff[weight1; tree1]] =
     if[less[weight1; weight2];
        (Huff[weight1; tree1] Huff[weight2; tree2] . remainder);
        (Huff[weight2; tree2] . Insert[remainder; Huff[weight1; tree1]])];

: *Combine[t1; t2] is the combination of the weighted trees t1 and t2 resulting*
: *from hanging t1 and t2 from a common root, and adding their weights.*

   Combine[Huff[weight1; tree1]; Huff[weight2; tree2]] =
     Huff[add[weight1; weight2]; (tree1 . tree2)].

9.3. Quicksort

The following equational program sorts a list of integers by the Quicksort procedure [Ho62, AHU74]. This program may also be translated easily into LISP. The fundamental idea behind Quicksort is that we may sort a list l by choosing a value i (usually the first value in l) splitting l into the lists $l_<$, $l_=$, and $l_>$ of elements $<i$, $=i$, and $>i$, respectively. Then, sort $l_<$ and $l_>$ ($l_=$ is already sorted), and append them to get the sorted version of l. Quicksort sorts a list of n elements in time $O(n\log n)$ on the average.

Symbols

: *List construction operators*
   cons: 2;
   nil: 0;

: *List manipulation operators*
   smaller, larger: 2;
   append: 2;
   sort: 1;

: *Logical and arithmetic operators and symbols*
   if: 3;

less: 2;
include integer_numerals, truth_values.

For all i, j, a, b, rem:

  sort[()] = ();

  sort[(i . rem)] = append[sort[smaller[i; rem]]; append[(i); sort[larger[i; rem]]]];

: smaller[i; a] is a list of the elements of a smaller than or equal to the integer i.

  smaller[i; ()] = ();

  smaller[i; (j . rem)] = if[less[i; j]; smaller[i; rem]; (j . smaller[i; rem])];

: larger[i; a] is a list of the elements of a larger than the integer i.

  larger[i; ()] = ();

  larger[i; (j . rem)] = if[less[i; j]; (j . larger[i; rem]); larger[i; rem]];

: append[a; b] is the concatenation of the lists a and b.

  append[(); a] = a;

  append[(i . rem); a] = (i . append[rem; a]);

: if, less, and greater are the standard logical and arithmetic operations.

  if[true; a; b] = a; if[false; a; b] = b;

  include lessint.

9.4. A Toy Theorem Prover

The fact that sorting a list l with an equational program is equivalent to proving $sort[l] = l'$ based on certain assumptions, leads one to consider the similarity between sorting by exchanges, and proving equalities based on commutativity and associativity. Given the axioms $x+y = y+x$ and $(x+y)+z = x+(y+z)$, we quickly learn to recognize that for any two additive expressions, E_1 and E_2, containing the same summands possibly in a different order, $E_1 = E_2$. One way to formalize that insight is to give a procedure that takes such E_1 and E_2 as inputs, checks whether they are indeed equal up to commutativity and associativity, and produces the proof of equality if there is one. The proof of equality of two terms by commutativity and associativity amounts to a sorting of the summands in one or both terms, with each application of the commutativity axiom corresponding to an interchange.

In the following program, *compare*[*a*;*b*] takes two additive expressions *a* and *b*, and produces a proof that *a*=*b* from commutativity and associativity, if such a proof exists. Additive expressions are constructed from numbered variables, with *v*[*i*] representing the *i*th variable v_i, and the syntactic binary operator *plus*. Proofs are represented by lists of expressions, with the convention that each expression in the list transforms into the next one by one application of commutativity or associativity to some subexpression. Since equality is symmetric, proofs are correct whether they are read forwards or backwards. The proof of *a*=*b* starts by proving *a*=*a'*, where *a'* has the same variables as *a*, combined in the standard form $v_{i_1}+(v_{i_2}+ \cdots (v_{i_{n-1}}+v_{i_n}) \cdots)$, with $i_j \leqslant i_{j+1}$. This proof of *a*=*a'* is the value of *stand*[*a*]. A similar proof of *b*=*b'* is produced by *stand*[*b*]. Finally, *stand*[*a*] is concatenated with the reversal of *stand*[*b*]. If the standard forms of *a* and *b* are not syntactically identical, then there is a false step in the middle of the concatenated proofs, and that step is marked with the special operator *falsestep*[].

The interesting part of the procedure above is the *stand* operation, proving equality of a term with its standard form. That proof works recursively on an expression *a*+*b*, first standardizing *a* and *b* individually, then applying the following transformations to combine the standardized a and b into a single standard form.

1. $(v_i+a)+(v_j+b)$ *associates to* $v_i+(a+(v_j+b))$ *when* $i \leqslant j$

2. $(v_i+a)+(v_j+b)$ *commutes to* $(v_j+b)+(v_i+a)$ *associates to* $v_j+(b+(v_i+a))$ *when* $i > j$

3. $(v_i+a)+v_j$ *associates to* $v_i+(a+v_j)$ *when* $i \leqslant j$

4. $(v_i+a)+v_j$ *commutes to* $v_j+(v_i+a)$ *when* $i > j$

5. $v_i+(v_j+b)$ *associates to* $(v_i+v_j)+b$

    commutes to $(v_j+v_i)+b$ *associates to* $v_j+(v_i+b)$ *when* $i > j$

6. v_i+v_j *commutes to* v_j+v_i *when* $i > j$

In cases 1-3 above, more transformations must be applied to subexpressions. In the following program, the *merge* operator performs the transformations described above.

Symbols

: Constructors for lists
   cons: 2;
   nil: 0;
   include integer_numerals;

: Constructors for additive expressions
   plus: 2;
   v: 1;

: Errors in proofs
   falsestep: 0;

: Operators for testing and proving equality under commutativity, associativity
   compare: 2;
   stand: 1;
   merge: 1;
   plusp: 2;
   appendp: 2;

: Standard list and arithmetic operators

addend: 2;
if: 3;
and: 2;
less: 2;
equ: 2;
include truth_values.

For all a, b, c, d, i, j, rem, rem1, rem2:

compare[a; b] = appendp[stand[a]; stand[b]];

stand[v[i]] = (v[i]);

stand[plus[a; b]] = merge[plusp[stand[a]; stand[b]]];

merge[(a b . rem)] = (a . merge[(b . rem)]);

merge[(a)] = merge[a];

: Case 6
  merge[plus[v[i]; v[j]]] =

    if[less[j; i];
:   *commute vi and vj*
        (plus[v[i]; v[j]]   plus[v[j]; v[i]]);

:   *else*
:   *no change*
        (plus[v[i]; v[j]])];

: Case 5
  merge[plus[v[i]; plus[v[j]; b]]] =

    if[less[j; i];
        (plus[v[i]; plus[v[j]; b]]
:   *associate vi with vj*
        plus[plus[v[i]; v[j]]; b]
:   *commute vi and vj*
        plus[plus[v[j]; v[i]]; b] .
:   *associate vi with b*
        plusp[(v[j]); merge[plus[v[i]; b]]]);

:   *else*
:   *no change*
        plusp[(v[i]); merge[plus[v[j]; b]]]];

merge[plus[plus[v[i]; a]; v[j]]] =

　　　　if[less[j; i];
: Case 4
　　　　(plus[plus[v[i]; a]; v[j]] .
:　　　　　　　　　　　　　　*commute vi+a and vj*
　　　　　plusp[(v[j]); merge[plus[v[i]; a]]]);

:　　　*else*
: Case 3
　　　　(plus[plus[v[i]; a]; v[j]] .
:　　　　　　　　　　　　　　*associate a with vj*
　　　　　plusp[(v[i]); merge[plus[a; v[j]]]])];

merge[plus[plus[v[i]; a]; plus[v[j]; b]]] =

　　　　if[less[j; i];
: Case 2
　　　　(plus[plus[v[i]; a]; plus[v[j]; b]]
:　　　　　　　　　　　　*commute vi+a and vj+b*
　　　　　plus[plus[v[j]; b]; plus[v[i]; a]] .
:　　　　　　　　　　　　　*associate b with vi+a*
　　　　　plusp[(v[j]); merge[plus[b; plus[v[i]; a]]]]);

:　　　*else*
: Case 1
　　　　(plus[plus[v[i]; a]; plus[v[j]; b]] .
:　　　　　　　　　　　　　*associate a with vj+b*
　　　　　plusp[(v[i]); merge[plus[a; plus[v[j]; b]]]])];

: plusp[p; q] transforms proofs p of E1=F1 and q of E2=F2 into a proof
: of plus[E1; E2] = plus[F1; F2].

　plusp[(a); rem] = plusp[a; rem];

　plusp[(a b . rem1); (c . rem2)] = (plus[a; c] . plusp[(b . rem1); (c . rem2)]);

　plusp[a; ()] = ()
　　where a is either v[i] or plus[b; c] end or end where;

　plusp[a; (b . rem)] = (plus[a; b] . plusp[a; rem])
　　where a is either v[i] or plus[b; c] end or end where;

: appendp[p; q] appends proofs p and the reversal of q, coalescing the last lines
: if they are the same, and indicating an error otherwise.

appendp[(a); (b)] = if[equ[a; b]; (a); (a falsestep[] b)];

appendp[(a b . rem); c] = (a . appendp[(b . rem); c]);

appendp[(a); (b c . rem)] = addend[appendp[(a); (c . rem)]; b];

: addend[l; a] adds the element a to the end of the list l.

addend[(); a] = (a);

addend[(a . rem); b] = (a . addend[rem; b]);

: equ is extended to additive terms, as a test for syntactic equality.

equ[v[i]; v[j]] = equ[i; j];

equ[plus[a; b]; plus[c; d]] = and[equ[a; c]; equ[b; d]];

equ[v[i]; plus[c; d]] = false;

equ[plus[a; b]; v[j]] = false;

include equint;

: if, and, less are standard operators.

if[true; a; b] = a; if[false; a; b] = b;

and[a; b] = if[a; b; false];

include lessint.

9.5. An Unusual Adder

The following example gives a rather obtuse way to add two numbers. The intent of the example is to demonstrate a programming technique supported by the equation interpreter, but *not* by LISP, involving the definition of infinite structures. We hope that this silly example will clarify the technique, while more substantial examples in Sections 9.7, 15.3 and 15.4 will show its value in solving problems elegantly. The addition program below uses an infinite list of infinite lists, in which the ith member of the jth list is the integer $i+j$. In order to add two nonnegative integers, we select the answer out of this infinite addition table. The outermost evaluation strategy guarantees that only a finite portion of the table will actually be produced, so that the computation will terminate.

Symbols

: List constructors.
  cons: 2;
  nil: 0;
  include integer_numerals;

: List utilities.
  element: 2;
  first; 1;
  tail: 1;
  inclist: 1;

: Standard arithmetic operators.
  add, subtract, equ: 2;
  if: 3;
  include truth_values;

: Unusual integer list, addition table and operator.
  intlist: 0;
  addtable: 0;
  weirdadd: 2.

For all

  first[(x . l)] = x;

  tail[(x . l)] = l;

  element[i; l] = if[equ[i; 0];
          first[l];
          element[subtract[i; 1]; tail[l]]];

  weirdadd[i; j] = element[i; element[j; addtable[]]];

  addtable[] = (intlist[] . inclist[addtable[]]);

intlist[] = (0 . inclist[intlist[]]);

inclist[i] = add[i; 1] where i is in integer_numerals end where;
inclist[(i . l)] = (inclist[i] . inclist[l]);

include addint, subint, equint.

9.6. Arbitrary-Precision Integer Operations

The equation interpreter implementation provides the usual integer operations as primitives, when these operations are applied to integers that may be represented in single precision, and when the result of the operation is also single precision. In order to provide arbitrary precision integer operations, we extend these primitive sets of equations with some additional explicit equations.

The following equations define arbitrary-precision arithmetic on positive integers in a straightforward way. A large base is chosen, for example base 2^{15}=32768, and the constructor *extend* is used to represent large numbers, with the understanding that *extend*(x, i) represents $x*base+i$, for $0 \leqslant i < base$. *longadd* and *longmult* are the binary operators for addition and multiplication. Addition follows the grade school algorithm of adding digits from right to left, keeping track of a carry. Multiplication also follows the usual algorithm for hand calculation, adding up partial products produced by multiplying one digit of the second multiplicand with the entire first multiplicand.

Symbols

: Constructors for arbitrary-precision integers.
  extend: 2;
  include integer_numerals;

: Base for arithmetic.

base: 0;

: Single precision arithmetic operators.
  add: 2;
  multiply: 2;

: Arbitrary-precision arithmetic operators.
  longadd: 2;
  longmult: 2;

: Operators used in defining the arithmetic operators.
  sum: 3;
  acarry: 3;
  carryadd: 3;
  prod: 3;
  mcarry: 3;
  carrymult: 3.

For all x, y, z, i, j, k:

base() = 32768;

longadd(x, y) = carryadd(x, y, 0);

carryadd(i, j, k) = if(equ(acarry(i, j, k), 0),
                       sum(i, j, k),
                       extend(acarry(i, j, k), sum(i, j, k)))
          where i, j are in integer_numerals end where;

carryadd(extend(x, i), j, k) = carryadd(extend(x, i), extend(0, j), k)
          where j is in integer_numerals end where;

carryadd(i, extend(y, j), k) = carryadd(extend(0, i), extend(y, j), k)
          where i is in integer_numerals end where;

carryadd(extend(x, i), extend(y, j), k) =
          extend(longadd(x, y, acarry(i, j, k)), sum(i, j, k));

sum(i, j, k) = mod(add(i, add(j, k)), base());

acarry(i, j, k) = div(add(i, add(j, k)), base());

longmult(x, j) = carrymult(x, j, 0)
          where j is in integer_numerals end where;

longmult(x, extend(y, j)) =

longadd(carrymult(x, j, 0), extend(longmult(x, y), 0));

carrymult(i, j, k) = if(equ(mcarry(i, j, k), 0),
  prod(i, j, k),
  extend(mcarry(i, j, k), prod(i, j, k))
  where i is in integer_numerals end where;

carrymult(extend(x, i), j, k) =
  extend(carrymult(x, j, mcarry(i, j, k)), prod(i, j, k));

prod(i, j, k) = mod(multiply(i, multiply(j, k)), base());

mcarry(i, j, k) = div(multiply(i, multiply(j, k)), base());

include addint, divint, modint, multint.

The simple equational program above has several objectionable qualities. First, in order to make the operations *sum*, *acarry*, *prod*, and *mcarry* really work, we must choose a base much smaller than the largest integer representable in single precision. In particular, to allow evaluation of *prod* and *mcarry* in all cases, the base used by the program may not exceed the *square root* of full single precision. This use of a small base doubles the sizes of multiple-precision integer representations. By redefining the offending operators, we may allow full use of single precision, but only at the cost of a substantial additional time overhead. For example, *sum* would have to be defined as

sum(i, j, k) = addmod(i, addmod(j, k, base()), base());

addmod(i, j, k) = if(less(i, subtract(k, j)),
  add(i, j),
  add(subtract(max(i, j), k), min(i, j)));

and *prod* would be even more complex, because of the possibility of zeroes. Even if we accept the reduced base for arithmetic, extra time is required to add or multiply two single-precision numbers with a single-precision result, since we must check for the nonexistent carry. Finally, it is distasteful to introduce new operators *longadd* and *longmult* when our intuitive idea is to extend *add* and *multiply*.

In order to avoid these objections, we need a slightly better support from the predefined operations *add* and *multiply*. When faced with an expression $add\,(\alpha,\beta)$, where α and β are single-precision numerals, but their sum requires double precision, the current version of the equation interpreter merely declines to reduce. In order to support multiple-precision arithmetic cleanly and efficiently, the implementation must be modified so that *add* and *multiply* produce results whenever their arguments are single-precision numerals, even if the results require double precision. The double precision results will be represented by use of the *extend* operator in the program above. The only technical problem to be solved in providing this greater support is the syntactic one: what status does the *extend* operator have - need it be declared by the user? This syntactic problem is a special case of a very general need for modular constructs, including facilities to combine sets of equations and to hide certain internally meaningful symbols from the user. Rather than solve the special case, we have postponed this important improvement until the general problem of modularity is solved (see Section 14).

Given an appropriate improvement to the predefined arithmetic operations, arbitrary precision may be provided by the following equational program. *lowdigit* picks off the lowest order digit of an extended-precision numeral, *highdigits* produces all but the lowest order digit.

Symbols

: *Constructors for arbitrary-precision integers.*
   extend: 2;
   include integer_numerals;

: Arithmetic operators.
  add: 2;
  multiply: 2;

: Operators used in defining the arithmetic operators.
  lowdigit: 1;
  highdigits: 1.

For all x, y, z, i, j, k:

  add(extend(x, i), extend(y, j)) = add(extend(add(x, y), 0), add(i, j));

  add(extend(x, i), j) = extend(add(x, highdigits(add(i, j))), lowdigit(add(i, j)))
               where j is in integer_numerals end where;

  add(i, extend(y, j)) = extend(add(y, highdigits(add(i, j))), lowdigit(add(i, j)))
               where i is in integer_numerals end where;

  lowdigit(extend(x, i)) = i;

  highdigits(extend(x, i)) = x;

  multiply(x, extend(y, j)) = add(multiply(x, j), extend(multiply(x, y), 0));

  multiply(extend(x, i), j) = add(multiply(i, j), extend(multiply(x, j), 0))
               where j is in integer_numerals end where;

  include addint, multint.

This improved equational program answers all of the objections to the first one, and is substantially simpler. Notice that, whenever an operation is applied to single-precision arguments, yielding a single-precision result, only the predefined equations for the operation are applied, so there is no additional time overhead for those operations. Negative integers may be handled through a *negate* operator, or by negating *every* digit in the representation of a negative number. The second solution wastes one bit in each digit, but is more compact for single-precision negative numbers, and avoids additional time overhead for operations on single-precision negative numbers.

9.7. Exact Addition of Real Numbers

Another interesting example of programming with infinite lists involves *exact* computations on the *constructive real numbers* [Bi67, Br79, My72]. In principle, a constructive real number is a program enumerating a sequence of rational intervals converging to a real number. Explicit use of these intervals is quite clumsy compared to the more intuitive representation of reals as infinite decimals. Unfortunately, addition is not computable over infinite decimals. Suppose we try to add $0.99 \cdots$ to $1.00 \cdots$. No matter how many digits of the two summands we have seen, we cannot decide for sure whether the sum should be $1. \cdots$ or $2. \cdots$. If the sequence of 9s in the first summand ever drops to a lower digit, then the sum *must* be of the form $1. \cdots$; if the sequence of 0s in the second summand ever rises to a higher digit, then the sum *must* be of the form $2. \cdots$. As long as the 9s and 0s continue, we cannot reliably produce the first digit of the sum. Ironically, in exactly the case where we can *never* decide whether to use $1. \cdots$ or $2. \cdots$, either one would be right, since $1.99 \cdots = 2.00 \cdots$. One aspect of the problem is that conventional infinite decimal notation allows multiple representations of certain numbers, such as $1.99 \cdots = 2.00 \cdots$, but requires a unique representation of others, such as $0.11 \cdots$. The solution is to generalize the notation so that *every* number has multiple representations, by allowing individual digits to be negative as well as positive. This idea was proposed for bit-serial operations on varying-precision real numbers [Av61, At75, OI79].

Let the infinite list of integers $(d_0 \, d_1 \, d_2 \cdots)$, be used to represent the real number $\sum_{i=0}^{\infty} d_i * 10^{-i}$. d_0 is the integer part, and there is an implicit decimal point between d_0 and d_1. In conventional base 10 notation, each d_i for $i \geqslant 1$ would be limited to the range $[0,9]$. Suppose that the range $[-9,+9]$ is used instead ($[-5,+5]$ suffices, in fact, but leads to a clumsier program). As a result, *every* real number has more than one representation. In particular, the intervals corresponding to finite decimals *overlap*, so that every real number is in the interior of arbitrarily small intervals. For a conventional finite decimal a, let $\mathbf{I}_{0,9}(a)$ denote the interval of real numbers having conventional representations beginning with a. Similarly $\mathbf{I}_{-9,9}(a)$ denotes the interval of real numbers having extended representations beginning with a, where a is a finite decimal with digits from -9 to 9.

The problem with the conventional notation is that certain real numbers do not lie in the interiors of any small intervals $\mathbf{I}_{0,9}(a)$, but only on the endpoints. When generating the decimal expansion of a real number x, it is not safe to specify an interval with x at an endpoint, since an arbitrarily small correction to x may take us out of that interval. For example, 1.1 is only an endpoint of the intervals $\mathbf{I}_{0,9}(1.1) = [1.1, 1.2]$, $\mathbf{I}_{0,9}(1.10) = [1.1, 1.11]$, $\mathbf{I}_{0,9}(1.100) = [1, 1.101]$, etc., and the smallest interval $\mathbf{I}_{0,9}(a)$ with 1 in its interior is $\mathbf{I}_{0,9}(1) = [1,2]$. On the other hand, 1.1 is in the interior of each interval $\mathbf{I}_{-9,9}(1.1) = [1, 1.2]$, $\mathbf{I}_{-9,9}(1.10) = [1.09, 1.11]$, $\mathbf{I}_{-9,9}(1.100) = [1.009, 1.101]$, etc., because the larger number of digits stretches these intervals to twice the width of the conventional ones, yielding enough overlaps of intervals to avoid the singularities of the conventional notation.

The notation described above is a *fixed point* notation. Infinite *floating point* decimals may also be defined, allowing d_0 to be restricted to the range $[-9,+9]$ as well. Such an extension of the notation makes the programs for arithmetic operations more complex, but does not introduce any essential new ideas. Conventional computer arithmetic on real numbers truncates the infinite representation of a real to some finite precision. The equation interpreter is capable of handling infinite lists, so, except for the final output, it may manipulate exact real numbers.

In order to program addition of infinite-precision real numbers, as described above, we mimic a program in which the two input numbers are presented to a process called *addlist*, which merely adds corresponding elements in the input lists to produce the output list. Notice that the output from *addlist* represents the real sum of the two inputs, but has digits in the range [−18,+18]. The output from *addlist* goes to a process called *compress*, which restores the list elements to the range −9 to +9. The output from *compress* is the desired result. The function *add* is defined by the composition of *addlist* and *compress*. Notice that, while *addlist* produces one output digit for every input pair, *compress* must see more than one input digit in order to produce a single output digit. Looking at d_i and d_{i+1}, where d_i has already been compressed to the range [−8,+8], *compress* adjusts d_{i+1} into the range [−8,+8] by adding or subtracting 10, if necessary, and compensating by adjusting d_i by ±1. Notice that it is important to first place a digit in [−8,+8], so that it may be used in the adjustment of the next digit and stay in [−9,+9].

In order to use the addition procedure, we need to provide some interesting definitions of infinite-precision real numbers, and also a function called *standard* to produce the output in conventional base-10 with finite precision. *standard* takes two arguments: a single integer i, and an infinite-precision real r. The result is the standard base-10 representation of r to i significant digits. Notice that *standard* may require $i+1$ digits of input in order to produce the first digit of output.

Symbols

: *List constructors*
  cons: 2;
  nil: 0;

: *List manipulation operators*
  first: 1;
  tail: 1;

: *Real arithmetic operator*
  add: 2;

: *Other operators needed in the definitions*
  addlist: 2;
  compress: 1;
  stneg, stpos: 3;
  revneg, revpos: 2;
  rotate: 1;

: *Input and output operators*
  repeat: 2;
  standard: 2;

: *Standard arithmetic and logical operators and symbols.*
  if: 3;
  equ, less, greater: 2;
  include integer_numerals, truth_values.

For all x, y, i, j, k, l, a, b:

: *add is extended to infinite-precision real numbers.*

   add[(i . x); (j . y)] = compress[addlist[(i . x); (j . y)]];

: *addlist adds corresponding elements of infinite lists.*

   addlist[(i . x); (j . y)] = (add[i; j] . addlist[x; y]);

: *compress normalizes an infinite list of digits in the range [-18, +18]*
: *into the range [-9, +9].*

   compress[(i j . x)] =
        if[less[j; -8]; (subtract[i; 1] . compress[(add[j; 10] . x)]);
        if[greater[j; 8]; (add[i; 1] . compress[(subtract[j; 10] . x)]);
          (i . compress[(j . x)])]];

: *repeat[x; y] is the infinite extension of the decimal expansion x*
: *by repeating the finite sequence y.*

   repeat[(i . x); y] = (i . repeat[x; y]);

   repeat[(); y] = (first[y] . repeat[(); rotate[y]]);

: *rotate[y] rotates the first element of the list y to the end.*

   rotate[(i)] = (i);

   rotate[(i j . x)] = (j . rotate[(i . x)]);

: *standard[i; a] is the normal base 10 expansion of the first i digits of a.*

   standard[j; (i . a)] = if[equ[j; 0]; ();
                 if[equ[i; 0]; (0 . standard[subtract[j; 1]; a]);
                 if[less[i; 0]; stneg[j; (i . a); ()];
                   stpos[j; (i . a); ()]]]];

: *stneg[i; a; b] translates the first i digits of a into normal base 10 notation,*
:   *backwards, and appends b, assuming that a is part of a negative number.*
: *stpos[i; a; b] does the same thing for positive numbers.*

   stneg[j; (i . a); b] = if[equ[j; 0];
              revneg[b; ()];
              stneg[subtract[j; 1]; a; (i . b)]];

   stpos[j; (i . a); b] = if[equ[j; 0];
              revpos[b; ()];
              stpos[subtract[j; 1]; a; (i . b)]];

: *revneg[a; b] reverses the finite decimal expansion a, borrowing and carrying so as*
:   *to make each digit nonpositive, finally appending the list b.*
: *revpos[a; b] does the same, making each digit nonnegative.*

   revneg[(); b] = b;

   revneg[(i . a); b] = if[less[i; 1];
              revneg[a; (i . b)];
              revneg[(add[first[a]; 1] . tail[a]);
                (add[i; -10] . b)]];

   revpos[(); b] = b;

revpos[(i . a); b] = if[less[i; 0];
                     revpos[(add[first[a]; -1] . tail[a]);
                          (add[i; 10] . b)];
                     revpos[a; (i . b)]];

: first, tail, if, add, subtract, equ, less, are standard list,
: conditional, and arithmetic operators.

first[(i . a)] = i; tail[(i . a)] = a;

if[true; x; y] = x;   if[false; x; y] = y;

greater[i; j] = less[subtract[0; i]; subtract[0; j]]
     where i, j are in integer_numerals end where;

include addint, subint, equint, lessint.

In this example, producing output in standard form was much more difficult than performing the addition. Other arithmetic operations, however, such as multiplication, are much more difficult to program.

9.8. Polynomial Addition

Polynomial addition is a commonplace program in LISP, with polynomials represented by lists of coefficients. The equation interpreter allows polynomial sums to be computed in the same notation that we normally use to write polynomials, with no distinction between the operator *add* that applies to integer numerals, the operator *add* that applies to polynomials, and the operator *add* used to construct polynomials. In LISP, the first would be *PLUS*, the second a user defined function, perhaps called *POLYPLUS* and the third would be encoded by a particular use of *cons*.

In effect, the equational programs shown below for "adding polynomials" are really just simplifying polynomial expressions into a natural canonical form. The *Horner—rule form* for a polynomial of degree n in the variable X is

$c_0 + X*(c_1 + X* \cdots + X*c_n \cdots)$. The list $(c_0 \, c_1 \cdots c_n)$, typically used to represent the same polynomial in LISP, is a very simple encoding of the Horner-rule form. In the equation interpreter, we may use the Horner-rule form literally. The resulting program simplifies terms of the form $\pi_1 + \pi_2$, where each of π_1 and π_2 is in Horner-rule form, to an equivalent Horner-rule form. Notice that the symbol *add* in the following programs may be an *active* symbol or a static constructor for polynomials, depending on context. Also, notice that the variable X over which the polynomials are expressed is *not* a variable with respect to the equational program, but an atomic_symbol.

Symbols

> add: 2;
> multiply: 2;
> include integer_numerals, atomic_symbols.

For all i, j, a, b:

> add(add(i, multiply(X, a)), add(j, multiply(X, b))) =
>   add(add(i, j), multiply(X, add(a, b)))
>   where i, j are in integer_numerals end where;
>
> add(i, add(j, multiply(X, b))) =
>   add(add(i, j), multiply(X, b))
>   where i, j are in integer_numerals end where;
>
> add(add(i, multiply(X, a)), j) =
>   add(add(i, j), multiply(X, a))
>   where i, j are in integer_numerals end where;

> *include addint.*

The program above is satisfyingly intuitive, but does not remove high-order 0 coefficients. Thus, $(1 + X*(2 + X*3)) + (1 + X*(2 + X*-3))$ reduces to $2 + X*(4 + X*0)$ instead of the more helpful $2 + X*4$. Getting rid of the high-order zeroes is tricky, since the natural equations $X*0 = 0$ and $a + 0 = a$ suffer from overlaps with the other equations. One solution, show below, is to check for zeroes *before* construct-

ing a Horner-rule form, rather than eliminating them afterwards.

Symbols

> add: 2;
> multiply: 2;
>
> if: 3;
> equ: 2;
> and: 2;
> include integer_numerals, atomic_symbols, truth_values.

For all i, j, a, b, c, d:

> add(add(i, a), add(j, b)) = add(add(i, j), add(a, b))
>   where i, j are in integer_numerals,
>   a, b are multiply(c, d)
>   end where;
>
> add(i, add(j, b)) = add(add(i, j), b)
>   where i, j are in integer_numerals,
>   b is multiply(c, d)
>   end where;
>
> add(add(i, a), j) = add(add(i, j), a)
>   where i, j are in integer_numerals,
>   a is multiply(c, d)
>   end where;
>
> add(multiply(X, a), multiply(X, b)) =
>   if(equ(add(a,b), 0), 0, multiply(X, add(a, b)));
>
> equ(add(i, multiply(X, a)), add(j, multiply(X, b))) =
>   and(equ(i, j), equ(a, b))
>   where i, j are in integer_numerals end where;
>
> equ(i, add(j, multiply(X, b))) = false
>   where i, j are in integer_numerals end where;
>
> equ(add(i, multiply(X, a)), j) = false
>   where i, j are in integer_numerals end where;
>
> if(true, a, b) = a; if(false, a, b) = b;
>
> and(a, b) = if(a, b, false);
>
> include addint, equint.

It is amusing to consider other natural forms of polynomials, such as the *power−series* form, $c_0*X^0+c_1*X^1+\cdots+c_n$. This corresponds to the representation of polynomials as lists of exponent-coefficient pairs. For dense polynomials, the exponents waste space, but for sparse polynomials the omission of internal zeroes may make up for the inclusion of exponents, as in $1+X^{100}$. A nice equational programming challenge is to produce an elegant program for addition of polynomials in power-series form.

9.9. The Combinator Calculus

Weak reduction in the combinator calculus [CF58, St72] is a natural sort of computation to describe with equations. The following equations use the *Lambda* syntax of Section 4.3 to allow the abbreviation

$$(a_1\ a_2\ \cdots\ a_n)$$

for the expression

$$AP(AP(\ \cdots\ AP(a_1, a_2),\ \cdots\ ), a_n)$$

The symbol *Lambda* from Section 4.3 is not used in the combinator calculus.
Symbols
  AP: 2;
  S, K, I: 0;
  include atomic_symbols.
For all x, y, z:
  (S x y z) = (x z (y z));
  (K x y) = x;

(I x) = *x*.

This example, and the polynomial addition of Section 9.8, differ from the first ones in that the only symbol that can construct complex expressions, *AP*, appears (implicitly) at the head of left-hand sides of equations. In many interesting systems of terms, there are one or more symbols that do not appear at the heads of left-hand sides, so that they may be used to construct structures that are stable with respect to reduction. These stable structures may be analyzed and rearranged by other operators. For example, in LISP, the symbol *cons* is a constructor, and an expression made up only of *cons* and atomic symbols (i.e., an S-expression), is always in normal form. It is helpful to notice the existence of constructors when they occur, but the example above illustrates the usefulness of allowing systems without constructors. The use of constructors is discussed further in Section 12.1.

9.10. Beta Reduction in the Lambda Calculus

This example should only be read by a user with previous knowledge of the lambda calculus. The reader needs to read de Bruijn's article [deB72] in order to understand the treatment of variables. The object is to reduce an arbitrary lambda term to normal form by a sequence of β-reductions. A number of rather tricky problems are encountered, but some of the usual problems encountered by other implementations of β-reduction are avoided by use of the equation interpreter. This example uses the Lambda notation of Section 4.3.

The lambda calculus of Church [Ch41] presents several sticky problems for the design of an evaluator. First, the problem of capture of bound variables appears to require the use of the α-rule

$$\backslash x.E \;\rightarrow\; \backslash y.E[y/x]$$

to change bound variables. There is no simple way to generate the new variables needed for application of the α-rule in an equational program.   In more conventional languages, variable generation is simple, but its presence clutters up the program, and causes the outputs to be hard to read.

De Bruijn [deB72] gives a notation for lambda terms in which an occurrence of a bound variable is represented by the number of lambda bindings appearing between it and its binding occurrence. This notation allows a simple and elegant solution of the technical problem of capture, but provides an even less readable output. We represent each bound variable by a term $var[x,i]$, where x is the name of the variable and i is the de Bruijn number. The first set of equations below translates a lambda term in traditional notation into this modified de Bruijn notation. De Bruijn notation normally omits the name of the bound variable immediately after an occurrence of lambda, but we retain the name of the variable for readability. We write the de Bruijn form of a lambda binding as $\backslash\!:\!x.E$ (the x appears directly as an argument to the lambda) to distinguish from the traditional notation $\backslash x.E$ (in which the first argument to lambda is the singleton list containing x).

Symbols

: Operators constructing lambda expressions
  Lambda: 2;
  AP: 2;

: Constructors for lists
  cons: 2;
  nil: 0;

: var[x, i] represents the variable with de Bruijn number i, named x.
  var: 2;

: *bindvar carries binding instances of variables to the corresponding bound*
: *instances, computing de Bruijn numbers on the way.*
  bindvar: 3;

: *Arithmetical and logical operators and symbols*
  if: 3;
  equ: 2;
  add: 2;
  include atomic_symbols, truth_values, integer_numerals.

For all x, y, E, F, i, j:

: *Multiple-argument lambda bindings are broken into sequences of lambdas.*

  $\backslash x$ *y:rem.E* $=$ $\backslash x.\backslash y:rem.E;$

: *Single-argument lambda bindings are encoded in de Bruijn notation.*

  $\backslash x.E$ $=$ $\backslash :x.bindvar[E, x, 0];$

: *bindvar[E, x, i] attaches de Bruijn numbers to all free instances of the variable*
:   *x in the lambda-term E, assuming that E is embedded in exactly i*
:   *lambda bindings within the binding instance of x.*

  bindvar[x, y, i] $=$ *if[equ[x, y], var[x, i], x]*
               where x is in atomic_symbols end where;

  bindvar[var[x, j], y, i] $=$ *var[x, j];*

  bindvar[(E F), y, i] $=$ *(bindvar[E, y, i] bindvar[F, y, i]);*

  bindvar[$\backslash$:x.E, y, i] $=$ $\backslash :x.bindvar[E, y, add[i, 1]]$
              where x is in atomic_symbols end where;

: *if is the standard conditional function, equ the standard equality test, and add*
: *the standard addition operator on integers.*

  if[true, E, F] $=$ *E; if[false, E, F]* $=$ *F;*

  include equatom, addint, equint.

In order to perform evaluation of a lambda term in de Bruijn notation, the transformation described above must be done logically prior to the actual β-

reduction steps. In principle, equations for de Bruijn notation and β-reduction could be combined into one specification, but it seems to be rather difficult to avoid overlapping left-hand sides in such a combined specification (see Section 5, restriction 4). At any rate, it makes logical sense to think of the transformation to de Bruijn notation as a syntactic preprocessing step, rather than part of the semantics of β-reduction. Therefore, we built a custom syntactic preprocessor for the β-reduction equations. After executing

loadsyntax Lambda

int.in (the syntactic preprocessor for the command *ei*) is the shell script:

#! /bin/sh

SYSTEM/Syntax/Outersynt/Lambda/int.in SYSTEM |

SYSTEM/Syntax/Common/int.in.trans SYSTEM |

SYSTEM/Syntax/Common/int.in.fin SYSTEM ;

where *SYSTEM* is the directory containing equational interpreter system libraries, differing in different installations. we edited *int.in* to look like

#! /bin/sh

SYSTEM/Syntax/Outersynt/Lambda/int.in SYSTEM |

SYSTEM/Syntax/Common/int.in.trans SYSTEM |

SYSTEM/Syntax/Common/int.in.fin SYSTEM |

DEBRUIJN/interpreter;

where *DEBRUIJN* is the directory in which we constructed the transformation to de Bruijn notation. We did not change *pre.in* (the syntactic preprocessor for *ep*) or *int.out* (the pretty-printer for *ei*).

Even with the elegant de Bruijn notation, two technical problems remain. First, the official definition of β-reduction:

$$(\backslash x.E \ F) \ \rightarrow E[F/x]$$

cannot be written as a single equation, since the equation interpreter has no notation for syntactic substitution (see [Kl80a] for a theoretical discussion of term rewriting systems with substitution). The obvious solution to this problem is to introduce a symbol for substitution, and define its operation recursively with equations. A nice version of this solution is given by Staples [St79], along with a proof that leftmost-outermost evaluation is optimal for his rules. For notational economy, we take advantage of the fact that the lambda term $\backslash x.E$ may be used to represent syntactic substitution, so that no explicit symbol for substitution is required. Combining this observation with Staples' rules, we produced the following recursive version of β-reduction:

$$(\backslash x.x \ G) \ \rightarrow G$$

$$(\backslash x.y \ G) \ \rightarrow y \ \textit{where x and y are different variables}$$

$$(\backslash x. (E \ F) \ G) \ \rightarrow ((\backslash x.E \ G) \ (\backslash x.F \ G))$$

$$(\backslash x.\backslash y.E \ G) \ \rightarrow (\backslash y. (\backslash x.E \ G))$$

These rules may be translated straightforwardly into the de Bruijn notation, and written as equations, using a conditional function and equality test to combine the first two rules into one equation. In the de Bruijn form, occurrences of lambda must be annotated with integers indicating how many other instances of lambda have been passed in applications of the fourth rule above. Otherwise, there would be no way to recognize the identity of the two instances of the same variable in the first rule. Initially and finally, all of these integer labels on lambdas will be 0, only in intermediate steps of substitution will they acquire higher values.

Unfortunately, the left-hand side of the third rule overlaps itself, violating restriction 4 of Section 5. To avoid this overlap, we introduce a second application operator, *IAP*, to distinguish applications that are not the heads of rules. The third rule above is restricted to the case where E is applied to F by *IAP*. Since $\x.(E\ F)$ is applied to G by the usual application operator, *AP*, there is no overlap. Interestingly, Staples introduced essentially the same restriction in a different notation because, without the restriction, leftmost-outermost reduction is not optimal. This technique for avoiding overlap is discussed in Section 12.4. [OS84] develops these ideas for evaluating lambda-terms more thoroughly, but not in the notation of the equation interpreter. All of the observations above lead to the following equations.

Symbols

: Constructors for lists
  cons: 2;
  nil: 0;

: Constructors for lambda-terms
: IAP represents an application that is known to be inert (cannot become the head
: of a redex as the result of reductions in the subtree below).
  Lambda: 2;
  AP: 2;
  IAP: 2;
  var: 2;

  incvars: 2;

: Arithmetical and logical operators
  if: 3;

add: 2;
equ: 2;
less: 2;
include atomic_symbols, truth_values, integer_numerals.

For all x, y, z, E, F, G, i, j:

: Detect inert applications and mark them with IAP.

> *(x E) = IAP[x, E] where x is either*
> > *var[y, i]*
> > *or IAP[F, G]*
> > *or in atomic_symbols*
> > *end or*
> *end where;*

: \x:i.E represents a lambda expression that has passed by i other instances of
:   lambda. It is necessary to count such passings in order to recognize instances
:   of the bound variable corresponding to the x above. Only active instances of
:   lambda, that is, ones that are actually applied to something, are given an
:   integer tag of this sort.

> *(\:x.E F) = (\x:0.E F)*
> > *where x is in atomic_symbols end where;*

> *(\y:i.var[x, j] E) = if[equ[i, j], E,*
> > *if[less[i, j], var[x, add[j, -1]],*
> > > *var[x, j]]]*
> > *where i is in integer_numerals end where;*

> *(\y:i.x E) = x where x is in atomic_symbols,*
> > *i is in integer_numerals*
> > *end where;*

> *(\y:i.IAP[E, F] G) = ((\y:i.E G) (\y:i.F G))*
> > *where i is in integer_numerals end where;*

> *(\y:i.\:z.E F) = (\:z.(\y:add[i, 1].E F))*
> > *where i is in integer_numerals end where;*

incvars[var[x, i], j] = if[less[i, j], var[x, i], var[x, add[i, 1]]];

incvars[x, i] = x where x is either in atomic_symbols
> > > *or in integer_numerals*
> > > *or in truth_values*
> > > *or in character_strings*
> > *end or*
> *end where;*

incvars[IAP[E, F], i] = IAP[incvars[E, i], incvars[F, i]];

incvars[\x:t.E, i] = \x:incvars[t, i]. incvars[E, add[i, 1]];

if[true, x, y] = x; if[false, x, y] = y;

include equint, addint, lessint.

Certain other approaches to the lambda calculus, such as the evaluation strategy in LISP, avoid some of the notational problems associated with overlapping left-hand sides by using an evaluation operator. Essentially, such techniques reduce *eval*[E] to the normal form of E, rather than reducing E itself. Such a solution could be programmed with equations, but it introduces two more problems, both of which exist in standard implementations of LISP. Notice that the outermost evaluation strategy used by the equation interpreter exempted us from worrying about cases, such as $(\x.y (\x. (xx)\x. (xx)))$, which have a normal form, but also an infinite sequence of reductions. Implementations of the lambda calculus using an evaluation operator must explicitly program leftmost-outermost evaluation, else they will compute infinitely on such examples without producing the normal form. Also, in terms, such as $\x. (\y.yz)$, whose normal forms contain lambdas (in this case, the normal form is $\x.z$), it is very easy to neglect to evaluate the body of the unreduced lambda binding. Using rules that reduce lambda terms directly puts the onus on the equation interpreter to make sure that these rules are applied wherever possible.

9.11. Lucid

Lucid is a programming language designed by Ashcroft and Wadge [AW76, AW77] to mimic procedural computation with nonprocedural semantics. Early attempts to construct interpreters [Ca76] and compilers [Ho78] encountered serious difficulties. The following set of equations, adapted from [HO82b], produce a Lucid interpreter directly, using the *Standmath* syntax of Section 4.1. A trivial Lucid program, itself consisting of equations, is appended to the end of the equations that define Lucid. Evaluation of the expression *output* () produces the result of running the Lucid program. Even though convenience and performance considerations require the eventual production of a hand-crafted Lucid interpreter, such as the one in [Ca76], the ability to define and experiment with the Lucid language in the simple and relatively transparent form below would certainly have been helpful in the early stages of Lucid development.

: Equations for the programming language Lucid, plus a Lucid
: program generating a list of integers.

Symbols

: Lucid symbols
  NOT: 1;
  OR: 2;
  add: 2;
  equ: 2;
  if: 3;

  first: 1;
  next: 1;
  asa: 2;
  latest: 1;
  latestinv: 1;
  fby: 2;

  include integer_numerals, truth_values;
: symbols in the Lucid program
  intlist: 0;
  output: 0.

For all W, X, Y, Z:

: Definitions of the Lucid operators

NOT(true) = *false;*

NOT(false) = *true;*

NOT(fby(W, X)) = *fby(NOT(first(W)), NOT(X));*

NOT(latest(X)) = *latest(NOT(X));*

OR(true, X) = *true;*

OR(false, X) = *X;*

OR(fby(W, X), fby(Y, Z)) =
  fby(OR(first(W), first(Y)), OR(X, Z));

OR(fby(W, X), latest(Y)) =
  fby(OR(first(W), latest(Y)), OR(X, latest(Y)));

OR(latest(X), fby(Y, Z)) =
  fby(OR(latest(X), first(Y)), OR(latest(X), Z));

OR(fby(W, X), false) = *fby(W, X);*

OR(latest(X), latest(Y)) = *latest(OR(X, Y));*

OR(latest(X), false) = *latest(X);*

if(true, Y, Z) = *Y;*

if(false, Y, Z) = *Z;*

if(fby(W, X), Y, Z) = *fby(if(first(W), Y, Z), if(X, Y, Z));*

if(latest(X), Y, Z) = *latest(if(X, Y, Z));*

first(X) = *X*
  where X is either in truth_values
                        or in integer_numerals
          end or
  end where;

first(fby(X, Y)) = *first(X);*

first(latest(X)) = *latest(X);*

next(X) = *X*

where X is either in truth_values
             or in integer_numerals
          end or
     end where;

$next(fby(X, Y)) = Y;$

$next(latest(X)) = latest(X);$

$asa(X, Y) = if(first(Y), first(X), asa(next(X), next(Y)));$

$latestinv(X) = X$
     where X is either in truth_values
                or in integer_numerals
             end or
     end where;

$latestinv(fby(X, Y)) = latestinv(X);$

$latestinv(latest(X)) = X;$

$add(fby(W, X), fby(Y, Z)) =$
     $fby(add(first(W), first(Y)), add(X, Z));$

$add(fby(W, X), latest(Y)) =$
     $fby(add(first(W), latest(Y)), add(X, latest(Y)));$

$add(latest(X), fby(Y, Z)) =$
     $fby(add(latest(X), first(Y)), add(latest(X), Z));$

$add(fby(W, X), Y) =$
     $fby(add(first(W), Y), add(X, Y))$
     where Y is in integer_numerals end where;

$add(X, fby(Y, Z)) =$
     $fby(add(X, first(Y)), add(X, Z))$
     where X is in integer_numerals end where;

$add(latest(X), latest(Y)) = latest(add(X, Y));$

$add(latest(X), Y) = latest(add(X, Y))$
     where Y is in integer_numerals end where;

add(X, latest(Y)) = latest(add(X, Y))
  where X is in integer_numerals end where;

equ(fby(W, X), fby(Y, Z)) =
  fby(equ(first(W), first(Y)), equ(X, Z));

equ(fby(W, X), latest(Y)) =
  fby(equ(first(W), latest(Y)), equ(X, latest(Y)));

equ(latest(X), fby(Y, Z)) =
  fby(equ(latest(X), first(Y)), equ(latest(X), Z));

equ(fby(W, X), Y) =
  fby(equ(first(W), Y), equ(X, Y))
  where Y is in integer_numerals end where;

equ(X, fby(Y, Z)) =
  fby(equ(X, first(Y)), equ(X, Z))
  where X is in integer_numerals end where;

equ(latest(X), latest(Y)) = latest(equ(X, Y));

equ(latest(X), Y) = latest(equ(X, Y))
  where Y is in integer_numerals end where;

equ(X, latest(Y)) = latest(equ(X, Y))
  where X is in integer_numerals end where;

include addint, equint;

: A trivial Lucid program

intlist() = fby(0, add(intlist(), 1));

output() = fby(first(intlist()),
            fby(first(next(intlist())),
              first(next(next(intlist()))))).

The equational program given above differs from other Lucid interpreters in one significant way, and two superficial ways. First and most significant, the *OR* operator defined above is not as powerful as the *OR* operator in Lucid, because it fails to satisfy the equation *OR* (*X*,*true*)=*true*, when *X* cannot be evaluated to a truth value. The weakening of the *OR* operator is required by restrictions 3 and 5 of Section 5. These restrictions will be relaxed in later versions of the equation interpreter, allowing a full implementation of the Lucid *OR*. Second, the variable *INPUT*, which in Lucid is implicitly defined to be the sequence of values in the input file of the Lucid program when it runs, is not definable until run time, so it cannot be given in the equations above. In order to mimic the input behavior of Lucid, the equation interpreter would have to be used with a syntactic preprocessor to embed given inputs within the term to be evaluated. Interactive input would require an interactive interface to the equation interpreter. Such an interactive interface does not exist in the current version, but is a likely addition in later versions (see Section 15.3). Finally, of the many primitive arithmetic and logical operations of Lucid, only *add*, *equ*, *OR*, and *if* have been given above. To include other such operations requires duplicating the equations distributing primitive operations over *fby* and *latest*. With a large set of primitives, these equations would become unacceptably unwieldy. A truly satisfying equational implementation of Lucid would have to encode primitive operations as nullary symbols, and use an application operator similar to the one in the *Curry* inner syntax of Section 4.4 in order to give only one set of distributive equations.

10. Errors, Failures, and Diagnostic Aids

In the interest of truth in software advertising, exceptional cases in the equation interpreter are divided into two classes: *errors* and *failures*. *Errors* are definite mistakes on the part of the user resulting from violations of reasonable and conceptually necessary constraints on processing. *Failures* are the fault of the interpreter itself, and include exhaustion of resources and exceeding of arbitrary limits. Each message on an exceptional case is produced on the UNIX standard error file, begins with the appropriate word *"Error"* or *"Failure"*, and ends with an identifying message number, intended to help in maintenance. An attempt is made to explain the error or failure so that the user may correct or avoid it. The eventual goal of the project is that the only type of failure occurring in the reduction of a term to normal form will be exhaustion of the total space resources. Currently, the interpreter will fail when presented with individual input symbols that are too long, but it will not fail due to overflow of a value during reduction. There are also some possible failures in the syntactic preprocessing and output pretty-printing steps that result in messages from *yacc* (the UNIX parser generator) rather than from the equational interpreter system. These failures apparently are all the result of overflow of some allocated space, particularly the *yacc* parsing stack. Occasionally, running of a large problem, or of too many problems simultaneously, will cause an overflow of some UNIX limits, such as the limit on the number of processes that may run concurrently.

Because of the layered modular design of the interpreter, different sorts of errors may be reported at different levels of processing, and, regrettably, in slightly different forms. For the preprocessor (*ep*), the important levels are 1) context-free syntactic analysis, 2) context-sensitive syntactic analysis, and 3) semantic processing. For the interpreter (*ei*), only levels 1 and 3 are relevant. Sections 10.1 through 10.3 describe the sorts of messages produced at each of these levels.

10.1. Context-Free Syntactic Errors and Failures

Context-free syntactic errors in preprocessor input may involve the general syntax of definitions, described in Section 3, or one of the specific syntaxes for terms described in Section 4. Context-free errors in interpreter input may only involve a specific term syntax. Error messages relating to a specific term syntax always include the name of the syntax being used. Error detection is based on the parsing strategy used by *yacc* [Jo78]. Each error message includes a statement of the syntactic restriction most likely to cause that sort of parsing failure. The parser makes no attempt to recover from an error, so only the first syntactic error is likely to be reported. It is possible that an error in a term will be detected as an error in the general syntax of definitions, and vice versa. Error messages are particularly opaque when the wrong syntactic preprocessor was loaded by the last invocation of loadsyntax, so the user should always pay attention to the name of the syntax in use. *Yacc* failures are possible in the syntactic preprocessing, either from parser stack overflow, or from an individual symbol being too long.

10.2. Context-Sensitive Syntactic Errors and Failures

Context-sensitive errors are only relevant to preprocessor input. They all involve inconsistent use of symbols. The three types of misuse are: 1) repeated declaration of the same symbol; 2) use of a declared symbol with the wrong arity; 3) attempt to include a class of symbols or equations that does not exist; 4) repetition of a variable symbol on the left-hand side of an equation; 5) appearance of a variable on the right-hand side of an equation that does not appear on the left.

Context-sensitive syntactic preprocessing may fail due to exhaustion of space resources, or to an individual symbol being too long for the current version. The second sort of failure will be avoided in later versions. In order to produce a lexicon presenting all of the symbols used in an equational program, see Section 10.4 below.

10.3. Semantic Errors and Failures

The only semantic failure in the interpreter is exhaustion of total space resource. Other semantic errors and failures are only relevant to preprocessor input. The simplest such error is use of a symbol from one of the classes *integer_numerals*, *atomic_symbols*, *truth_values*, or *characters*, without a declaration of that class. In future versions, these errors will be classified as context-sensitive syntactic errors. The more interesting errors are violations of restrictions 3, 4, and 5 from Section 5. Violations of these restrictions always involve nontrivial overlayings of parts of left-hand sides of equations. In addition to describing which restriction was violated, and naming the violating equations, the preprocessor tries to report the location of the overlap by naming the critical symbol involved. This is probably the weakest part of the error reporting, and future versions will try to provide more graphic reports for semantic errors. Notice that restriction 5 (left-sequentiality) will be removed in later versions. To specify the offending equations, the preprocessor numbers all equations, including predefined classes (counting 1 for each class), and reports equations by number. In order to be sure of the numbering used by the preprocessor, and in order to get a more graphic view of the terms in the tree representation used by the preprocessor, the user should see Section 10.5 below.

10.4. Producing a Lexicon to Detect Inappropriate Uses of Symbols (*el*)

After executing

>   *ep Equnsdir*

the user may produce a lexicon listing in separate categories

1)   all declared literal symbols

2)   all declared literal symbols not appearing in equations

3)   all atomic symbols appearing in equations

4)   all characters appearing in equations

5)   all truth values appearing in equations.

Empty categories are omitted, and symbols within a category are given in alphabetical order. A lexicon is produced on the standard output by typing

>   *el Equnsdir*

el stands for equational lexicon. The lexicon is intended to be used to discover accidental misspellings and omissions that may cause a symbol to belong to a category other than the one intended. Each lexicon is headed by the date and time of the last invocation of *ep*. Changes to definitions after the given date and time will not be reflected in the lexicon.

10.5. Producing a Graphic Display of Equations In Tree Form (*es*)

In order to understand the semantic errors described in Section 10.3, it is useful to see a set of equations in the same form that the preprocessor sees. Not only is this internal form tree-structured, rather than linear, but there may be literal symbols appearing in the internal form that are only implicit in the given definitions, such as the symbol *cons*, which appears implicitly in the *LISP.M* expression (*a b c*).

The user may also use the tree-structured form of the terms in his equations to verify that the matching of parentheses and brackets in his definitions agrees with his original intent. To generate a tree-structured display of equations on the standard output, type

> *es Equnsdir*

es stands for equation show. Unfortunately, the more mnemonic abbreviations are already used for other commands. *es* may only be used after running *ep* on the same directory. The output from *es* lists the equations in the order given by the user, with the sequential numbers used in error and failure reports from the preprocessor. Each term in an equation is displayed by listing the symbols in the term in preorder, and using indentation to indicate the tree structure. Variables on the left-hand sides of equations are replaced by descriptions of their ranges, in pointed brackets ($<>$), and variables on the right-hand sides are replaced by the addresses of the corresponding variables on the left-hand sides. Representations of predefined classes of equations are displayed, as well as equations given explicitly by the user. For example, the following definitions

Symbols

> *f, g: 2;*
> *h: 1;*
>
> *include atomic_symbols.*

For all x, y, z:

> *f(g(x, y), a) = h(y) where x is in atomic_symbols end where;*
> *include equatom.*

produce the listing:

Listing of equational definitions processed on Apr 19 at 15:43

1:
  f
    g
      <atomic_symbol>
      <anything>
    a
  =
  h
    variable 1 2

2:
  equ
    <atomic_symbol>
    <atomic_symbol>
  =
  e
    variable 1
    variable 2

Notice that, on the left-hand side of equation 1, the variable x is replaced by *<atomic_symbol>*, and the variable y is replaced by *<anything>*, representing the fact that any term may be substituted for y. On the right-hand side, y is replaced by

    variable 1 2

indicating that the corresponding y on the left-hand side is the 2nd son of the 1st son of the root of the term. The date and time at the top refer to the time of invocation of *ep*. The user should check that this time agrees with his memory. Changes to definitions after the given date and time are not reflected in the display.

10.6. Trace Output (*et*)

A primitive form of trace output is available, which displays for each reduction step the starting term, the redex, the number of the equational rule applied, and the reductum. In order to produce trace output, invoke the equation interpreter with the option *t* as

   ei Equnsdir t <input

where *Equnsdir* is the directory containing the equational definitions, and *input* is a file containing the term to be reduced. Since *ei* uses purely positional notation for its parameters, *Equnsdir* may not be omitted. The invocation of *ei* above produces a file *Equnsdir/trace.inter* containing a complete trace of the reduction of the input term to normal form. To view the trace output on the screen, type

   et Equnsdir

(*Equnsdir* defaults to *.*). *et* stands for equational trace. The trace listing is headed by the date and time of the invocation of *ei* resulting in that trace.   The user should check that the given time agrees with his memory.

10.7. Miscellaneous Restrictions

Literal symbols are limited to arities no greater than 10, and all symbols are limited to lengths no greater than 20 in the current version.

11. History of the Equation Interpreter Project

The theoretical foundations of the project come from the dissertation "Reduction Strategies in Subtree Replacement Systems," presented by Michael O'Donnell at Cornell University in 1976. The same material is available in the monograph *Computing in Systems Described by Equations* [O'D77]. There, the fundamental restrictions 1-4 on the left-hand sides of equations in Section 5 were presented, and shown to be sufficient for guaranteeing uniqueness of normal forms. In addition, outermost reduction strategies were shown to terminate whenever possible, and conditions were given for the sufficiency of leftmost-outermost reductions. A proof of optimality for a class of reduction strategies was claimed there, but shown incorrect by Berry and Lévy [BL79, O'D79]. Huet and Lévy later gave a correct treatment of essentially the same optimality issue [HL79].

In the theoretical monograph cited above, O'Donnell asserted that "a good programmer should be able to design efficient implementations of the abstract computations" described and studied in the monograph. In 1978, Christoph Hoffmann and O'Donnell decided to demonstrate that such an implementation is feasible and valuable. The original intent was to use the equations for formal specifications of interpreters for a nonprocedural programming languages. For example, the equations that McCarthy gave to define LISP [McC60] could be given, and the equation processor should automatically produce a LISP interpreter exactly faithful to those specifications. Preliminary experience indicated that such applications were severely handicapped in performance. On the other hand, when essentially the same computation was defined directly by a set of equations, the equation interpreter was reasonably competitive with conventional LISP. So, the emphasis of the project changed from interpreter generation to programming directly with equations.

From early experience, the project goal became the production of a usable interpreter of equations with very strict adherence to the semantics given in Section 1, and performance reasonably competitive with conventional LISP interpreters. The specification of such an interpreter was given in [HO82b], and the key implementation problems were discussed there. Since the natural way of defining a single function might involve a large number of equations, the second goal requires that the interpreter have little or no runtime penalty for the number of equations given. Thus, sequential checking for applicability of the first equation, then the second, etc. was ruled out, and pattern matching in trees was identified as the key algorithmic problem for the project. The overhead of pattern matching appears to be the aspect of the interpreter that must compete with the rather slight overhead of maintaining the recursion stack in LISP. Some promising algorithms for tree pattern matching were developed in [HO82a].

In 1979 Giovanni Sacco, a graduate student, produced the first experimentally usable version of the interpreter in CDC Pascal, and introduced some table-compression techniques which, without affecting the theoretical worst case for pattern matching, improved performance substantially on example problems. Hoffmann ported Sacco's implementation to the Siemens computer at the University of Kiel, Germany in 1980. Hoffmann and O'Donnell used Sacco's implementation for informal experiments with LISP, the Combinator Calculus, and the Lambda Calculus. These experiments led to the decision to emphasize programming with equations over interpreter generation. These experiments also demonstrated the inadequacy of any single notation for all problems, and motivated the library of syntaxes provided by the current version. Another graduate student,

Paul Golick, transferred the implementation to UNIX on the VAX, and rewrote the run-time portion of the interpreter (*ei* in the current version) in 1980. During 1982 and Spring of 1983, O'Donnell took over the implementation effort and produced the current version of the system. The final year of work involved informal experiments with three different pattern matching techniques, and reconfiguration of the implementation to allow easy substitution of different concrete syntaxes.

Experience with the interpreter comes from the interpreter implementation itself, from two projects done in the advanced compiler course at Purdue University, and form a course in Logic Programming at the Johns Hopkins University. O'Donnell used the equation interpreter to define the non-context-free syntactic analysis for itself, gaining useful informal experience in the applicability of the interpreter to syntactic problems. In 1982, Hoffmann supervised a class project which installed another experimental pattern-matching algorithm in the interpreter, and used the equation interpreter to define a Pascal interpreter. In 1983, Hoffmann supervised another class project using the equation interpreter to define type checking in a Pascal compiler. These two projects generated more information on the suitability of various pattern-matching algorithms, and on the applicability of equations to programming language problems. In 1983, O'Donnell assigned students in a Logic Programming course to a number of smaller projects in equational programming. One of these projects found the first natural example of a theoretical combinatorial explosion in one of the pattern-matching algorithms.

12. Low-Level Programming Techniques

Compared to the syntactic restrictions of conventional languages like PASCAL, the restrictions on equations described in Section 5 are a bit subtle. We believe that the additional study needed to understand the restrictions is justified for several reasons. First, the restrictions are similar in flavor to those imposed by deterministic parsing strategies such as *LR* and *LALR*, and perhaps even a bit simpler. The trouble taken to satisfy the restrictions is rewarded by the guarantee that the resulting program produces the same result, independently of the order of evaluation. This reward should become very significant on parallel hardware of the future, where the trouble of insuring order-independence in a procedural program may be immense. Finally, there are disciplined styles of programming with equations that can avoid errors, and techniques for correcting the errors when they occur. A few such techniques are given in this section; we anticipate that a sizable collection will result from a few years of experience.

12.1. A Disciplined Programming Style Based on Constructor Functions

In many applications of equational programming, the function symbols may be partitioned into two classes:

1. constructor symbols, used to build up static data objects, and

2. defined symbols, used to perform computations on the data objects.

For example, in LISP M-expressions, the atomic symbols, *nil*, and the binary symbol *cons*, are constructors, and all metafunction symbols are defined symbols. Technically, a *constructor* is a symbol that never appears as the outermost symbol on the left-hand side of an equation, and a *defined symbol* is one that does appear as the outermost symbol on a left-hand side. The *constructor discipline* consists of never allowing a defined symbol to appear on a left-hand side, except as the outermost symbol. An equational program that respects the constructor discipline clearly satisfies the nonoverlapping restriction 4 of Section 5.

Example 12.1.1

The following set of equations, in standard mathematical notation, does not respect the constructor discipline, although it does not contain an overlap.

Symbols

> *f: 1;*
> *g: 2;*

> *include atomic_symbols.*

For all x:

> $f(g(a, x)) = g(a, f(x));$

> $g(b, x) = a.$

The symbol g is a defined symbol, because it appears outermost on the left-hand side of the second equation, but g also appears in a nonoutermost position on the left-hand side of the first equation. On the other hand, the following set of equations accomplishes the same result, but respects the constructor discipline.

For all x:

> $f(h(x)) = g(a, f(x));$

> $g(a, x) = h(x);$

> $g(b, x) = a.$

Here, h, a, and b are constructors, f and g are defined symbols. Neither f nor g appears on a left-hand side except as the outermost symbol. The occurrences of f and g on the right-hand sides are irrelevant to the constructor discipline.

☐

The constructor discipline avoids violations of the nonoverlapping restriction 4, but it does not prevent violations of restriction 3, which prohibits two different left-hand sides from matching the same term. For example, $f(a,x)=a$ and $f(x,a)=a$ violate restriction 3, although the defined symbol f does not appear on a left-hand side except in the outermost position.

When the constructor discipline is applied, the appearance of a defined symbol in a normal form is usually taken to indicate an error, either in the equations or in the input term. Many other research projects, particularly in the area of abstract data types, require the constructor discipline, and sometimes require that defined symbols do not appear in normal forms [GH78]. The latter requirement is often called *sufficient completeness*.

It is possible to translate every equational program satisfying restrictions 1-4 (i.e., the *regular term reduction systems*) into an equational program that respects the constructor discipline. The idea, described by Satish Thatte in [Th85], is to create two versions, f and f', of each defined symbol that appears in a nonouter-most position on a left-hand side. f remains a defined symbol, while f' becomes a constructor. Every offending occurrence of f (i.e., nonoutermost on a left-hand side) is replaced by f'. In addition, equations are added to transform every f that heads a subterm *not* matching a left-hand side into f'.

Example 12.1.2

Applying the procedure described above to the first equational program in Example 12.1.1 yields the following program.

For all x:

$$f(g'(a,x)) = g(a, f(x));$$
$$g(a, x) = g'(a, x);$$

$g(b, x) = a.$

☐

In the worst case, this procedure could increase the size of the program quadratically, although worst cases do not seem to arise naturally. At any rate, the constructor discipline should probably be enforced by the programmer as he programs, rather than added on to a given program. In Section 12.4 we show how to use a similar procedure to eliminate overlaps.

The constructor discipline is rather sensitive to the syntactic form that is actually used by the equation interpreter.

Example 12.1.3

Consider the following program, given in Lambda notation.

Symbols
  AP: 2;

  include atomic_symbols.

For all x, y:

  (REFLECT (CONS x y)) = (CONS (REFLECT x) (REFLECT y));

  (REFLECT x) = x where x is in atomic_symbols end where.

Recall that this is equivalent to the standard mathematical notation:

For all x, y:

  AP(REFLECT, AP(AP(CONS, x), y)) =

    AP(AP(CONS, AP(REFLECT, x)), AP(REFLECT, y));

  AP(REFLECT, x) = x where x is in atomic_symbols end where.

This program does not respect the constructor discipline, as the defined symbol *AP* appears twice in nonoutermost positions in the left-hand side of the first equation. As long as no inputs will contain the symbols *REFLECT* or *CONS* except applied (using *AP*) to precisely one or two arguments, respectively, the same results may be obtained by the following un-Curried program in standard mathematical notation.

For all x, y:

   REFLECT(CONS(x, y)) = CONS(REFLECT(x), REFLECT(y));

   REFLECT(x) = x where x is in atomic_symbols end where.

The last program respects the constructor discipline.

☐

Example 12.1.4

Weak reduction in the combinator calculus [Sc24, St72] may be programmed in Lambda notation as follows.

Symbols

   AP: 2;
   include atomic_symbols.

For all x, y, z:

   (S x y z) = (x z (y z));

   (K x) = x.

As in the first program of example 12.2.1, the constructor discipline does not hold, because of the implicit occurrences of the defined symbol *AP* in nonoutermost positions of the first left-hand side. The left-hand sides may be un-Curried to

$S(x, y, z)$

$K(x)$

The latter program respects the constructor discipline, with S and K being defined symbols, and no constructors mentioned in the left-hand sides. The right-hand sides cannot be meaningfully un-Curried, without extending the notation to allow variables standing for functions.

☐

One is tempted to take a symbol in Curried notation as a defined symbol when it appears leftmost on a left-hand side of an equation. Unfortunately, this natural attempt to extend the constructor discipline systematically to Curried notation fails to guarantee the nonoverlapping property.

Example 12.1.5
In the following program, given in Lambda notation, the symbol P appears only leftmost in left-hand sides of equations.

Symbols
  AP: 2;

  include atomic_symbols.

For all x, y, z:

  $(P \; x \; y) = Q;$

  $(P \; x \; y \; z) = R.$

The two left-hand sides overlap, however, and $(PQQQ)$ has the two different normal forms QQ and R.

☐

Informally, the overlap violation above appears to translate to a violation of restriction 3 in an un-Curried notation. Formalization of this observation would require a treatment of function symbols with varying arities. The appropriate formalization *for this case* is not hard to construct, but other useful syntactic transformations besides Currying may arise, and might require totally different formalisms to relate them to the constructor discipline.

Because of the sensitivity of the constructor discipline to syntactic assumptions, and because the enforcement of this discipline may lead to longer and less clear equational programs, the equation interpreter does not enforce such a discipline. Whenever a particular problem lends itself to a solution respecting the constructor discipline, we recommend that the programmer enforce it on himself, and document the distinction between constructors and defined symbols. So far, most examples of equational programs that have been run on the interpreter have respected the constructor discipline, and the examples of nonoverlapping equations *not* based on constructors have been few, and often hard to construct. So, experience to date fails to give strong support for the utility of the greater generality of nonoverlapping equations. We expect that future versions of the interpreter will enforce even weaker restrictions, based on the Knuth-Bendix closure algorithm [KB70], and that substantial examples of programs requiring this extra generality will arise. Further research is required to adapt the Knuth-Bendix procedure, which was designed for reduction systems in which every term has a normal form, to nonterminating systems.

12.2. Simulation of LISP Conditionals

The effort expended in designing and implementing the equation interpreter would be wasted if the result were merely a syntactic variant of LISP. For the many problems, and portions of problems, however, for which LISP-style programming is appropriate, a programmer may benefit from learning how to apply an analogous

style to equational programming. The paradigm of LISP programming is the
recursive definition of a function, based on a conditional expression. The general
form, presented in informal notation, looks like

$$f[x] = \quad \textit{if } P_1[x] \textit{ then } E_1$$

$$\textit{else if } P_2[x] \textit{ then } E_2$$

$$\cdot$$
$$\cdot$$
$$\cdot$$

$$\textit{else if } P_n[x] \textit{ then } E_n$$

$$\textit{else} \qquad E_{n+1}$$

where $P_1[x]$ is usually "x *is nil*", or occasionally "x *is atomic*", and $P_2, \cdots, P_n$
require more and more structure for x. In order to program the same computation
for the equation interpreter, each line of the conditional is expressed as a separate
equation. The conditions $P_1, \cdots, P_n$ are expressed implicitly in the structure of
the arguments to f on the left-hand sides of the equations, and occasionally in syntactic restrictions on the variables. Since there is no order for the equations, the
effect of the order of conditional clauses must be produced by letting each condition include the negation of all previous conditions. As long as the conditions deal
only with the structure of the argument, rather than computed qualities of its
value, this translation will produce a more readable form than LISP syntax, and
the incorporation of negations of previous conditions will not require expansion of
the size of the program. The else clause must be translated into an equation that
applies precisely in those cases where no other condition holds. Expressing this
condition explicitly involves some extra trouble for the programmer, but has the
benefit of clarifying the case analysis, and illuminating omissions that might be
more easily overlooked in the conditional form. If the programmer accidentally

provides two equations that could apply in the same case, the interpreter detects a violation of restriction 3. If he neglects to cover some case, the first time that a program execution encounters such a case, the offending application of f will appear unreduced in the output, displaying the omission very clearly.

Example 12.2.1

Consider the following informal definition of a function that flattens a binary tree into a long right branch, with the same atomic symbols hanging off in the same order.

flat[x] =   *if x is atomic   then x*

           else if car[x] is atomic then cons[car[x]; flat[cdr[x]]]

           else flat[cons[car[car[x]]; cons[cdr[car[x]]; cdr[x]]]]

The actual LISP program, using the usual abbreviations for compositions of *car* and *cdr*, follows.

```
(DEF '((FLAT (LAMBDA (X)
        (COND
            ((ATOM X)          X)
            ((ATOM (CAR X)) (CONS (CAR X) (FLAT (CDR X))))
            (T (FLAT (CONS (CAAR X) (CONS (CDAR X) (CDR X)))))
)    ))   )    )
```

The same computation is described by the following equational program, using LISP.M notation.

Symbols

  flat: 1;
  cons: 2;
  nil: 0;

  include atomic_symbols.

For all x:

flat[x] = *x where x is in atomic_symbols end where;*

flat[(x . y)] = *(x . flat[y]) where x is in atomic_symbols end where;*

flat[((x . y) . z)] = *flat[(x . (y . z))].*

☐

When conditions in a LISP program refer to predicates that must actually be computed from the arguments to a function, rather than to the structure of the arguments, the programmer must use a corresponding conditional function in the equational program. The translation from LISP syntax for a conditional function to the LISP.M notation for the equation interpreter is utterly trivial.

12.3. Two Approaches to Errors and Exceptional Conditions

The equation interpreter has no built-in concept of a run-time error. There are failures at run-time, due to insufficient space resources, but no exceptional condition caused by application of a function to inappropriate arguments is detected. We designed the interpreter this way, not because we believe that run-time error detection is undesirable, but rather because it is completely separated from the other fundamental implementation issues. We decided to provide an environment in which different ways of handling errors and exceptions may be tried, rather than committing to a particular one. If errors are only reported to the outside world, then the reporting mechanism is properly one for a syntactic postprocessor. Certain normal forms, such as *car*[()] in LISP, are perfectly acceptable to the equation interpreter, but might be reported as errors when detected by a postprocessor. Total support of this approach to errors may require a mechanism for halting evaluation before a normal form is reached, but that mechanism will be provided in future versions as a general augmentation of the interface (see Section 15.3), allowing the interpreter to act in parallel with other components. No specific effort should be required for error detection.

If a programmer wishes to detect and react to errors and exceptional conditions within an equational program, two basic strategies suggest themselves. In the first strategy, exception detection is provided by special functions that inspect a structure to determine that it may be manipulated in a certain way, before that manipulation is attempted. In the other strategy, special symbols are defined to represent erroneous conditions. Reaction to exceptions is programmed by the way these special symbols propagate through an evaluation. We chose to provide a setting in which many strategies can be tested, rather than preferring one.

Example 12.3.1

Consider a table of name-value pairs, implemented as a list of ordered pairs. The table is intended to represent a function from some name space to values, but occasionally certain names may be accidentally omitted, or entered more than once. In a program for a function to look up the value associated with a given name, it may be necessary to check that the name occurs precisely once. The following programs all use LISP.M notation. The first applies the strategy of providing checking functions. Efficiency has been ignored in the interest of clarifying the fundamental issue.

Symbols

```
cons: 2;
nil:  0;
occurs: 2;
legmap: 2;
lookup: 2;
add: 2;
equ: 2;
if: 3;
```

include atomic_symbols, integer_numerals, truth_values.

For all m, n, l, v:

occurs[m; ()] = 0;

occurs[m; ((n . v) . l)] =
if[equ[m; n]; add[occurs[m; l]; 1]; occurs[m; l]];

legmap[m; l] = equ[occurs[m; l]; 1];

lookup[m; ((n . v) . l)] =
if[equ[m; n]; v; lookup[m; l]];

if[true; m; n] = m;   if[false; m; n] = n;

include equint, addint, equatom.

When *lookup*[*m;l*] is used in a larger program, the programmer will have to test *legmap*[*m;l*] first, if there is any chance that *m* is not associated uniquely in *l*. Essentially the same facility is provided by the following program, which applies the strategy of producing special symbols to represent errors.

Symbols
  cons: 2;
  nil: 0;

  lookup: 2;

  undefined, overdefined: 0;

  if: 3;
  equ: 2;

  include atomic_symbols, truth_values.

For all m, n, l, v:

  lookup[m; ()] = undefined[];

  lookup[m; ((n . v) . l)] =
    if[equ[m; n];
        if[equ[lookup[m; l]; undefined[]]; v; overdefined[]];
        lookup[m; l]];

  if[true; m; n] = m; if[false; m; n] = n;

  include equatom.

☐

Either strategy may be adapted to produce more or less information about the precise form of an error or exceptional occurrence. There appears to be no technical reason to prefer one to the other. The choice must depend on the programmer's taste. It is probably foolish to mix the two strategies within one program.

12.4. Repairing Overlaps and Nonsequential Constructs

When a set of logically correct equations is rejected by the equation interpreter because of overlapping left-hand sides, there are two general techniques that may succeed in removing the overlap, without starting from scratch. The first, and simplest, is to generalize the equation whose left-hand side applies outermost in the offending case, so that the overlap no longer involves explicitly-given symbols, but only an instance of a variable.

Example 12.4.1

Consider lists of elements in LISP.M notation, where a special element *missing*, different from *nil*, is to be ignored whenever it appears as a member of a list. Such a *missing* element would allow recursive deletion of elements from a list in an especially simple way. The equation defining the behavior of *missing* may easily overlap with other equations.

Symbols

    cons: 2;
    nil: 0;

    missing: 0;

: *mirror[l] is l concatenated with its own reversal.*
    mirror: 1;

    include atomic_symbols.

For all l, 11, x:

  (missing[] . l) = l;

  mirror[l] = append[l; reverse[l]] where l is either ()
                                    or (x . 11)
                            end or
                    end where;

The two equations in the fragment above overlap in the term

  mirror[(missing[] . l)]

This overlap may be avoided by deleting the *where* clause on the second equation, and allowing the mirror operation to apply to elements other than lists, perhaps with meaningless results. Of course, the first equation will certainly overlap with other equations defining, for example, *reverse* and *append*, and these overlaps will require other avoidance techniques.

☐

The technique of generalization, shown above, only works when unnecessarily restrictive equations have led to overlap. More often, overlaps may be removed by restricting the equation whose left-hand side appears innermost in the offending case, either by giving more structure to the left-hand side, or by adding extra symbols to differentiate different instances of the same operation. The second method seems to be unavoidable in some cases, but it regrettably decreases the readability and generality of the program.

Example 12.4.2

Consider an unusual setting for list manipulation, based on an associative concatenation operator *cat*, instead of the constructor *cons* of LISP. An atomic symbol *a* is identified with the singleton list containing only *a*. The following program, given in standard mathematical notation, enforces the associativity of *cat* by always associating to the right, and defines reversal as well.

Symbols

  cat: 2;

  reverse: 1;

  include atomic_symbols.

For all x, y, z:

  cat(cat(x, y), z) = cat(x, cat(y, z))
    where x is in atomic_symbols end where;

  reverse(cat(x, y)) = cat(reverse(y), reverse(x));

  reverse(x) = x where x is in atomic_symbols end where.

The restriction of x in the first equation to be an atomic symbol prevents a self-overlap of the form *cat* (*cat* (*cat* (*A*,*B*),*C*),*D*), but there is still an overlap between the first and second equations in the form *reverse* (*cat* (*cat* (*A*,*B*),*C*)). The same effect may be achieved, without overlap, by restricting the variable x to atomic symbols in the second equation as well. This correction achieves the right output, but incurs a quadratic cost for *reverse*, because of the reassociation of *cat*s implied by it. See Section 16.1 for a more thorough development of this novel approach to list manipulation, achieving the linear reversal cost that was probably intended by the program above.

☐

Example 12.4.3

In order to approach an implementation of the lambda calculus, one might take the Curried notation in which binary application is the only operation, and add a syntactic substitution operator. The following program defines substitution, and for

the sake of simplicity only the identity function, using standard mathematical notation. *subst* (x,y,z) is intended to denote the result of substituting x for each
occurrence of y in z.

Symbols

> *AP: 2;*
> *I: 0;*
> *subst: 3;*
>
> *if: 3;*
> *equ: 2;*
>
> *include atomic_symbols, truth_values.*

For all w, x, y, z:

> *AP(I(), x) = x;*
>
> *subst(w, x, y) = if(equ(x, y), w, y)*
>   *where y is in atomic_symbols end where;*
>
> *subst(w, x, AP(y, z)) = AP(subst(w, x, y), subst(w, x, z));*
>
> *if(true, x, y) = x; if(false, x, y) = false;*
>
> *include equatom.*

The first and third equations overlap in the form *subst* $(A,B,AP(I,C))$. In order
to avoid this overlap, change nonoutermost occurrences of the symbol *AP* on left-
hand sides (there is only one in this example, in the third equation) into a new
symbol, *IAP* (*I*nert *AP*plication). Two additional equations are required to convert *AP* to *IAP* when appropriate.

For all w, x, y, z:

> *AP(I(), x) = x;*
>
> *subst(w, x, y) = if(equ(x, y), w, y)*
>   *where y is in atomic_symbols end where;*
>
> *subst(w, x, IAP(y, z)) = AP(subst(w, x, y), subst(w, x, z));*

AP(x, y) = IAP(x, y) where x is in atomic_symbols end where;

AP(IAP(x, y)) = IAP(IAP(x, y));

if(true, x, y) = x; if(false, x, y) = false;

include equatom.

Notice that *IAP* is never used on the right-hand side. Essentially, the use of *IAP* enforces innermost evaluation in those cases where left-hand sides used to overlap.

□

The technique of adding symbols to avoid overlap, illustrated in Example 12.4.3, is essentially the same idea as that used by Thatte [Th85] to translate nonoverlapping equations into the constructor discipline (see Section 12.1). Example 16.3.3 shows how the same technique was used independently by Hoffmann, who thought of overlap as a potential inconsistency in a concurrent program, and used locks to avoid the inconsistency.

When a logically correct set of equations is rejected by the equation interpreter because of a failure of left-sequentiality, the first thing to try is reordering the arguments to offending functions. If the program is part of a polished product, the reordering may be accomplished in syntactic pre- and postprocessors. If the trouble of modifying the syntactic processors is too great, the user, regrettably, must get accustomed to seeing the arguments in the new order.

Example 12.4.4

Consider a program generalizing the LISP functions *car* and *cdr* to allow an arbitrarily long path to a selected subtree. *select*[*t*;*p*] is intended to select the subtree of *t* reached by the path *p* from the root of *t*. Paths are presented as lists of atomic symbols *L* and *R*, representing left and right branches, respectively.

Symbols

   cons: 2;
   nil: 0;

   select: 2;

   include atomic_symbols.

For all x, y, p:

   select[x; ()] = x;

   select[(x . y); (L . p)] = select[x; p];

   select[(x . y); (R . p)] = select[y; p].

Left-sequentiality fails for the program above because, after seeing the symbol *select*, there is no way to decide whether or not to inspect the first argument, seeking a *cons*, or the second argument, seeking (). Only after seeing the second argument, and determining whether or not it is (), can the interpreter know whether or not the first argument is relevant. Left-sequentiality is restored merely by reversing the arguments to select.

For all x, y, p:

   select[(); x] = x;

   select[(L . p); (x . y)] = select[p; x];

   select[(R . p); (x . y)] = select[p; y].

☐

     Failures of left-sequentiality may also be repaired by artificially forcing the interpreter to inspect an argument position, by replacing the variable with a disjunction of all possible forms substituted for that variable. This technique degrades the clarity of the program, and risks the omission of some possible form. In the worst case, the forced inspection of an ill-defined argument could lead to an unnecessary infinite computation.

Example 12.4.5

The first program of Example 12.4.4 may also be repaired by replacing the first equation,

$\quad$ *select[x; ()] = x;*

with the two equations,

$\quad$ *select[x; ()] = x where x is in atomic_symbols end where;*
$\quad$ *select[(x . y); ()] = (x . y);*

or, equivalently, by qualifying the variable *x* to be

$\quad\quad$ *either (y . z) or in atomic_symbols end or*

☐

Whenever permutation of arguments restores left-sequentiality, that method is preferred to the forced inspection. In some cases, however, argument permutation fails where forced inspection succeeds.

Example 12.4.6

The parallel *or* function may be defined by
Symbols
$\quad$ *or: 2;*
$\quad$ *include truth_values.*
For all x:
$\quad$ *or(true, x) = true;*
$\quad$ *or(x, true) = true;*

or(false, false) = false.

Left-sequentiality fails because of the first two equations. If the second equation is changed to

or(false, true) = true;

then left-sequentiality is restored. The *or* operator in the modified equations is sometimes called the *conditional or*. The results are the same as long as evaluation of the first argument to *or* terminates, but arbitrarily much effort may be wasted evaluating the first argument when the second is *true*. In the worst case, evaluation of the first argument might never terminate, so the final answer of *true* would never be discovered.

□

13. Use of Equations for Syntactic Manipulations

While computer programming in general remains something of a black art, certain special problem areas have been reduced to a disciplined state where a competent person who has learned the right techniques may be confident of success. In particular, the use of finite-state lexical analyzers and push-down parses, generated automatically from regular expressions and context-free grammars, has reduced the syntactic analysis of programming languages, and other artificially designed languages, to a reliable discipline [AU72]. The grammatical approach to syntactic analysis is also beneficial because the grammatical notation is reasonably self-documenting - sufficiently so that the same grammar may be used as input to an automatic parser generator, and as appendix to a programmer's manual, providing a reliable standard of reference to settle subtle syntactic issues that are not explained sufficiently in the text of the manual. Beyond context-free manipulations, the best-known contender for formal generation of language processors is the *attribute grammar* [Kn68, AU72]. An attribute grammar is a context-free grammar in which each nonterminal symbol may have attribute values associated with it, and each production is augmented with a description of how attributes of nonterminals in that production may be computed from one another. Although they have proved very useful in producing countless compilers, interpreters, and other language processors, attribute grammars have not provided a transparency of notation comparable to that of context-free grammars, especially when, as is usually the case, actual computation of one attribute from another is described in a conventional programming language, such as C.

Linguists who seek formal descriptions of natural languages have tried to boost the power of context-free grammars with *transformational grammars*

[Ch65]. A transformational grammar, like an attribute grammar, contains a context-free grammar, but the context-free grammar is used to produce a tree, which is then transformed by schematically presented transformation rules. The parse tree produced by the context-free grammar is called the *surface structure*, and the result of the transformations is called the *deep structure* of an input string of symbols. A number of different formal definitions of transformational grammar have been proposed, all of them suffering from complex mechanisms for controlling the way in which tree transformations are applied. We propose the equation interpreter as a suitable mechanism for the transformational portion of transformational grammars. By enforcing the confluence property, the equation interpreter finesses the complex control mechanisms, and returns to a notation that has the potential for self-documenting qualities analogous to those of context-free grammars. The concepts of surface structure, which captures the syntactic structure of the source text, without trivial lexical details, and deep structure, which is still essentially syntactic, but which captures the structure of the syntactic concepts described by the source text, rather than the structure of the text itself, appear to be very useful ones in the methodology of automatic syntactic analysis. The analysis into surface and deep structures should be viewed as a refinement of the idea of *abstract syntax* - syntax in tree form freed of purely lexical issues - which has already proved a useful organizing concept for language design [McC62, La65].

In this section, we propose that the concept of *abstract syntax* be made an explicit part of the implementation of syntactic processors, as well as a design concept. Rather than extend the traditional formalisms for context-free grammars, we develop a slightly different notation, clearly as strong in its power to define sets of strings, and better suited to the larger context of regular/context-free/equational processing.

13.1 An Improved Notation for Context-Free Grammars

The tremendous success of context-free grammars as understandable notations for syntactic structure comes from their close connection to natural concepts of type structure. By making the connection even closer, we believe that clarity can be improved, and deeper structural issues separated more cleanly from superficial lexical ones. The first step is to start, not with source text, which is a concrete realization of a conceptual structure, but with the conceptual structure itself. By "conceptual structure," we mean what a number of programming language designers have called *abstract syntax* [McC62, La65], and what Curry and Feys called *formal objects* or *Obs* [CF58]. We do *not* intend meanings or semantic structures: rather abstract, but syntactic, mental forms that are represented straightforwardly by source texts. Just as programming language design should start with the design of the abstract syntax, and seek the most convenient way to represent that abstract syntax in text, the formal description of a language should first define the abstract structure of the language, then its concrete textual realization. Abstract syntaxes are defined by type assignments.

Definition 13.1.1

Let Σ be an alphabet on which an abstract term is to be built, and let Γ_0 be a set of primitive types used to describe the uses of symbols in Σ.

A *flat type* over Γ_0 is either a primitive type $t \in \Gamma_0$, or

$s_1 \times \cdots \times s_n \rightarrow t$ where $s_1, \cdots s_n, t \in \Gamma_0$.

The set of all flat types over Γ_0 is called Γ.

A *type assignment* to Σ is a binary relation $\tau \subseteq \Sigma \times \Gamma$.

For $f \in \Sigma$, when τ is understood, $f:t_1, \cdots, t_n$ means that $f \tau t_i$ for $i \in [1,n]$. Usually τ is a function, so $n=1$.

The *typed language* of Σ and τ, denoted Σ_τ, is the set of all terms built from symbols in Σ, respecting the types assigned by τ. Formally,

If $(f,t) \in \tau$ for $t \in \Gamma_0$ then f is in the typed language of Σ and τ, and f has type t (i.e., f is a constant symbol of type t).

If $E_1, \cdots, E_n$ are in the typed language of Σ and τ, with types $s_1, \cdots, s_n \in \Gamma_0$, and if $f:s_1 \times \cdots \times s_n \rightarrow t$, then $f(E_1, \cdots, E_n)$ is in the typed language of Σ and τ with type t.

τ is extended so that $E \tau t$, also written $E:t$, if t is the type of an arbitrary term $E \in \Sigma_\tau$.

☐

$f(E_1, \cdots, E_n)$ denotes an abstract term, or tree, with f at the head or root, and subterms $E_1, \cdots, E_n$ attached to the root in order. In particular, $f(E_1, \cdots, E_n)$ does *not* denote a particular string of characters including parentheses and commas.

Abstract syntaxes are merely the typed languages of typed alphabets as described above. These languages might naturally be called *regular tree languages*, because they can be recognized by nondeterministic finite automata running from the root to the leaves of a tree, splitting at each interior node to cover all of the sons (a different next state may be specified for each son), and accepting when *every* leaf yields an accepting state [Th73]. All of the technical devices of this section are found in earlier theoretical literature on tree automata and grammars [Th73], but we believe that the particular combination here is worthy of consideration for practical purposes.

Type assignments are almost context-free grammars, they merely lack the terminal symbols. Each primitive type t may be interpreted as a nonterminal symbol N_t in the context-free grammar, and the type assignment $f:s_1 \times \cdots \times s_n \to t$ corresponds to the production $N_t \to N_{s_1} \cdots N_{s_n}$. Notice that the type assignment has one piece of information lacking in the context-free production - the name f. Names for context-free productions clarify the parse trees, and make issues such as ambiguity less muddy. The terminal symbols, giving the actual strings in the context-free language, are given separately from the type assignment. This separation has the advantage of allowing different concrete notations to be associated with the same abstract syntax for different purposes (e.g., internal storage, display on various output devices - the translation from a low-level assembly code to binary machine code might even be represented as another notation for the assembly code). Separation also clarifies the distinction between essential structure and superficial typography. We do not suggest that typography is unimportant compared to the structure, merely that it is helpful to know the difference.

The following definition introduces all of the formal concepts needed to define context-free languages in a way that separates essential issues from typographical ones, and that makes the relationship between strings and their abstract syntax trees more explicit and more flexible than in traditional grammatical notation. The idea is to define the abstract syntax trees first, by introducing the symbols that may appear at nodes of the trees, and assigning a type to each. Legitimate abstract syntaxes are merely the well-typed terms built from those symbols. Next, each symbol in the abstract syntax is associated with one or more notational schemata, showing how that symbol is denoted in the concrete syntax, as a string of characters. Auxiliary symbols may be used to control the selection of a notational schema when a single abstract symbol has several possible denotations. This control facility does not allow new sets of strings to be defined, but it does allow a given set of strings to be associated with abstract syntax trees in more ways than can be done by traditional grammar-driven parsing.

The design of this definition was determined by three criteria.

1.   The resulting notation must handle common syntactic examples from the compiler literature in a natural way.

2.   The translations defined by the notation must be closed under homomorphic (structure-preserving) encodings of terms. For example, if it is possible to make terms built out of the binary function symbol f correspond to strings in a particular way, then the same correspondence must be possible when $f(x,y)$ is systematically encoded as $apply(apply(f,x),y)$, an encoding called *Currying*. If this criterion were not satisfied, a user might have to redesign the abstract syntax in order to achieve typographical goals. The whole point of the new notation is to avoid such interference between levels.

3.   A natural subset of the new notation must equal the power of *syntax−directed translation schemata* [Ir61, LS68, AU72].

Definition 13.1.2

Let *cat* be a binary symbol indicating concatenation. $cat(\alpha,\beta)$ is abbreviated $\alpha\beta$. Let $V=\{x_1,x_2,\cdots\}$ be a set of formal variables, $V\cap\Sigma=\phi$. Let Δ be a finite alphabet of *auxiliary symbols*, $S\in\Delta$ a designated *start symbol*. A *notational specification* for a type assignment τ to *abstract alphabet* Σ in *concrete alphabet* Ω with auxiliary alphabet Δ is a binary relation $\eta\subseteq(((\Sigma\cup V)_{\tau'}\cup\{empty\})\times\Delta)\times(\{cat\}\cup\Omega^*\cup(V\times\Delta))_\psi$, where τ' is τ augmented so that each variable in V has every type in Γ_0 (i.e., a variable may occur anywhere in

a term), and ψ is the type assignment such that each word in Ω^*, and each annotated variable in $\mathbf{V} \times \Delta$, is a single nullary symbol of type $STRING$, and cat is of
type $STRING \times STRING \rightarrow STRING$. $empty$ denotes the empty term, without
even a head symbol. Without loss of generality, the variables on the left-hand term
in the η relation are always $x_1, \cdots, x_n$, in order from left to right. Notational
specifications are described by productions of the form

E^A is denoted F,

indicating that $<E,A>\eta F$. Within F, the auxiliary symbols are given as superscripts on the variables. When the same pair $<E,A>$ is related by η to several
expressions $F_1, \cdots, F_m$, the m elements of the relation are described in the form
E^A is denoted E_1 or $\cdots$ or E_m. Multiple superscripts indicate that any of the
superscripts listed may be used. If only one element of Δ may appear on a particular symbol, then the superscript may be omitted.

A $context-free$ notational specification is one in which the η relation is restricted
so that when $<E,A>\eta F$, no variable occurs more than once in F.

A $simple$ notational specification is a context-free notational specification in which
the η relation is further restricted so that when $<E,A>\eta F$, the variables
$x_1, \cdots, x_n$ occur in order from left to right in E, possibly with omissions, but
without repetitions.

Each notational specification η defines an $interpretation$ $\bar{\eta} \subseteq (\Sigma_t \times \Delta) \times \Omega^*$, associating trees (abstract syntax) with strings of symbols (concrete syntax). The interpre-
tation is defined by

$<E,A>\eta\alpha \implies <E,A>\bar{\eta}\alpha$ when E contains no variables.

$<E[x_1, \cdots, x_m], A>\eta\alpha[<x_1, B_1>, \cdots, <x_n, B_n>]$ &

$\quad <E_1, B_1>\bar{\eta}\beta_1$ & $\cdots$ & $<E_m, B_m>\bar{\eta}\beta_m$ &

$$<empty,B_{m+1}>\overline{\eta}\beta_{m+1} \ \& \ \cdots \ \& \ <empty,B_n>\overline{\eta}\beta_n$$
$$\Rightarrow f(E_1,\cdots,E_m)\overline{\eta}\alpha[\beta_1,\cdots,\beta_n]$$

$F\overline{\eta}\alpha$ abbreviates $<F,S>\overline{\eta}\alpha$, where S is the start symbol.

The *string language* of a notational specification η at type t is
$\{\alpha \in \Omega^* | \ \exists F \in \Sigma_\tau \ (F,t) \in \tau \ \& \ F\overline{\eta}\alpha\}$.

☐

The formal definition above is intuitively much simpler than it looks. Notational specifications give nondeterministic translations between terms and strings in a schematic style using formal variables. The intent of a single production is that the terms represented by the variables in any instance of that production should be translated first, then those translations should be combined as shown in the production. In most cases, the left-hand side of a production is of the simple form $f(x_1,\cdots,x_n)$. This form is enough to satisfy design criterion 1 above. The more complex terms allowed on left-hand sides of productions are required to satisfy criterion 2, and the *empty* left-hand sides are required for criterion 3. Greater experience with the notation is required in order to judge whether the added generality is worth the trouble in understanding its definition.

The string languages of context-free notational specifications and simple notational specifications are precisely the context-free languages, but notational specifications offer more flexibility than context-free grammars for defining tree-string relations. Since the relation between the parse tree and a string has a practical importance far beyond the set of parsable strings, this added flexibility appears to be worth the increase in complexity of the specifications, even if it is never used to define a non-context-free language. The type-notation pairs defined here are more powerful than the *syntax−directed translation schemata* of Aho and Ullmann [AU72] when the abstract-syntax trees are encoded as strings in postorder. Context-free notational specifications are equivalent in power to syntax-directed translation schemata, and simple notational specifications are equivalent in power to *simple syntax−directed translation schemata* and to *pushdown transducers*. Independently of the theoretical power involved, the notation of this section should be preferred to that of syntax-directed translation schemata, since it makes the intuitive tree structure of the abstract syntax explicit, rather than encoding it into a string. Notice that auxiliary symbols are equivalent to a restricted use of *inherited attributes* in attribute grammars. Since these attributes are chosen from a finite alphabet, they do not increase the power of the formalism as a language definer.

A notational specification is generally not acceptable unless it is *complete*, that is, every abstract term in the typed language has at least one denotation. Completeness is easy to detect automatically. Unfortunately, *ambiguity*, that is, the existence of two or more denotations for the same abstract term, is equivalent to ambiguity in context-free grammars, which is undecidable. For generating parsers, ambiguity is deadly, since the result of parsing is not well-defined. Just as with context-free grammars, we should probably enforce stronger decidable sufficient conditions for nonambiguity. For unparsers, ambiguity is usually undesirable, but it might be occasionally useful when there is no practical need to distinguish between two abstract terms.

Every context-free grammar decomposes naturally into a type assignment and a simple context-free notational specification, with a trivial Δ, and η a function. The natural decomposition is unique except for ordering of the arguments to each function symbol, and choice of names for the function symbols. Similarly, every context-free type-notation pair defines a unique natural context-free grammar.

Example 13.1.1

Consider a context-free grammar for arithmetic expressions.

$S \rightarrow N$

$S \rightarrow S + S$

$S \rightarrow S*S$

$S \rightarrow (S)$

$N \rightarrow 0|1|2|3|4|5|6|7|8|9$

$N \rightarrow N0|N1| \cdots |N9$

This grammar decomposes naturally into the type assignment

$numeral : N \rightarrow S$

$plus : S \times S \rightarrow S$

$times : S \times S \rightarrow S$

$paren : S \rightarrow S$

$digit 0 : N \cdots digit 9 : N$

$extend 0 : N \rightarrow N \cdots extend 9 : N \rightarrow N$

and the context-free notational specification

$numeral(x_1)$ *is denoted* x_1

$plus(x_1, x_2)$ *is denoted* $x_1 + x_2$

$times(x_1, x_2)$ *is denoted* $x_1 * x_2$

$paren(x_1)$ *is denoted* (x_1)

$digit 0$ *is denoted* $0 \cdots digit 9$ *is denoted* 9

$extend 0(x_1)$ *is denoted* $x_1 0 \cdots extend 9(x_1)$ *is denoted* $x_1 9$

The type-notation pair derived above is not the most intuitive one for arithmetic expressions, because the *paren* symbol has no semantic content, but is an artifact of the form of the grammar. To obtain a more intuitive notational specification, for the type assignment that omits *paren*, delete the *paren* line from the notational specification above, and replace the *plus* and *times* lines by the following.

plus (x_1, x_2) *is denoted* $x_1 + x_2$ *or* $(x_1 + x_2)$

times (x_1, x_2) *is denoted* $x_1 * x_2$ *or* $(x_1 * x_2)$

The auxiliary alphabet Δ is still trivial, but the notational relation η is no longer a function.

$\square$

The auxiliary symbols in Δ are not strictly necessary for defining an arbitrary context-free language, but they allow technical aspects of the parsing mechanism to be isolated in the notational specification, instead of complicating the type assignment. For example, the extra nonterminal symbols often introduced into grammars to enforce precedence conditions should not be treated as separate types, but merely as parsing information attached to a single type.

Example 13.1.2

The grammar of Example 13.1.1 is ambiguous. For example, $1+2*3$ may be parsed as *plus* $(1, times\,(2,3))$, or *times* $(plus\,(1,2),3)$. The usual way to avoid the ambiguity in the context-free grammar is to expand the set of nonterminal symbols as follows.

$S \rightarrow S + T$

$S \rightarrow T$

$T \rightarrow T * R$

$T \to R$

$R \to (S)$

$R \to N$

$N \to 0|1|2|3|4|5|6|7|8|9$

$N \to N0|N1| \cdots |N9$

This grammar gives precedence to ∗ over +, and associates sequences of the same operation to the left. The direct translation of this grammar yields the following type assignment and notational specification.

$plus: S \times T \to S$

$summand: T \to S$

$times: T \times R \to T$

$multiplicand: R \to T$

$paren: R \to S$

$numeral: N \to R$

$digit\,0: N \quad \cdots \quad digit\,9: N$

$extend\,0: N \to N \quad \cdots \quad extend\,9: N \to N$

$plus\,(x_1, x_2)$ is denoted $x_1 + x_2$

$summand\,(x_1)$ is denoted x_1

$times\,(x_1, x_2)$ is denoted $x_1 * x_2$

$multiplicand\,(x_1)$ is denoted x_1

$paren\,(x_1)$ is denoted (x_1)

$numeral\,(x_1)$ is denoted x_1

$digit\,0$ is denoted $0 \quad \cdots \quad digit\,9$ is denoted 9

extend$0(x_1)$ *is denoted* $x_1 0$ $\cdots$ *extend*$9(x_1)$ *is denoted* $x_1 9$

As well as *paren*, we now have the semantically superfluous symbols *summand* and *multiplicand*, and types T and R that are semantically equivalent to S. In order to keep the abstract syntax of the second part of Example 13.1.1, while avoiding ambiguity, the parsing information given by these semantically superfluous symbols and types should be encoded into auxiliary symbols S, T, R as follows.

plus$: S \times S \rightarrow S$

times$: S \times S \rightarrow S$

numeral$: N \rightarrow S$

digit$0: N$ $\cdots$ *digit*$9: N$

extend$0: N \rightarrow N$ $\cdots$ *extend*$9: N \rightarrow N$

plus$(x_1, x_2)^S$ *is denoted* $x_1^S + x_2^T$ *or* $(x_1^S + x_2^T)$

plus$(x_1, x_2)^{T,R}$ *is denoted* $(x_1^S + x_2^T)$

times$(x_1, x_2)^{S,T}$ *is denoted* $x_1^T * x_2^R$ *or* $(x_1^T * x_2^R)$

times$(x_1, x_2)^R$ *is denoted* $x_1^T * x_2^R$

numeral$(x_1)^{S,T,R}$ *is denoted* x_1

digit0 *is denoted* 0 $\cdots$ *digit*9 *is denoted* 9

extend$0(x_1)$ *is denoted* $x_1 0$ $\cdots$ *extend*$9(x_1)$ *is denoted* $x_1 9$

□

Non-context-free notational specifications allow matching of labels at the beginning and end of bracketed sections. For example, to define procedure definitions in a conventional programming language so that the name of a procedure appears at the end of its body, as well as in the heading, use the following notational specification:

procedure (x_1, x_2, x_3) *is denoted PROCEDURE* $x_1(x_2); x_3$ *END* $\{x_1\}$

Given current software that is available off-the-shelf, the best thing to do with a context-free type-notation pair is probably to convert it into a context-free grammar, and apply the usual parsing techniques. The new notation does not show to greatest advantage under such usage, since the tricks that are required to avoid parsing conflicts may complicate the grammar by introducing otherwise unnecessary auxiliary symbols. It is probably not a good idea to try to parse with non-context-free type-notation pairs, although unparsing is no problem.

The ideal application of type-notation pairs depends on future availability of *structure—editor* generators, as an alternative to parsers [MvD82, Re84]. Structure editors are fruits of the observation that source text was developed for particular input techniques, such as the use of punched cards, involving substantial off-line preparation before each submission. During the off-line work, a user needs to work with a presentation of his program that is simultaneously machine-readable and human-readable. With highly interactive input techniques, based on video terminals, there is no more requirement that what the user types correspond character by character to what he sees on the screen. Structure editors let short sequences of keystrokes produce simple manipulations of tree structures (i.e., abstract syntaxes), and instantly display the current structure on the screen. The process that must be automated is *unparsing*, a process technically much simpler than parsing, and immune to the problems of nondeterminism that arise in general context-free parsing. Type assignments are ideal for defining the internal structures to be manipulated by structure editors. The notational components still need strengthening to deal with the two-dimensional nature of the video display. Unparsing is easy even for non-context-free type-notation pairs.

13.2. Terms Representing the Syntax of Terms

When equations are used to perform syntactic processing, we often need a way to distinguish different levels of meaning. For example, there is no way to write an equational program translating an arbitrary list of the form $(F \ A_1 \ \cdots \ A_n)$ to $F[A_1, \cdots, A_n]$. We might be tempted to write

$$translate[(x \ . \ y)] = x[transargs[y]],$$

but F is a nullary symbol in the first instance, and an n-ary function symbol in the second. Also, the use of the variable x in place of a function symbol on the right-hand side is not allowed. Yet, the translation described above is a very natural part of a translation of LISP programs into equational programs. The problem is, that the symbol *translate* is defined above as if it operates on the objects *denoted by* S-expressions, when, in fact, it is supposed to operate on the expressions themselves. Consider the further trouble we would have with a syntactic processor that counts the number of leaves in an arithmetic expression. We might write

$$count\_leaves\,(add\,(x,y)) = add\,(count\_leaves\,(x),\ count\_leaves\,(y)).$$

Technically, this equation overlaps with the defining equations for *add*. Intuitively, it is a monster.

To achieve sufficient transformational power for the LISP example, and to avoid the confusion of the *add* example, we need a notation for explicitly describing other notations -- terms denoting terms. As long as we accept some equations on terms, we are in trouble letting terms stand for themselves. Rather, we need explicit functions whose use is to construct terms. One natural set of functions for this purpose uses list notation based on *nil* and *cons*, as in LISP, plus *atomic_symbols* as names of symbols within the terms being described, unary functions *litsym*, *atomsym*, *intnum*, *truthsym*, and *char* to construct symbols of various types from their names, and *multiap* to apply a function symbol syntactically to a list of argument terms.

Example 13.2.1

Using the notation defined above, we may translate LISP S-expressions to the functional terms that they often represent. We must translate *multiap*[*litsym*[*cons*]; (*atomsym*[*F*] . ···)] to *multiap*[*litsym*[*F*]; (···)]. This may be accomplished naturally by the following equational program.

Symbols

: Constructors for terms
   nil: 0;
   cons: 2;
   litsym, atomsym, intnum, truthsym, char: 1;
   multiap: 2;
   include atomic_symbols;

: Translating operators
   translate: 1;
   transargs: 1.

For all x, y:

   translate[litsym[x]]   = litsym[x];
   translate[atomsym[x]] = atomsym[x];
   translate[intnum[x]]   = intnum[x];
   translate[truthsym[x]] = truthsym[x];
   translate[char[x]]   = char[x];

   translate[multiap[litsym[cons]; (atomsym[x] . y)]] =
      multiap[litsym[x]; transargs[y]];

   transargs[()] = ();

   transargs[(x . y)] = (translate[x] . transargs[y]).

Similarly, the leaf counting program becomes

Symbols

: Constructors for terms
  nil: 0;
  cons: 2;
  litsym, intnum: 1;
  multiap: 2;
  include atomic_symbols;

: Counting operator
  count: 1;

: Arithmetic operator
  add: 2.

For all x, y:

  count[intnum[x]] = 1;

  count[multiap[litsym[add]; (x y)]] = add[count[x]; count[y]].

☐

The examples above are not appealing to the eye, but the potential for confusion is so great that precision seems to be worth more than beauty in this case. Special denotations involving quote marks might be introduced, but they should be taken as abbreviations for an explicit form for denoting syntax, such as the one described above.

In order to apply an equational program to perform a syntactic manipulation, the term to be manipulated should be in an explicitly syntactic form. Yet, the initial production of that term as input, and the final output form for it, are unlikely to be explicitly syntactic themselves. For example, one use of the translation of S-expressions to functional forms is to take an S-expression, translate it into a functional form, evaluate the functional form, then translate back to an S-expression. The user who presents the initial S-expression only wants to have it evaluated, so he should not need to be aware of the syntactic translations, and should be allowed to present the S-expression in its usual form. In order to evaluate the functional form, it must not be given as explicit syntax, else it will not be understood by an evaluator of functional forms. From these considerations, we seem to need transformers in and out of explicit syntactic forms. These translators cannot be defined by the equation interpreter, without getting into an infinite regress, since the transformation of a term into its explicit syntactic form is itself a syntactic transformation. So, the implementation of the equation interpreter includes two programs called *syntax* and *content*. *syntax* transforms a term into its explicit syntactic form, and *content* transforms an explicit syntactic form into the term that it denotes. Thus, the *syntax* of $(A \cdot B)$ is

$$multiap[litsym[cons]; (atomsym[A] \, atomsym[B])],$$

and the *content* of

$$multiap[litsym[f]; (atomsym[A] \, intnum[22] \, atomsym[B])]$$

is $f[A; 22; B]$.

13.3. Example: Type-Checking in a Term Language

A typical problem in non-context-free syntactic processing is type checking, where the types of certain symbols are given by declarations lexically distant from the occurrences of the symbols themselves. While the most popular application of type checking occurs in processing conventional programming languages, such as Pascal, the essential ideas can be understood more easily by considering a simpler language, consisting of declarations followed by a single term. An advanced compiler class taught by Christoph Hoffmann constructed a full type checker for Pascal in 1983. Substantial extra effort was required to enforce declare-before-use and similar restrictions included in the design of Pascal mostly to simplify conventional compiler implementations.

We present the term language in the type-notation form of Section 13.1, and assume that some mechanism is already available to translate from concrete syntax to abstract syntax. The type S denotes a list of declarations paired with a term, E denotes a term, D a declaration, A an atomic symbol and T a type. EL, DL, and TL denote lists of declarations, terms, and types, respectively. S, E, and T are also used as auxiliary symbols, corresponding intuitively to their uses as types. The auxiliary symbol P indicates a type occurring within the left-hand side of a functional type, and so needing to be parenthesized if it is a functional type itself, EC and DC indicate nonempty lists of terms and declarations, respectively.

$typed\_term:DL \times E \rightarrow S$

$cons:D \times DL \rightarrow DL$, $E \times EL \rightarrow EL$, $T \times TL \rightarrow TL$

$nil:DL,EL,TL$

$declaration:A \times T \rightarrow D$

$type:A \rightarrow T$

$function:T \times TL \rightarrow T$

$term:A \rightarrow E$

$multiap:E \times EL \rightarrow E$

$typed\_term(dl,e)$ is denoted $dl^{DC}.e$

$cons\,(d,dl)^{DC}$ is denoted d; dl^{DC} or $d\ dl^{N}$

$declaration\,(a,t)$ is denoted $a:t^{T}$

$type\,(a)^{T,P}$ is denoted a

$function\,(t,tl)^{T}$ is denoted $tl^{TC} \rightarrow t$

$function\,(t,tl)^{P}$ is denoted $(tl^{TC} \rightarrow t)$

$cons\,(t,tl)^{TC}$ is denoted $t^{P} \times tl^{TC}$ or $t\ tl^{N}$

$term\,(a)^{E,P}$ is denoted a

$multiap\,(e,el)^{E}$ is denoted $e^{P}\,(el^{EC})$

$multiap\,(e,el)^{P}$ is denoted $(e^{P})\,(el^{EC})$

$cons\,(e,el)^{EC}$ is denoted e,el^{EC} or $e\ el^{N}$

nil^{N} is denoted ϵ

The operator *multiap* above applies a function, which may be given by an arbitrarily complex term, to a list of arguments. *term* constructs a primitive term, and *type* a primitive type, from an atomic symbol that is intended to be the name of the term or type. $function\,(t,tl)$ represents the type of functions whose arguments are of the types listed in tl, and whose result is of type t. The denotational specifications above produce the minimum parenthesization needed to avoid ambiguity. The empty list is denoted by the empty string. A typical element of the language above is given by the concrete form

$f : t \times t \rightarrow t$;

$g : (t \times t \rightarrow t) \times t \rightarrow t \rightarrow t$;

$a : t$.

$f(a, (g(f, a))(a))$

and the abstract form, given in LISP.M notation,

typed_term[
  (
    declaration[*f*;*function*[*type*[*t*],(*type*[*t*] *type*[*t*])]]

    declaration[
      g,
      function[
        function[*type*[*t*],(*type*[*t*])];
        (*function*[*type*[*t*],(*type*[*t*] *type*[*t*])],*type*[*t*])
      ]
    ]

    declaration[*a*,*type*[*t*]]
  );

    multiap[
      term[*f*];
      (
        term[*a*]

        multiap[
          multiap[*term*[*g*],(*term*[*f*] *term*[*a*])];
            (*term*[*a*])]
)
    ]
]

Although the presentation of the abstract syntax above is not very readable for even moderate sized declarations and terms, it has the flexibility needed to describe a wide class of computations on the terms.   The substantial *ad hoc* extensions to the concrete syntax that would be required to denote portions of well-formed expressions, and to present equations with variables, would end up being more confusing than the general abstract form. In particular, the distinction between semantic function application, involving the operators performing the type checking, and syntactic function application in the term being checked, requires some departure from conventional concrete notation. So, even though it is a very poor *display* notation, the abstract syntax may be a good *internal* notation for defining computations.

The following equational program uses the LISP.M notation to define type checking for the typed terms described above. We assume that equations are given defining operations on symbol tables, as described in Section 16.3.

: check[typed_term[dl; e]] evaluates to true if the term e is type correct
: with respect to the declarations in dl.

Symbols:

: constructors for typed terms
: declaration[a;t] declares the atomic symbol a to have type t
: type[a] is a primitive type named by the atomic symbol a
: function[t;tl] is the type of functions with argument types given
:   by the list tl, and value of type t
: term[a] is a primitive term named by the atomic symbol a
: multiap[e;el] is a term with head function symbol e applied to the list of
:   arguments el
   typed_term: 2;
   declaration: 2;
   type: 1;
   function: 2;
   term: 1;
   multiap: 2;

: standard list constructors
   cons: 2;
   nil: 0;

: type manipulating operations
   typeof: 2;
   typelist: 2;
   resulttype: 2;
   argtypes: 2;

: primitive symbol table operations
   entertable: 3;

emptytable: 0;
lookup: 2;

: special type-checking operations
  check: 1;
  buildtable: 1;
  looklist: 2;
  checkargs: 2;
  typecheck: 2;

: standard logical symbols
  equ: 2;
  and: 2;
  include truth_values;

: atomic symbols used to identify type, constant, and function symbols
  include atomic_symbols.

For all d, dl, e, el, t, t1, t2, tl, tl1, tl2, a, a1, a2, st, b:

: To check a typed term, build a symbol table from the declarations,
: then check the term against the symbol table.

  check[typed_term[dl,e]] = typecheck[buildtable[dl]; e];

: The symbol table is built by the natural iteration through the list of
: declarations.

  buildtable[()] = emptytable[];

  buildtable[(declaration[a;t] : dl)] = entertable[buildtable[dl]; a; t];

: Final type checking goes recursively through the term. Whenever a
: function application is encountered, the type of the function is computed and
: checked for consistency with the types of the arguments.

  typecheck[st; ()] = true;

  typecheck[st; (e . el)] = and[typecheck[st; e]; typecheck[st; el]];

  typecheck[st; term[a]] = true;

  typecheck[st; multiap[e; el]] =
    and[and[typecheck[st; e];
        typecheck[st; el]];
      checkargs[argtypes[typeof[st; el]]; typelist[st; el]]];

  typelist[st; ()] = ();

typelist[st; (e . el)] = (typeof[st; e] . typelist[st; el]);

typeof[st; term[a]] = lookup[st; a];

typeof[st; multiap[e; el]] = resulttype[typeof[st; e]];

resulttype[function[t; tl]] = t;

argtypes[function[t; tl]] = tl;

checkargs[(); ()] = true;

checkargs[(); (t . tl)] = false;

checkargs[(t . tl); ()] = false;

checkargs[(t1 . tl1); (t2 . tl2)] = and[equ[t1; t2]; checkargs[tl1; tl2]];

: Assume that equations are given for entertable, lookup.

: The standard equality test on atomic symbols is extended to type
: expressions by the natural recursion.

equ[type[a1]; type[a2]] = equ[a1; a2];

equ[function[t1; tl1]; function[t2; tl2]] =
*   and[equ[t1; t2]; checkargs[tl1; tl2]];*

equ[function[t; tl]; type[a]] = false;

equ[type[a]; function[t; tl]] = false;

include equatom;

: and is the standard boolean function.

and[true; true] = true;

and[true; b] = b.

The equations above may easily be augmented to report conflicts and omissions in the declarations. If type checking is to be followed by some sort of semantic processing, such as interpreting or translating the term, it may be useful to attach types (or other information from a symbol table) to the symbols in a term, so that the semantic processing does not need the symbol table. This technique was used in the implementation of the equation interpreter itself: each variable symbol in a left-hand side term is annotated to indicate the allowable substitutions for that variable, and each variable in a right-hand side term is annotated to show its address on the corresponding left-hand side. These annotations provide precisely the information needed by the semantic portion of the interpreter. To illustrate the technique, we present equations annotating each symbol in a typed term with its type.

: typenotes[st; e] annotates each symbol in the term e with the type assigned to it
: by the symbol table st. Type conflicts are marked for debugging purposes.

Symbols:

: constructors for types and terms used as in the previous program
   type: 1;
   function: 2;
   term: 1;
   multiap: 2;

: extra constructors for annotated terms
: aterm[a;t] is a primitive term named by the atomic symbol a of type t
: typeconflict[e] marks the term e as having a typeconflict in the application
:   of its head function symbol to inappropriate arguments
   aterm: 2;
   typeconflict: 1;

: standard list constructors
   cons: 2;
   nil: 0;

: type manipulating operations
   typeof: 2;
   typelist: 2;
   resulttype: 2;
   argtypes: 2;

: primitive symbol table operations
   lookup: 2;

: special type-checking operations

looklist: 2;
checkargs: 2;
typenotes: 2;

: standard logical symbols
equ: 2;
and: 2;
if: 3;
include truth_values;

: atomic symbols are used to identify type, constant, and function symbols
include atomic_symbols.

For all d, dl, e, el, t, t1, t2, tl, tl1, tl2, a, a1, a2, st, b:

: Annotation goes recursively through the term. Whenever a function
: application is encountered, the type of the function is computed and checked
: for consistency with the types of the arguments.

typenotes[st; ()] = ();

typenotes[st; (e . el)] = (typenotes[st; e] . typenotes[st; el]);

typenotes[st; term[a]] = aterm[a; typeof[st; a]];

typenotes[st; multiap[e; el]] =
if[checkargs[argtypes[typeof[st; e]]; typelist[st; el]];
multiap[typenotes[st; e]; typenotes[st; el]];
typeconflict[multiap[typenotes[st; e]; typenotes[st; el]]]];

: Assume that equations are given for entertable, lookup.
: Equations for the remaining operations are the same as in the previous program.

if(true, x, y) = x; if(false, x, y) = y.

14. Modular Construction of Equational Definitions

The equational programming language, although its concepts are far from being primitive operations on conventional computing machines, is not really a high-level language. Rather, it is the assembly language for an unusual abstract machine. The problem is that the set of equations constituting a program has no structure to help in organizing and understanding it. In order to be suitable for solving any but rather small problems, the equational programming language needs constructs that allow decomposition of a solution into manageable components, or modules, with semantically elegant combining operations. In particular, different sets of equations, presented separately, must be combinable other than by textual concatenation, and the combining operation must protect the programmer from accidental coincidence of symbols in different components. Furthermore, sets of equations must be parameterized to allow variations on a single concept (e.g., recursion over a tree structure) to be produced from a single definition, rather than being generated individually. In this chapter, we define a speculative set of combining operations for equational programs, and discuss possible means of implementation. None of these features has been implemented for the equational programming language, although some similarly motivated features are implemented in OBJ [BG77, Go84]. Libraries of predefined equations cannot be integrated well into the equation interpreter until some good structuring constructs are implemented.

In order to combine sets of equations in coherent ways, we need to design the combining operations in terms of the *meanings* of equational programs, rather than their texts. Based on the scenario of Section 1, the meaning of an equational program should be characterized by three things:

1.   the language of terms over which equations are given;

2.   a class of models of that language;

3.   the subset of terms that are considered simple, or transparent, enough to be allowed as output.

Items 1 and 2 are standard concepts from universal algebra. For equational programming, the information in 2 may be given equivalently as a *congruence relation* on terms, but extensions to other logical languages might need the greater generality of classes of models. In any case, the use of classes of models is better in keeping with the intuitive spirit of our computing scenario.

Definition 14.1

Let Σ be a ranked alphabet, $\rho(a)$ the rank of $a \in \Sigma$, $\Sigma_\#$ the set of terms over Σ.

A *model* of Σ is a pair $<U,\psi>$, where U, the *universe*, is any set, and ψ is a mapping from Σ to functions over U with $\psi(a):U^{\rho(a)} \to U$.

ψ extends naturally to $\Sigma_\#$ by $\psi(f(E_1, \cdots, E_n)) = (\psi(f))(\psi(E_1), \cdots \psi(E_n))$.

A model $<U,\psi>$ *satisfies* an equation $E=F$, written $<U,\psi> \models E=F$, if $\psi(E)=\psi(F)$.

A set **W** of models *satisfies* a set E of equations, written $\mathbf{W} \models E$, if $<U,\psi> \models E=F$ for all $<U,\psi> \in \mathbf{W}$, $E=F \in E$.

The set of *models* of a set E of equations, written *Mod*(E), is $\{<U,\psi> | <U,\psi> \models E\}$.

The set of *normal forms* of a set E of equations, written *Norm*(E), is $\{E \in \Sigma_\# | \mathbf{V} F=G \in E$ F *is not a subterm of* $E\}$.

A *computational world* is a triple $<\Sigma, \mathbf{W}, N>$, where Σ is a ranked alphabet, **W** is a class of models of Σ, and $N \subseteq \Sigma_\#$. N is called the *output set*.

The *world* of a set of equations E over Σ, written *World*(E), is

$<\Sigma, Mod(E), Norm(E)>$.

☐

The function *World* assigns meanings to equational programs by letting Σ be the ranked alphabet defined by the *Symbols* section, and taking *World*(E) where E is the set of all instances of equations in the program. The computing scenario of Section 1 may be formalized by requiring, on input E, an output $F \in Norm(E)$ such that $Mod(E) \models E=F$. In principle, we would like separate control of the models and the output terms, but the pragmatic restriction that output terms must be precisely the *normal forms* -- terms with no instances of left-hand sides of equations -- limits us to constructs that generate both of these components of program meanings in ways that make them compatible with the evaluation mechanism of reduction. Notice that uniqueness of normal forms means that there may not be two different terms $F_1, F_2 \in \Sigma_\#$ with $\mathbf{W} \models F_1=F_2$, i.e, there must exist at least one model in $\mathbf{W}$ in which $\psi(F_1) \neq \psi(F_2)$.

Explicit presentation of an equational program is one way to specify a computational world, the purpose of this section is to explore others. Because this aspect of our study of equational logic programming is quite new and primitive, we do not try to build a convenient notation for users yet. Rather, we explore constructs that are both meaningful and implementable, and leave the design of good syntax for them to the future. The OBJ project has gone much farther in the user-level design of constructs for structured definition of equational programs, and the constructs proposed here are inspired by that work [BG77, Go84]. Our problem is to determine how well such constructs can be implemented in a form consistent with our computational techniques. In particular, we prefer implementations in which all of the work associated with the structuring constructs is done during the preprocessing of equations, so that the resulting interpreter is of the same sort that we derive directly from a set of equations.

The most obvious way of constructing a computational world is to combine the information in two others.

Definition 14.2

Given two ranked alphabets $\Sigma_1 \subseteq \Sigma_2$, and a model $<U,\psi>$ of Σ_2, we may restrict this model naturally to a model of Σ_1 by restricting ψ to Σ_1. When two classes of models, W_1 and W_2, are given over different alphabets, Σ_1 and Σ_2, the *intersection* $W_1 \cap W_2$ is the set of all models of $\Sigma_1 \cup \Sigma_2$ whose restrictions to Σ_1 and Σ_2 are in W_1 and W_2, respectively. In the case where $\Sigma_1 = \Sigma_2$, this specializes naturally to the conventional set-theoretic intersection.

Given two computational worlds, $<\Sigma_1, W_1, N_1>$ and $<\Sigma_2, W_2, N_2>$, the *sum* $<\Sigma_1, W_1, N_1> + <\Sigma_2, W_2, N_2>$ is $<\Sigma_1 \cup \Sigma_2, W_1 \cap W_2, N_1 \cup N_2>$.

$\square$

The sum described above is similar to the *enrich* operation of [BG77], except that enrich requires one of its arguments to be given by explicit equations. The sum of computational worlds corresponds roughly to concatenation of two sets of equations. Even this simple combining form cannot be implemented by simple-minded textual concatenation, because a variable in one program may be a defined symbol in the other. If an equational program is syntactically cooked into a form where each instance of a variable is marked unambiguously as such, then concatenation of cooked forms will often accomplish the sum of worlds. The equation interpreter is implemented in such a way that the cooked form is created explicitly, and may provide the basis for a very simple implementation of the sum. For greater efficiency, we would like to implement the sum at the level of the pattern-matching tables that drive the interpreter. Such an implementation depends critically on the choice of pattern matching technique (see Section 18.2).

The concatenation of syntactically cooked programs described above succeeds only when the combined equations satisfy the restrictions of Section 5. Certainly, this need not be the case, since the sum of computational worlds with unique normal forms may *not* have unique normal forms. For example, combining the singleton sets $\{a=b\}$ and $\{a=c\}$ fails to preserve uniqueness of normal forms. This problem is inherent in the semantics of the sum, and can only be solved completely by an implementation that deals with indeterminate programs. Unfortunately, there are cases where the semantics of the sum does maintain uniqueness of normal forms, but the concatenation of equations fails nonetheless.

Example 14.1

Consider the following two sets of equations:

1. $\{f(g(x))=a \ , \ a=b\}$

2. $\{g(c)=c \ , \ b=a\}$

Each of these sets individually has unique normal forms, and every reduction sequence terminates. Their sum has uniqueness of normal forms, but not finite termination. Notice that, in the sum, the unique normal form of $f(g(c))$ is $f(c)$, but there is also an infinite reduction $f(g(c))=a=b=a \cdots$. The combined set of equations cannot be processed by the equation interpreter, because of the overlap between $f(g(x))$ and $g(c)$.

This failure to achieve an implementation of the sum in all semantically natural cases is a weakness of the current state of the equation interpreter. Of course, one may fiddle with the semantics of the sum to get any implementation to work, but we would rather seek implementation techniques that approach closer to the semantic ideal.

The sum allows for combining equational programs, but by itself is not very useful. We need a way of hiding certain symbols in a program, so that sums do not produce surprising results due to the accidental use of the same symbol in both summands. Other changes in notation will be required so that a module is not restricted to interact only with other modules using the same notational conventions. Both of these needs are satisfied by a single semantic construct.

Definition 14.3

Given a model $<U_1,\psi_1>$ over the alphabet Σ_1, a model $<U_2,\psi_2>$ over the alphabet Σ_2, and a relation $\delta \subseteq \Sigma_{1\#} \times \Sigma_{2\#}$, $<U_1,\psi_1> \delta <U_2,\psi_2>$ if

$$\forall E_1,F_1 \in \Sigma_{1\#}, E_2,F_2 \in \Sigma_{2\#} \quad E_1 \delta E_2 \ \& \ F_1 \delta F_2 \ \& \ \psi_1(E_1) = \psi_1(F_1) \implies \psi_2(E_2) = \psi_2(F_2)$$

For a set $\mathbf{W}$ of models over Σ_1, $\delta[\mathbf{W}]$ is the set of all models over Σ_2 that are in the δ relation to some member of $\mathbf{W}$.

For a subset $N \subseteq \Sigma_{1\#}$, $\delta[N]$ is the set of all terms in $\Sigma_{2\#}$ that are not in the δ relation to any term not in N.

Given a computational world $<\Sigma_1,\mathbf{W},N>$, an alphabet Σ_2, and a relation $\delta \subseteq \Sigma_{1\#} \times \Sigma_{2\#}$, the *syntactic transform* $\sigma[<\Sigma_1,\mathbf{W},N>, \delta, \Sigma_2]$ is $<\Sigma_2, \delta[\mathbf{W}], \delta[N]>$.

□

The syntactic transform defined above may accomplish hiding of symbols, by letting $\Sigma_2 \subseteq \Sigma_1$, with δ the equality relation restricted to Σ_2. A change of notation, for example letting $f(x,y,z)$ represent $g(x,h(y,z))$, is accomplished by a δ relating each term E to the result E' of replacing every subterm of the form $g(F_1,h(F_2,F_3))$ with the form $f(F_1,F_2,F_3)$. The syntactic transform is similar to the *derive* operator of [BG77].

The syntactic transform for symbol hiding may be implemented by renaming the symbols in $\Sigma_1 - \Sigma_2$ in such a way that they can never coincide with names produced elsewhere. Other syntactic transforms require different implementations depending on the characteristics of the δ relation. Suppose δ is a partial function, defined by a set of equations suitable for the equation interpreter. Add to the equations defining δ the equation

$\delta(v) = v$ *where v is a variable symbol.*

The resulting equational program may be used to transform equations for $<\Sigma_1,\mathbf{W},N>$ into equations defining $\sigma[<\Sigma_1,\mathbf{W},N>, \delta, \Sigma_2]$. If the transformation eliminates all instances of symbols not in Σ_2, and produces equations satisfying the restrictions of Section 5, then we have an implementation of the syntactically transformed world. We have not yet determined how easy or hard it is to produce definitions of useful δs allowing for this sort of transformation.

If δ is a *one−to−one* correspondence between some subset of $\Sigma_{1\#}$ and a subset of $\Sigma_{2\#}$, and if δ and δ^{-1} can be programmed nicely, then the syntactic transform may be implemented by applying δ^{-1} to the input, applying an existing program for $<\Sigma_1,\mathbf{W},N>$ to that result, and finally applying δ. If δ is defined by an equational program, and if the result of reversing each equation satisfies the restrictions of Section 5, then we may use those reversals as a program for δ^{-1}. Alternatively, given equational programs for δ and δ^{-1} we may try to verify that they are inverses by applying the program for δ^{-1} to the right-hand sides of equations in the program for δ, to see if we can derive the corresponding left-hand sides. Further study is required to determine whether either of these techniques works often enough to be useful. In any case, the last two techniques produce something more complex than a single equational program, raising the question of how to continue combining their results by more applications of sum and syntactic transform.

15. High-Level Programming Techniques

This section treats high-level programming concepts that fit naturally on the evaluation mechanism of the equation interpreter. The current version of the interpreter does not provide any special syntax to support these techniques, but future work may lead to convenient syntaxes for applying them.

15.1. Concurrency

Although the current implementation of the equation interpreter runs on conventional sequential computing machines, some qualities of equational logic show interesting potential for implementation on parallel machines of the future. Even with a sequential implementation, the ability to express programming concepts based on concurrent computations gives a conceptual advantage. There are three distinguishable sources of concurrent programming power in a reduction-based evaluation for equational logic, two of which are provided by the current implementation.

The simplest source of concurrent programming power arises from the possibility of evaluating independent subexpressions concurrently. Roughly speaking, this means that several, or all, of the arguments to a function may be evaluated simultaneously (in general, evaluation of a single argument may be partial instead of complete). This potential concurrency arises simply from the absence of side-effects in equational evaluation, and is the same as the potential concurrency in Functional Programming languages [Ba78]. A genuinely parallel implementation of the equational interpreter might realize a substantial advantage from such concurrency. There is also a definite conceptual advantage to the programmer in *knowing* that order of evaluation of arguments is irrelevant to the final result. In most cases, however, no style of programming is supported that could not translate quite simply into sequential evaluation in some particular order.

Concurrent evaluation of independent subexpressions becomes an essential feature when it is possible to reach a normal form without completing all of the evaluations of subexpressions, and when there is no way *a priori* to determine how much evaluation of which subexpressions is required. The most natural example of this behavior is in the *parallel or*, defined by the equations:

or(true, x) = *true;*

or(x, true) = *true;*

or(false, false) = *false.*

Intuitively, it seems *essential* to evaluate the arguments of the *or* concurrently, since one of them might evaluate to *true* while the other evaluation fails to terminate. In the presence of other equations defining other computable functions, there is no way to predict which of the arguments will evaluate to a truth value. Translation of the intuitively concurrent evaluation of an expression containing *or*s into a sequential computation requires a rather elaborate mechanism for explicitly interleaving evaluation steps on the two arguments of an *or*. The current implementation of the equation interpreter does not support the essential concurrency involved in the parallel *or*, due to the restriction number 5 of Section 5 (left-sequentiality). Section 19 presents evidence that the parallel *or* cannot be satisfactorily simulated by the sequentializable definitions allowed by the current implementation. Future versions will support the parallel *or*, and similar definitions. The basis of the implementation is a multitasking simulation of concurrency on a sequential machine. We do not know yet how small the overhead of the multitasking can be, and that stage of the project awaits a careful study of the concrete details involved. The general problems of supporting this sort of concurrency on conventional sequential machines are discussed in Section 18.3.

The final source of concurrent behavior is easily overlooked, but is arguably the most useful of them all. This sort of concurrency results from the outermost, or "lazy", evaluation strategy, that allows nested subexpressions to be reduced concurrently. Roughly, this means that evaluation of a function value may go on concurrently with evaluation of the arguments. Every piece of partial information about the arguments may immediately result in partial, or even complete, evaluation of a function value. As with the parallel *or*, this sort of concurrency translates into sequential behavior only at the cost of a careful interleaving of steps from the intuitively concurrent components of a computation. Unlike the unconstrained interleaving of the parallel *or*, the interleaving of nested evaluation steps is highly constrained by the need to generate enough information about arguments to allow an evaluation step on a function of those arguments. Nested concurrency is supported by the current version of the interpreter, as it depends only on the outermost evaluation strategy. It allows a style of programming based on pipelined coroutines, or more generally on dataflow graphs, as shown in Section 15.3.

15.2. Nondeterminism vs. Indeterminacy

Dijkstra argues eloquently [Di76] that programmers should not be required to specify details that are inessential to solving a given problem. Not only is inessential detail wasteful of programming time, it may have an adverse effect on the clarity of the program, by requiring a reader to separate the essential issues from the inessential. On this consideration, Dijkstra proposes a *nondeterministic* programming language, based on guarded commands. Not only are the computation steps nondeterministic, the final answer of a guarded-command program may not be uniquely determined by the inputs. This *indeterminacy* in the output is sometimes desirable in addition to nondeterminism in the computation steps, since many problems admit several acceptable answers.

The equation interpreter supports some of the advantages of nondeterministic specification of evaluation steps. Although the current implementation chooses, rather arbitrarily, to evaluate from left to right, the semantics of the language allow for any order of evaluation that finds a normal form. The presence or absence of real nondeterminism in the implementation is never visible to a user in the results of evaluation, since the restrictions of Section 5 guarantee uniqueness of the normal form, independently of order of evaluation. This guarantee of uniqueness is helpful in solving problems with uniquely determined answers, but it prevents taking full advantage of the simplifications allowed by nondeterministic and indeterminate programs for those problems with several acceptable answers. In particular, it prevents a satisfying implementation of guarded commands [Di76] by equations. The ideal facility would allow equational definitions with multiple normal forms, but recognize special cases where uniqueness is guaranteed.

There are no plans to introduce indeterminacy into the equation interpreter, not because of anything fundamentally repugnant about indeterminacy, but because the only simple way that we know to relax the uniqueness of normal forms causes other problems in the semantics of equational programming. The uniqueness of normal forms in equations satisfying the restrictions of Section 5 is a consequence of the Church-Rosser, or confluence, property. This property says that, whenever an expression A may reduce to two different expressions B and C, then there is another expression D to which both B and C reduce. The confluence property is required, not only to guarantee uniqueness of normal forms, but also to guarantee that some normal form will be found whenever such exists. The problem arises when some expression *A* reduces to normal form, and also has an infinite reduction sequence. The confluence property guarantees that, no matter how far we pursue the infinite path, it is still *possible* to reduce to the normal form. Without the confluence property, we may have such an *A*, and an expression *B* appearing on its infinite reduction sequence, but *B* may *not* be reducible to normal form. Yet, by the semantics of equational logic, *B* is equal to *A*, and therefore to any normal form of *A*. Figure 15.2.1 shows this situation graphically.

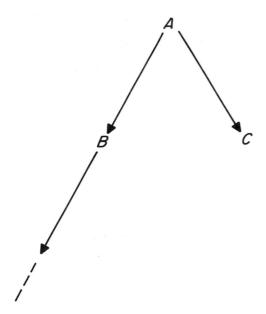

Figure 15.2.1

So, in a system of equations without the confluence property, there may be an expression *B* with a normal form, but the only way to find that normal form may require *backwards* reductions. All of the helpful theory used to find an efficient *forward* reduction to normal form fails to apply to backward reductions. It seems quite unlikely that a weaker condition than confluence can be designed to allow indeterminacy, but guarantee reductions to normal forms, so an indeterminate equation interpreter probably requires a substantial new concept in evaluation techniques. Even if such conditions are found, equational programming is probably the wrong setting for indeterminacy, since it would be impossible to have, for example, an expression α equal to each of the normal forms a and b, and an expression β equal to each of the normal forms b and c, without also having $\alpha = c$ and $\beta = a$. The computation techniques of reduction sequences could be applied to asymmetric congruence-like relations in order to produce indeterminacy, but such relations are not well established in logic, as is the symmetric congruence relation of equality.

15.3. Dataflow

The nested concurrency provided by outermost evaluation allows a very simple translation of dataflow programs into equational programs. A dataflow program [KM66] consists of a directed graph with an optional entry and an exit. The entry, if any, represents an *input sequence* of values, the exit an *output sequence*. Each edge in the graph represents a sequence of values communicated between two processes, represented by the nodes. In the semantics of a dataflow graph, the processes at the nodes are restricted to view their incoming sequences in order, and to produce each outgoing sequence in order, although several proposals for implementing them use numerical tags to simulate the order, and allow the actual time sequence to be different. A common kind of node, called a *copy node*, contains a process that merely copies its single incoming edge to each of its outgoing edges. It is easier for our purposes to group a copy node and its edges into one *multiedge* with a single head and several tails.

Every dataflow graph in which the node processes are all determinate as functions of their incoming sequences (i.e., they cannot make arbitrary or timing-dependent steps) may be translated easily into an equational program running on the equation interpreter. The basic idea is to use a convenient list notation, such as *LISP.M*, and replace each edge in the dataflow graph by a constant symbol, whose value will turn out to be the (possibly infinite) sequence of values transmitted through that edge. Each node becomes a set of function symbols, one for each outgoing edge, with arity equal to the number of incoming edges. Equations are written to define each node function. Finally, the connection structure of the dataflow graph is realized by a single defining equation for each of the edge constants. That is, if f is the function symbol representing a node with incoming edges a and b, and outgoing edge c, include the equation $c[] = f[a, b]$. In some cases structural equations may be condensed with some of the equations defining node processes. In particular, tree-shaped subgraphs of the dataflow graph may be condensed into single expressions, using edge names only to break loops. A single example should suffice to illustrate the technique.

Example 15.3.1

Consider the dataflow graph of Figure 15.3.1. The labels on edges and nodes indicate the corresponding constant and function symbols. Assuming that equations are given to define f, g, h, the following equations give the structure of the graph:

$a[] = f[input[], b[]];$

$b[] = g[a[]];$

$output[] = h[a[]; b[]].$

These equations may be condensed by eliminating either a or b (but not both),

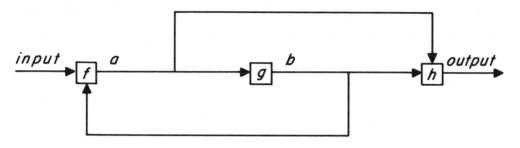

Figure 15.3.1

yielding

$b[] = g[f[input[]; b[]];$

$output[] = h[f[input[]; b[]]; b[]].$

or

$a[] = f[input[]; g[a[]]];$

$output[] = h[a[]; g[a[]]].$

□

In order to make use of the equational translation of a dataflow program, we also require a definition of *input*, and some mechanism for selecting the desired part of *output*, unless it is known to be finite (and even short). The idea of translating dataflow graphs into equations comes from Lucid [WA85].

For a more substantial example of dataflow programming, consider the prime number sieve of Eratosthenes. This elegant version of the prime number sieve is based on a dataflow program by McIlroy [Mc68, KM77]. The basic idea is to take the infinite list (2 3 4 ...), and remove all multiples of primes, in order to produce the infinite list of primes (the same one used to produce the multiples of primes that must be removed to produce itself). Figure 15.3.2 shows the dataflow graph corresponding to this idea, with each edge and node labelled by its corresponding symbol in the equational program.

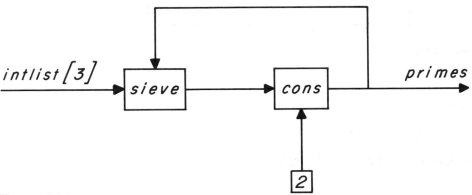

Figure 15.3.2

The following equational program captures the concept of the dataflow graph above, varying the notation a bit for clarity. Of course, in the equational program, it is essential to evaluate, not the infinite lists themselves, but an expression producing some finite sublist.

Example 15.3.1

: The following definitions are intended to allow production of lists of
: prime numbers. The list of the first i prime numbers is firstn[i; primes[]].

Symbols

: List construction and manipulation operators
  cons: 2;
  nil: 0;
  first: 1;
  tail: 1;
  firstn: 2;

: Logical and arithmetic operators
   if: 3;
   add, subtract, multiply, modulo, equ, less: 2;

: Operators associated with the prime sieve
   intlist: 1;
   sieve: 2;
   fact: 2;
   primes: 0;

: Primitive domains
   include integer_numerals, truth_values.

For all i, j, q, r:

: first[q] is the first element in the list q.
: tail[q] is the list of all but the first element in the list q.

   first[(i . q)] = i;   tail[(i . q)] = q;

: firstn[i; q] is the list of the first i elements in the list q.

   firstn[i; q] = if[equ[i; 0]; (); (first[q] . firstn[subtract[i; 1]; tail[q]])];

: if is the standard conditional function.

   if[true; i; j] = i; if[false; i; j] = j;

   include addint, multint, subint, modint, equint, lessint;

: intlist[i] is the infinite list (i i+1 i+2 ...).

   intlist[i] = (i . intlist[add[i; 1]]);

: The definitions of sieve and fact assume that r is given in increasing order, that
: r contains all of the prime numbers, and that r contains nothing less than 2.

: sieve[q; r] is the infinite list of those elements of the infinite list q that are
: not multiples of anything on the infinite list r.

   sieve[(i . q); r] = if[fact[i; r]; sieve[q; r]; (i . sieve[q; r])];

: fact[i; r] is true iff the infinite list r contains a nontrivial factor of i.

   fact[i; (j . r)] = if[less[i; multiply[j; j]];
                        false;
                        if[equ[modulo[i; j]; 0];

true;
fact[i; r]]];

: primes[] is the infinite list of prime numbers, (2 3 5 7 11 13 17 ...).

primes[] = (2 . sieve[intlist[3]; primes[]]).

The correct behavior of this dataflow program for primes depends on the not-so-obvious fact that there is always a prime between n and n^2. If not, the loop through the *sieve* and *cons* nodes would deadlock.

While the outermost evaluation strategy guarantees that the internal computations of an equational program will satisfy the semantics of an associated dataflow graph, there is still an interesting issue related to input to and output from the interpreter. At the abstract level, input is any expression, and output is a corresponding normal form. It is semantically legitimate to think of the input expression being provided instantaneously at the beginning of the computation, and the output expression being produced instantaneously at the end. An implementation following that idea strictly will not allow a dataflow behavior at the input and output interfaces of the interpreter. The all-at-once style of input and output forms a barrier to the composition of several equational programs, since it forces the, possibly very large, expressions transmitted between them to be produced totally, before the receiving program may start. In the worst case, an infinite term may be produced, even though only a finite part of it is required by the next step.

The current version of the equation interpreter incorporates a partial dataflow interface on output, but none on input. The output pretty-printers do not support incremental output, so a user may only benefit by using the internal form of output, or writing his own incremental pretty-printer. Interestingly, incremental output from the interpreter was *easier* to code than the all-at-once form. An output process drives the whole evaluation, by traversing the input expression. When it reaches a symbol that is stable -- that can clearly never change as a result of further reduction -- it outputs that symbol, and breaks the evaluation problem into several independent problems associated with the arguments to the stable symbol. Section 17.2 gives a careful definition of stability, and Section 18.2 describes how it is detected. When the output process finds an unstable symbol, it initiates evaluation, which proceeds only until that particular symbol is stable. The control structure described above is precisely the right one for outermost evaluation, even if incremental output is not desired.

In the computation described above, the interpreter program must contain an *a priori* choice of traversal order for expressions -- *leftmost* being the natural order given current typographical conventions. Leftmost production of an output expression would support natural incremental output of lists, using the conventional LISP notation. Since the essential data structure of the equation interpreter is trees, not lists, and there is no reason to expect *all* applications to respect a leftmost discipline, a future version of the interpreter should support a more flexible output interface. Probably the right way to achieve such an interface is to think of an interactive question-answer dialogue between the consumer of output and the interpreter. The precise design of the question-answer language requires further study, but it is likely to be something like the following. The output consumer possesses at least one, and probably several, cursors that point to particular subexpressions of the normal form expression coming from the interpreter. The output consumer may issue commands of the form "*move cursor x to α*", where α may be the father, or any specified son, of *x*'s current position. The interpreter does precisely enough evaluation to discover the new symbol under the cursor after each motion, and reports that symbol on its output. Thus, the order of traversal may be determined dynamically as a result of the symbols seen so far.

The question-answer output interface described above may also be used for the input interface, with the equation interpreter producing the questions, and some input process providing the answers. Such an interface will certainly allow connection of several equational programs in a generalized sort of pipeline. Another sort of input interface is likely to be more valuable, and also more difficult to construct. In order for equational programs to be used as interactive back ends behind structure editors, a purpose for which the equational programming style appears to be nicely suited as argued in Section 13, an incremental input interface must be provided in which the input process (essentially the user himself) determines the order in which the input expression is produced. Worse, existing portions of the input term may change. Changing input is substantially more difficult to accommodate than incrementally produced input. Besides requiring an efficient mechanism for incremental reevaluation, avoiding the reevaluation of unchanged portions of an expression, some adjustment of the output interface is required to notify the output consumer of changes as they occur. Apparently, the output consumer must be able to specify a region of interest, and be notified of whatever happens in that region of the expression. Further study is required to find a convenient representation of a region of interest, taking into account that the topology of the expression is subject to change as well as the symbol appearing at a particular node.

The incremental evaluation problem for equational programs appears to be substantially more difficult than that for attribute grammars [RTD83]. The elegance of Teitelbaum's and Reps' optimal reevaluation strategies for attribute grammars gives that formalism a strong edge in competition for beyond-context-free processing. Work is in progress to close that gap. The same factors that make incremental evaluation more difficult for equational programs will also make a good solution more valuable than that for attribute grammars. The optimal reevaluation strategy for attribute grammars treats attributes and the functions that compute one attribute from another as primitives. The reevaluation strategy only determines which attributes should be recomputed, it does not treat the problem of incremental reevaluation of an individual attribute with significant structure. Yet, one of the most critical performance issues for attribute reevaluation is avoidance of multiple copies and excess reevaluation of components of highly structured attributes, especially symbol tables. A lot of work on special cases of reevaluation of large, structured attributes is underway, but we are not aware of any thoroughly general approach. A good incremental evaluation strategy for equational programs will inherently solve the total problem, since the expression model of data underlying the equation interpreter makes all structure in data explicit, rather than allowing large structures to be treated as primitives.

All of the preceding discussion of input and output ignores the possibility of sharing of identical subexpressions in an expression. The equation interpreter could not achieve an acceptable performance in many cases without such sharing. Perhaps such sharing should be accommodated in the treatment of input and output as well, but careful thought is required to do so without distasteful complexity.

15.4. Dynamic Programming

Dynamic programming may be viewed as a general technique for transforming an inefficient recursive program into a more efficient one that stores some portion of the graph of the recursively defined function in an array, in order to avoid recomputation of function values that are used repeatedly. In a typical application of dynamic programming, the user must completely specify the way in which the graph of the function is to be arranged in an array, and the order in which the graph is to be computed. The latter task may be handled automatically by the equation interpreter. To illustrate this automation of part of the dynamic programming task, we give equations for the optimal matrix multiplication problem of [AHU74]. Instead of defining only a small finite part of the graph of the cost function, we define the infinite graph, and the outermost evaluation strategy of the equation interpreter guarantees that only the relevant part of the infinite graph is actually computed.

Example 15.4.1

The following equations solve the optimal matrix multiplication problem from The Design and Analysis of Computer Algorithms, by Aho, Hopcroft and Ullman, section 2.8. Given a sequence of matrix dimensions, $(d_0 \, d_1 \cdots d_m)$, the problem is to find the least cost for multiplying out a sequence of matrices $M_1 * M_2 * \cdots M_m$ where M_i is $d_{i-1} \times d_i$, assuming that multiplying an $i \times j$ matrix by a $j \times k$ matrix to get an $i \times k$ matrix costs $i * j * k$. There is an obvious, but exponentially inefficient recursive solution, expressed in a more liberal notation than that allowed by the equation interpreter:

$$cost[(d_0 \cdots d_m)] =$$
$$\min\{cost[(d_0 \cdots d_i)] + cost[(d_{i+1} \cdots d_m)] + d_0 * d_1 * d_m \,|\, 0 < i \leqslant m\}$$
$$cost[(d_0 d_1)] = 0$$

The problem with the recursive solution above is that certain values of the function *cost* are calculated repeatedly in the recursion. Dynamic programming yields a polynomial algorithm, by storing the values of *cost* in an array, and computing each required value only once. In the following equations, the function cost is represented by an infinite-dimensional infinite list giving the graph of the function:

costgraph[()] =
　(0 (cost[(1)] (cost[(1 1)] (cost[(1 1 1)] ...)
　　　　　　　　　　　　　(cost[(1 1 2)] ...)
　　　　　　　　　　　　　　...)*
　　　　　　　(cost[(1 2)] (cost[(1 2 1)] ...)
　　　　　　　　　　　　　(cost[(1 2 2)] ...)
　　　　　　　　　　　　　　...)*
　　　　　　　　...)*
　　　(cost[(2)] (cost[(2 1)] (cost[(2 1 1)] ...)
　　　　　　　　　　　　　　...)*
　　　　　　...)*
　...)*

That is, $cost[(d_0 \cdots d_m)]$ is the first element of the list which is element $d_m + 1$ of element $d_{m-1} + 1$ of ... element $d_0 + 1$ of *costgraph*[()]. $cost[(i)]$ is always 0, but explicit inclusion of these 0s simplifies the structure of costgraph. *costgraph*[*a*], for $a \neq ()$, is the fragment of *costgraph*[()] whose indexes are all prefixed by *a*.

Symbols

: operators directly related to the computation of cost
　cost: 1;
　costgraph: 1;
　costrow: 2;
　reccost: 1;
　subcosts: 2;

: list-manipulation, logical, and arithmetic operators

　cons: 2;
　nil: 0;
　min: 1;
　index: 2;
　length: 1;
　element: 2;
　firstn: 2;
　first: 1;
　tail: 1;
　aftern: 2;
　last: 1;
　addend: 2;
　if: 3;
　add: 2;

equ: 2;
less: 2;
subtract: 2;
multiply: 2;
include integer_numerals, truth_values.

For all a, b, i, j, k, x, y:

cost[a] = index[a; costgraph[()]];

: costgraph[a] is the infinite graph of the cost function for arguments starting
: with the prefix a.

costgraph[a] = (reccost[a] . costrow[a; 1]);

: costrow[a; i] is the infinite list
: (costgraph[ai] costgraph[ai+1] ...)
: where ai is a with i added on at the end.

costrow[a; i] =
(costgraph[addend[a; i]] . costrow[a; add[i; 1]]);

: reccost[a] has the same value as cost[a], but is defined by the recursive equations
: from the header.

reccost[(i j)] = 0; reccost[(i)] = 0; reccost[()] = 0;

reccost[(i j . a)] = min[subcosts[(i j . a); length[a]]]
where a is (k . b) end where;

: subcosts[a; i] is a finite list of the recursively computed costs of (d0 ... dm),
: fixing the last index removed at i, i-1, ... 1.

subcosts[a; i] =
if[equ[i; 0]; ();
(add[add[cost[firstn[add[i; 1]; a]]; cost[aftern[add[i; 1]; a]]];
multiply[multiply[first[a]; element[add[i; 1]; a]]; last[a]]])];

: Definitions of list-manipulation operators, logical and arithmetical operators.

min[(i)] = i;

min[(i . a)] = if[less[i; min[a]]; i; min[a]]
where a is (k . b) end where;

index[(); (x . b)] = x;

index[(i . a); x] = index[a; element[add[i; 1]; x]];

length[()] = 0;

length[(x . a)] = add[length[a]; 1];

element[i; (x . a)] = if[equ[i; 1]; x; element[subtract[i; 1]; a]];

firstn[i; a] = if[equ[i; 0]; (); (first[a] . firstn[subtract[i; 1]; tail[a]])];

first[(x . a)] = x; tail[(x . a)] = a;

aftern[i; a] = if[equ[i; 0]; a; aftern[subtract[i; 1]; tail[a]]];

last[(x)] = x;

last[(x y . a)] = last[(y . a)];

addend[(); y] = (y);

addend[(x . a); y] = (x . addend[a; y]);

if[true; x; y] = x;   if[false; x; y] = y;

include addint, equint, subint, multint.

☐

Although the algorithm in [AHU74] runs in time $O(n^3)$ on a problem of size n, the equation interpreter, running the equations above, takes time $O(n^4)$ because of the linear search required to look up elements of the graph of the cost function.   By structuring the graph as an appropriate search tree, the time could be reduced to $O(n^3 \log n)$, but there is no apparent way to achieve the cubic time bound, since the equation interpreter has no provision for constant-time array indexing.   Even the search-tree implementation requires some careful thought in the presence of infinite structures.   Section 16.3 shows how search tree operations may be defined by equations.

Avoidance of recomputation of function values in the example above depends on the sharing strategy of the equation interpreter, described in Section 18.4. A future version of the interpreter will provide, as an option, an alternate implementation of evaluation based on the congruence closure algorithm. [NO80, Ch80]. In that implementation, all recomputation will be avoided in every context, and the naive recursive equations can be used without the exponential cost.

16. Implementing Efficient Data Structures In Equational Programs

The usefulness of the equation interpreter in its current form is severely limited by the lack of carefully-designed data structures. Instead of providing many choices of data structures, the equation interpreter provides the raw materials from which different data structures may be built. In order to make the system usable for any but small problems, a library of predefined data structures must be built. The modular constructs from Section 14 will then be used to incorporate appropriate definitions of data structures into a program as they are needed. This section demonstrates the basic techniques used to define some popular efficient data structures.

16.1 Lists

Implementation of LISP-style lists in the equation interpreter is so straightforward that it is contained in several examples earlier in the text. We define the symbols *car*, *cdr*, *cons*, *nil*, *equ*, *atom*, and *null*, according to LISP usage, except that *nil* is not taken to be an atomic symbol.

Example 16.1.1

Symbols

: List constructors.
  cons: 2;
  nil: 0;
  include atomic_symbols;

: Selectors for the head, tail of a list.
  car, cdr: 1;

: Predicates on lists.
  equ: 2;
  atom: 1;
  null: 1;

: Boolean symbols.
  and: 2;
  include truth_values.

For all x, x1, x2, l, l1, l2:

  car[(x . l)] = x;

  cdr[(x . l)] = l;

  equ[(); ()] = true;

  equ[(x1 . l1); (x2 . l2)] = and[equ[x1; x2]; equ[l1; l2]];

  equ[(x1 . l1); x2] = false
       where x2 is either () or in atomic_symbols end or end where;

  equ[x1; x2] = false
     where x1 is in atomic_symbols, x2 is either () or (x . l) end or end where;

  equ[(); x2] = false
       where x2 is either (x . l) or in atomic_symbols end or end where;

  include equatom;

  atom[x] = true
       where x is in atomic_symbols end where;

  atom[()] = false;

  atom[(x . l)] = false;

  null[()] = true;

  null[(x . l)] = false;

  null[x] = false
       where x is in atomic_symbols end where;

  and[true; true] = true;

  and[true; false] = false;

  and[false; true] = false;

  and[false; false] = false.

□

The implementation of lists described above is sufficient for all programming in the style of pure LISP. It is not necessarily the implementation of choice for all list applications. The following equational program defines nonempty lists using *cat* (concatenate two lists) and *list* (create a list of one element) as constructors instead of *cons*. The resulting notation for lists no longer shows the LISP prejudice toward processing from first to last, so, instead of *car* and *cdr*, the four selectors *first*, *last*, *head* (all but the last), and *tail* (all but the first) are given. Since empty lists are not represented, it is appropriate to have the test *singleton* instead of *null*.

Example 16.1.2

Symbols

: List constructors.
  cat: 2;
  list: 1;
  include atomic_symbols;

: List selectors.
  first: 1;
  last: 1;
  head: 1;
  tail: 1;

: Predicates on lists.
  equ: 2;
  singleton: 1.

For all x, l1, l2, l3:

  first(list(x)) = x;

  first(cat(l1, l2)) = first(l1);

  last(list(x)) = x;

  last(cat(l1, l2)) = last(l2);

$head(cat(l1, cat(l2, l3))) = cat(l1, head(cat(l2, l3)));$

$head(cat(l1, list(x))) = l1;$

$tail(cat(cat(l1, l2), l3)) = cat(tail(cat(l1, l2)), l3);$

$tail(cat(list(x), l3) = l3;$

$equ(list(x1), list(x2)) = equ(x1, x2);$

$equ(l1, l2) = and(equ(first(l1), first(l2)), equ(tail(l1), tail(l2)))$
$\qquad\qquad where\ l1, l2\ are\ cat(l3, l4)\ end\ where;$

$equ(list(x), cat(l1, l2)) = false;$

$equ(cat(l1, l2), list(x)) = false;$

include equatom;

$singleton(list(x)) = true;$

$singleton(cat(l1, l2)) = false;$

: Use the same definition of and as in Example 16.1.1.

□

The *list-cat* representation of lists differs from the LISP version in making concatenation just as cheap as adding to the head, at the expense of an increase in the cost of producing the first element of a list. Perhaps more significant is the effect on infinite lists. A LISP list may only be infinite to the right, lists constructed from *cat* may have infinite heads as well as infinite tails, and even infinite intermediate segments.

The *list-cat* style of lists is symmetric with respect to treatment of the first and last elements, but it still makes production of intermediate elements more clumsy than *first*s and *last*s. A rather cute application of error markers, as described in Section 12.3, minimizes the clumsiness. In the following equations, *select* (*n,l*) selects, if possible, the *n*th element from the list *l*. *short* (*i*) reports that a list was short by *i* elements for the purpose of producing a specified element.

Example 16.1.3

select(n, list(x)) = *if(equ(n, 1), x, short(subtract(n, 1)));*

select(n, cat(l1, l2)) =
    if(tooshort(select(n, l1)),
        select(subtract(n, shortby(select(n, l1))), l2),
        select(n, l1));

tooshort(short(n)) = *true;*

tooshort(x) = *false*
    where x is in atomic_symbols end where;

shortby(short(n)) = *n;*

if(true, x, y) = *x; if(false, x, y)* = *y;*

include subint.

□

   In order to give similar treatment to all elements of a list, an extension to the *cat* notation is required. *listlnth* (*n,l*) marks the list *l* as having length *n*. As a special case, *listlnth* (1,*x*) represents the singleton list of *x*, replacing *list* (*x*) in the earlier examples. This variation implies a slightly different semantic view of lists, where a singleton list is the same thing as its sole element. Regrettably, an additional symbol *icat* (*i*nactive con*cat*enation) is required for concatenations that have already been associated with their lengths, in order to avoid an infinite computation for a concatenation. The following equations may be used to redefine *select* in the new notation.

Example 16.1.4

cat(listlnth(n1, l1), listlnth(n2, l2)) =
     listlnth(add(n1, n2), icat(listlnth(n1, l1), listlnth(n2, l2)));

select(n, listlnth(n1, l1)) = if(less(n1, n),
                               short(subtract(n, n1)),
                               select(n, l1));

select(1, x) = x where x is in atomic_symbols;

select(n, icat(listlnth(n1, l1), listlnth(n2, l2))) =
     if(less(n1, n),
        select(subtract(n, n1), listlnth(n2, l2)),
        select(n, l1)).

☐

In addition to its clumsiness, the *listlnth* notation suffers from an inability to deal
with any sort of infinite list.

Even using one of the variations of *cat* notation, provision should probably be
made for the empty list. The easiest way to add the empty list is to use the nullary
symbol *empty*, and allow any number of *empty*s to appear in a list, ignored by all
operations on that list. It is easy to modify the definitions of *first*, *last*, *head*, *tail*,
etc. to ignore *empty*s. The more efficient, but syntactically clumsier, solution is to
eliminate *empty* wherever it appears in a concatenation. Unfortunately, the obvious solution of adding the equations *cat(empty(), l) = l* and *cat(l, empty()) = l*
will not work because of the restrictions on left-hand sides of equations. First,
these two equations have a common instance in *cat(empty, empty)*. That problem
is easily avoided (at the cost of extra evaluation steps) by changing the second
equation to

$cat(l, empty()) = l$
    where l is either list(x) or cat(l1, l2) end or end where;

There is still a problem with overlap of the new equations with every other equation describing a function recursively by its effect on a concatenation, for instance the second equation in Example 16.1.2, $first(cat(l1, l2)) = first(l1)$. In order to avoid those overlaps, we must introduce the inactive concatenation symbol, *icat*, using it in place of *cat* as the list constructor, and adding the equations

$cat(empty(), l) = l;$

$cat(l, empty()) = l$
    where l is either list(x) or icat(l1, l2) end or end where;

$cat(l1, l2) = icat(l1, l2)$
    where l1, l2 is either list(x) or icat(l1, l2) end or end where.

This is another example of the last technique for removing overlaps described in Section 12.4

While the variations on list representation described above avoid a certain amount of unnecessary searching, and appear to have a heuristic value, their worst case operations involve complete linear searches. To improve on the worst case time for list operations, we must balance the tree representations of lists. Such balanced list representations may be derived by taking the search tree representations of Section 16.3, and omitting the keys.

16.2. Arrays

There is no way to implement arrays with constant access time in the equation interpreter. Such arrays could be provided as predefined objects with predefined operations, in the style of the arithmetic operations, but only at the cost of substantial increase to the conceptual complexity of storage management. Instead, we propose to implement arrays as balanced trees, accepting a logarithmic rather than constant access time. The following definitions implement one-dimensional arrays ranging over arbitrary subranges of the integers. Three constructors are used: *array*(i, j, a) denotes an array with indexes ranging from i to j, with contents described by a. In describing the contents, *arrbranch*$(a1, a2)$ denotes an array, or subarray, in which locations indexed by integers ending with binary bit 0 are given in $a1$, and those indexed by integers ending with binary bit 1 are given in $a2$. *arrelement*(x) denotes the single array element with value x. *element*(i, a) produces the element indexed by i in the array a, *constarry*(i, j, x) produces an array, indexed from i to j, containing $(j - i)+1$ copies of x. *update*(a, i, x) is the array a with the element indexed by i changed to the value x.

Example 16.2.1

Symbols

: Array constructors.
  array: 3;
  arrbranch: 2;
  arrelement: 1;

: Array selector.
  element: 2;

: Array initializer.
  constarray: 3;

: Array modifier.
  update: 3;

: Functions used internally for array computations.
  const: 2;

: Arithmetic operators for index computations.
  equ: 2;
  subtract, divide, modulo: 2;
  include integer_numerals, truth_values;
  if: 3.

For all i, j, k, a, a1, a2, x, y:

element (i, array (j, k, a)) = element (subtract (i, j), a);

element (i, arrbranch (a1, a2)) =
  if(equ (modulo (i, 2), 0),
    element (divide (i, 2), a1),
    element (divide (i, 2), a2));

element (0, arrelement (x)) = x;

constarray (i, j, x) = array (i, j, const (subtract (j, i), x));

const (i, x) = if(equ (i, 1),
        x,
          arrbranch (const (divide (i, 2), x),
              const (subtract (i, divide (i, 2)), x)));

update (array (i, j, a), k, x) = update (a, subtract (k, i), x);

update (arrbranch (a1, a2), i, x) =
  if(equ (modulo (i, 2), 0),
    arrbranch (update (a1, divide (i, 2), x), a2),
    arrbranch (a1, update (a2, divide (i, 2), x)));

update (arrelement (y), 0, x) = arrelement (x);

include equint, modint, divint, subint.

☐

In principle, the constructor *arrelement* is superfluous, and array elements could appear directly as arguments to *arrbranch*. In that case, the equation *element* $(0, arrelement (x)) = x$ would be replaced by *element* $(0, x) = x$, with a *where* clause restricting x to whatever syntactic forms were allowed for array elements. The version given above has the advantage of allowing any sorts of elements for arrays, including other arrays. Multidimensional arrays are easily represented by arrays whose elements are arrays of dimension one less.

Notice that the outermost evaluation strategy of the equation interpreter

causes *constarray* and *update* expressions to be worked out only as far as required
to accommodate *element* operations. So, some condensation of sparsely accessed
arrays is provided automatically. It is very tempting to allow the *element* operation to take a greater advantage of sparseness, using the equation
element $(i, const (j, x)) = x$. Unfortunately, this equation overlaps with the recursive definition of *const*, violating the syntactic restrictions of Section 5. In this
case, the violation is clearly benign, and future versions of the interpreter should
relax the restrictions to allow overlaps of this sort. Further research is required to
find an appropriate formal description of a useful class of benign overlaps. Such a
formalism will probably be based on the Knuth-Bendix closure algorithm [KB70],
extended to deal with possibly nonterminating reductions.

The explicit use of index bounds in *array* (i, j, a) prohibits infinite arrays, but
infinite arrays may be implemented with the *arrbranch* constructor, assuming that
the range always starts at 0. Arrays infinite on the left as well as the right are
easily provided by piecing together two *arrbranch* structures, and using an initial
comparison with 0 to direct operations to the appropriate portions.

In the array implementation described above, indexes are grouped in terms
according to their agreement on *low−order* bits. E.g., the even indexes all go to
the left of the first branch point, and the odd indexes go to the right. For applications involving only *element* and *update* operations, the order of indexes is
irrelevant, and this one was chosen for arithmetic simplicity. If other primitives,
operating on numerically contiguous sets of indexes, are desired, the definitions
may be modified to treat bits of an index from most significant to least significant,
at the price of slightly more complex arithmetic expressions in the definitions. This
rearrangement of indexes will also affect the benefits of sparse access by changing

the structure of contiguous elements in the data structure.

16.3. Search Trees and Tables.

The arrays of Section 16.2 avoid explicit mention of index values in the data structure by assuming that those values are chosen from a contiguous range. Sparseness in the use of the indexes may allow savings in space, due to the outermost evaluation strategy leaving some instances of *const* unevaluated, but the time cost of each *element* and *update* operation will be proportional to the logarithm of the total index range, no matter how sparsely that range is used. When the range of legal indexes is so great that even this logarithmic cost is not acceptable, balanced search trees should be used instead of arrays. At the cost of storing index values (usually called *keys* in this context) as well as element values, we can let the cost of access be proportional to the logarithm of the number of keys actually used, rather than the total range of keys. This section shows three alternative definitions of balanced search trees. The first two were developed by Christoph Hoffmann, and the description is adapted from [HO82b].

One popular balanced tree scheme that can be implemented by equations is based on 2−3 *trees*, a special case of *B−trees*. Informally, a 2-3 tree is a data structure with the following properties. In a 2-3 tree, there are 2−*nodes*, with two sons and 3−*nodes*, with three sons. A 2-node is labelled by a single key a, so that the keys labelling nodes in the left subtree are all smaller than a, and the keys labelling nodes in the right subtree are larger than a. A 3-node is labelled by two keys a and b, with $a < b$, so that the keys in the left subtree are all smaller than a, the keys in the middle subtree are between a and b, and the keys in the right subtree are larger than b. A *leaf* is a node whose subtrees are all empty. A 2-3 tree is perfectly balanced, i.e., the path lengths from the root to the leaves of the tree are all equal. Figure 16.3.1 below shows an example of a 2-3 tree. In this section, we will always show search trees as collections of keys only, with a membership test. It is straightforward to add arbitrary information associated with each key, and augment the membership test to produce that information. The augmentation is easy, but obscures the more interesting issues having to do with balancing the distribution of the keys, so it is omitted.

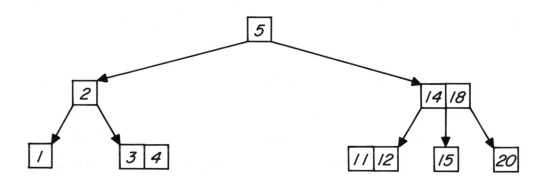

Figure 16.3.1

When inserting a new key k into a 2-3 tree, there are two cases to consider. If the proper place for inserting k is a 2-node leaf, then we simply convert the leaf to a 3-node. If the insertion should be made into a 3-node leaf, then we must somehow restructure parts of the tree to make space for k. The restructuring proceeds as follows. First form a 4-node, that is, a node with three keys a, b, and c, and four subtrees, as shown in Figure 16.3.2(a). Of course, if we begin with a leaf, then the subtrees are all empty. Now split the 4-node into three 2-nodes as shown in Figure 16.3.2(b). The key of the middle 2-node must be inserted into the node that is the former father of the 4-node, since, through the splitting, we have

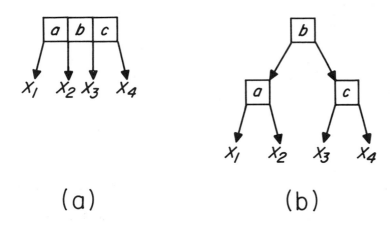

Figure 16.3.2

increased the number of sons. If the father node is a 2-node, then it becomes a 3-node, otherwise the splitting process is repeated on the father's level. If there is no father, i.e., if we have just split the tree root, then no further work is required. Note that without the insertion of the middle node into the father we would destroy the balance of the tree.

We denote a 2-3 tree by an expression *tree(t)*, where t represents the labelling and structure of the tree. A nonempty subtree with a 2-node root is written $t2(x1, l1, x2)$, where $x1$ and $x2$ represent its left and right subtrees, and $l1$ is the label of the node. Similarly, $t3(x1, l1, x2, l2, x3)$ denotes a 3-node with labels l1 and l2 and subtrees x1, x2, and x3. The constant e denotes the empty subtree.

Example 16.3.1

The 2-3 tree of Figure 16.3.1 is represented by

$$tree(t2(t2(t2(e(), 1, e()),$$
$$2,$$
$$t3(e(), 3, e(), 4, e())),$$
$$5,$$
$$t3(t3(e(), 11, e(), 12, e()),$$
$$14,$$
$$t2(e(), 15, e()),$$
$$18,$$
$$t2(e(), 20, e())))))$$

□

Now we program the insertion of a key k into a 2-3 tree $tree(x)$. Insertion of a key k proceeds by first locating the leaf in which to insert k. For this purpose, we must compare k to the labels of a node. If the comparison detects equality, then k is already in the tree and the insertion is done. Otherwise, the result of the comparison determines a subtree into which k is inserted.

Example 16.3.2

Symbols

: Constructors for search trees.
: tree, t2, and t3 are active symbols, as well as constructors.
  tree: 1;
  t2: 3;
  t3: 4;
  e: 0;
  include atomic_symbols, integer_numerals;

: Operations on search trees.
  insert: 2;
  member: 2;

: Symbols used in the definition of insert.
  put: 3;

: Arithmetic and logical operators.
  less: 2;
  equ: 2;
  if: 3.

For all k, l, l1, l2, x, x1, x2, x3, y:

: insert(k, x) inserts the key k in the tree x.

insert(k, tree(x)) = tree(insert(k, x));

insert(k, t2(x, l, y)) =
        if(equ(k, l), t2(x, l, y),
          if(less(k, l), t2(insert(k, x), l, y),
            t2(x, l, insert(k,y))));

insert(k, t3(x1, l1, x2, l2, x3)) =
        if(or(equ(k, l1), equ(k, l2)), t3(x1, l1, x2, l2, x3),
          if(less(k, l1), t3(insert(k, x1), l1, x2, l2, x3),
          if(less(k, l2), t3(x1, l1, insert(k, x2), l2, x3),
            t3(x1, l1, x2, l2, insert(k, x3)))));

insert(k, e()) = put(e(), k, e());

t2(put(x, k, y), l1, x2) = t3(x, k, y, l1, x2);

t2(x1, l1, put(x, k, y)) = t3(x1, l1, x, k, y);

t3(put(x, k, y), l1, x2, l2, x3) = put(t2(x, k, y), l1, t2(x2, l2, x3));

t3(x1, l1, put(x, k, y), l2, x3) = put(t2(x1, l1, x), k, t2(y, l2, x3));

t3(x1, l1, x2, l2, put(x, k, y)) = put(t2(x1, l1, x2), l2, t2(x, k, y));

tree(put(x, k, y)) = tree(t2(x, k, y));

if(true, x, y) = x; if(false, x, y) = y;

include lessint, equint;

: member(k, x) tests whether the key k occurs in the tree x.

member(k, l) = equ(k, l)
        where l is in atomic_symbols end where;

member(k, e()) = false;

member(k, tree(x)) = member(k, x);

member(k, t2(x1, l1, x2)) =
        if(less(k, l1),
          member(k, x1),

if(equ(k, l1),
  true,
  member(k, x2)));

member(k, t3(x1, l1, x2, l2, x3)) =
  if(less(k, l1),
    member(k, x1),
    if(equ(k, l1),
      true,
      if(less(k, l2),
        member(k, x2),
        if(equ(k, l2),
          true,
          member(k, x3))))).

☐

The equations of Example 16.3.2 contain a program for inserting a key into a 2-3 tree. Although the equations are very intuitive, they do not obey the restrictions of Section 5. For example, the second and fifth equations overlap in the expression

tree (ins (3, t2(put (e, 2,), 4, e ()))).

The problem arises conceptually because the described insertion proceeds in two phases: a traversal from the tree root to the insertion point, followed by a reverse traversal restructuring the nodes encountered up to the nearest 2-node, or up to the root if no 2-node is found. The overlap in the expression above corresponds to the competition between two insertions, one in the restructuring phase, when equation 5 applies, the other in the initial traversal, when equation 2 applies.

The problem can be solved in the traditional manner of setting locks to prevent the progress of subsequent insertions where they may interfere with previous updates which are not completed. This is easily done by indicating a locked node as *t2l*(...) instead of *t2*(...), and *t3l*(...) instead of *t3*(...). The equations for this solution are given below. Note that we force complete sequentiality of inser-

tions, because the root is locked in this solution. Notice also that the tree constructors $t2$ and $t3$, which were active in Example 16.3.2, are pure constructors in
Example 16.3.3. The new symbols $t2l$ and $t3l$ acquire the active role. Since the
symbols $t2$ and $t3$ may be thought of as being split into *active* versions, $t2l$ and
$t3l$, and *inactive* versions $t2$ and $t3$, this is another example of the last technique
of Section 12.4 for repairing overlaps, although it was originally thought of in
terms of record locking techniques from concurrent programming.

Example 16.3.3

Symbols

: Constructors for search trees.
   tree: 1;
   t2: 3;
   t3: 4;
   e: 0;
   include atomic_symbols, integer_numerals;

: Operations on search trees.
   insert: 2;
   member: 2;

: Symbols used in the definition of insert.
   put: 3;
   treel: 1;
   t2l: 3;
   t3l: 4;
   unlock: 1;

: Arithmetic and logical operators.
   less: 2;
   equ: 2;
   or: 2;
   if: 3.

For all k, l, l1, l2, x, x1, x2, x3, y:

: insert(k, x) inserts the key k in the tree x.

  insert(k, tree(x)) = treel(insert(k, x));

  insert(k, t2(x1, l1, x2)) =
     if(less(k, l1), t2l(insert(k, x1), l1, x2),

$$if(less(l1, k), t2l(x1, l1, insert(k, x2)),$$
$$\quad unlock(t2(x1, l1, x2))));$$

$$insert(k, t3(x1, l1, x2, l2, x3)) =$$
$$\quad if(or(equ(k, l1), equ(k, l2)), unlock(t3(x1, l1, x2, l2, x3)),$$
$$\quad if(less(k, l1), t3l(insert(k, x1), l1, x2, l2, x3),$$
$$\quad if(less(k, l2), t3l(x1, l1, insert(k, x2), l2, x3),$$
$$\quad\quad t3l(x1, l1, x2, l2, insert(k, x3))))));$$

$$insert(k, e()) = put(e(), k, e());$$

$$t2l(put(x, k, y), l1, x2) = unlock(t3(x, k, y, l1, x2));$$

$$t2l(x1, l1, put(x, k, y)) = unlock(t3(x1, l1, x, k, y));$$

$$t3l(put(x, k, y), l1, x2, l2, x3) = put(t2(x, k, y), l1, t2(x2, l2, x3));$$

$$t3l(x1, l1, put(x, k, y), l2, x3) = put(t2(x1, l1, x), k, t2(y, l2, x3));$$

$$t3l(x1, l1, x2, l2, put(x, k, y)) = put(t2(x1, l1, x2), l2, t2(x, k, y));$$

$$treel(put(x)) = tree(x);$$

$$t2l(unlock(x1), l1, x2) = unlock(t2(x1, l1, x2));$$

$$t2l(x1, l1, unlock(x2)) = unlock(t2(x1, l1, x2));$$

$$t3l(unlock(x1), l1, x2, l2, x3) = unlock(t3(x1, l1, x2, l2, x3));$$

$$t3l(x1, l1, unlock(x2), l2, x3) = unlock(t3(x1, l1, x2, l2, x3));$$

$$t3l(x1, l1, x2, l2, unlock(x3)) = unlock(t3(x1, l1, x2, l2, x3));$$

$$treel(unlock(x)) = tree(Xl);$$

$$or(true, x) = true;\ or(false, x) = x;$$

: The equations for if, equ, less, and member are the same as in Example 16.3.2.

☐

A different solution was proposed in [GS78], eliminating the need for locking the whole traversal path. The trick is to split the nodes encountered on the downward traversal if they do not permit the insertion of another key without splitting. Since a 3-node at the root of a 2-3 tree cannot be split on the way down without destroying the balance (there is no third key available), we must now deal with 2-3-4 trees, permitting 4-nodes also with three keys $l1$, $l2$ and $l3$, represented by $t4(x1, l1, x2, l2, x3, l3, x4)$

The equational program becomes a little more complex, since we have an additional node type. Nonetheless, 14 equations suffice. The transformations required to eliminate a 4-node as point of insertion are given by Figure 16.3.3. Mirror image cases have been omitted.

An equational definition of 2-3-4 tree insertion follows. Note that with this program we may insert keys in parallel without interference problems. Notice also that this solution respects the constructor discipline of Section 12.1.

Example 16.3.4

Symbols

: Constructors for search trees.
   tree: 1;
   t2: 3;
   t3: 4;
   e: 0;
   include atomic_symbols, integer_numerals;

: Operations on search trees.
   insert: 2;
   member: 2;

: Symbols used in the definition of insert.
   chk2: 5;
   chk3: 7;

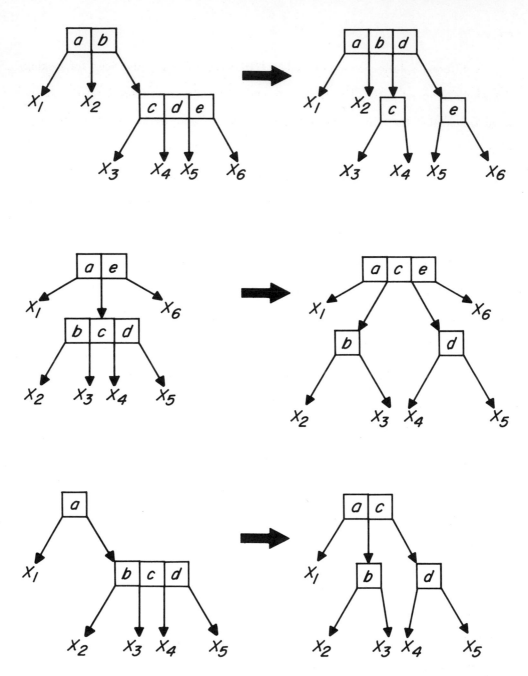

Figure 16.3.3

: Arithmetic and logical operators.
less: 2;
equ: 2;
or: 2;
if: 3.

For all k, l, l1, l2, x, x1, x2, x3, y:

: insert(k, x) inserts the key k in the tree x.

insert(k, tree(e())) = tree(t2(e(), k, e()));

insert(k, tree(t2(x1, l1, x2))) = tree(insert(k, t2(x1, l1, x2)));

insert(k, tree(t3(x1, l1, x2, l2, x3))) =
  tree(insert(k, t3(x1, l1, x2, l2, x3)));

insert(k, tree(t4(x1, l1, x2, l2, x3, l3, x4))) =
  tree(insert(k, t2(t2(x1, l1, x2), l2, t2(x3, l3, x4))));

insert(k, t2(x1, l1, x2)) =
  if(less(k, l1), chk2(k, x1, x2, l1, 1),
  if(less(l1, k), chk2(k, x2, x1, l1, 2),
    t2(x1, l1, x2)));

chk2(k, e(), y, l, i) =
    if(equ(i, 1),
      t3(e(), k, e(), l, e()),
      t3(e(), l, e(), k, e()));

chk2(k, t2(x1, l1, x2), y, l, i) =
    if(equ(i, 1),
      t2(insert(k, t2(x1,l1,x2)), l, y),
      t2(y, l, insert(k, t2(x1, l1, x2))));

chk2(k, t3(x1, l1, x2, l2, x3), y, l, i) =
    if(equ(i, 1), t2(insert(k, t3(x1, l1, x2, l2, x3)), l, y),
      t2(y, l, insert(k, t3(x1, l1, x2, l2, x3))));

chk2(k, t4(x1, l1, x2, l2, x3, l3, x4), y, l, i) =
  if(equ(k, l2),
    if(equ(i, 1),
      t2(t4(x1, l1, x2, l2, x3, l3, x4), l, y),
      t2(y, l, t4(x1, l1, x2, l2, x3, l3, x4))),
    if(less(k, l2),
    if(equ(i, 1),
      t3(insert(k, t2(x1, l1, x2)), l2, t2(x3, l3, x4), l, y)
      t3(y, l, insert(k, t2(x1, l1, x2)), l2, t2(x3, l3, x4))),
      if(equ(i, 1),

$t3(t2(x1, l1, x2), l2, insert(k, t2(x3, l3, x4)), l, y),$
$t3(y, l, t2(x1, l1, x2), l2, insert(k, t2(x3, l3, x4))))))));$

$insert(k, t3(x1, l1, x2, l2, x3)) =$
  $if(or(equ(k, l1), equ(k, l2)),$
    $t3(x1, l1, x2, l2, x3),$
    $if(less(k. l1),$
      $chk3(k, x1, x2, x3, l1, l2, 1),$
      $if(less(k, l2),$
        $chk3(k, x2, x1, x3, l1, l2, 2),$
        $chk3(k, x3, x1, x2, l1, l2, 3))));$

$chk3(k, e(), x, y, l, m, i) =$
  $if(equ(i, 1),$
    $t4(e(), k, e(), l, e(), m, e()),$
    $if(equ(i, 2),$
      $t4(e(), l, e(), k, e(), m, e()),$
      $t4(e(), l, e(), m, e(), k, e())));$

$chk3(k, t2(x1, l1, x2), x, y, l, m, i) =$
  $if(equ(i, 1),$
    $t3(insert(k, t2(x1, l1, x2)), l, x, m, y),$
    $if(equ(i, 2),$
      $t3(x, l, insert(k, t2(x1, l1, x2)), m, y),$
      $t3(x, l, y, m, insert(k, t2(x1, l1, x2)))));$

$chk3(k, t3(x1, l1, x2, l2, x3), x, y, l, m, i) =$
  $if(equ(i, 1),$
    $t3(insert(k, t3(x1, l1, x2, l2, x3)), l, x, m, y),$
    $if(equ(i, 2),$
      $t3(x, l, insert(k, t3(x1, l1, x2, l2, x3), m, y),$
      $t3(x, l, y, m, insert(k, t3(x1, l1, x2, l2, x3)))));$

$chk3(k, t4(x1, l1, x2, l2, x3, l3, x4), x, y, l, m, i) =$
  $if(equ(k, l2),$
    $if(equ(i, 1),$
      $t3(t4(x1, l1, x2, l2, x3, l3, x4), l, x, m, y),$
      $if(equ(i, 2),$
        $t3(x, l, t4(x1, l1, x2, l2, x3, l3, x4), m, y),$
        $t3(x, l, y, m, t4(x1, l1, x2, l2, x3, l3, x4)))),$
      $if(less(k, l2),$
        $if(equ(i, 1),$
          $t4(insert(k, t2(x1, l1, x2)), l2,$
            $t2(X3, L3, X4), L, X, M, Y),$
          $if(equ(i, 2),$
            $t4(x, l, insert(k, t2(x1, l1, x2)),$
              $l2, t2(x3, l3, x4), m, y),$
            $t4(x, l, y, m, insert(k, t2(x1, l1, x2)),$

$$l2, t2(x3, l3, x4)))),$$
$$if(equ(i, 1),$$
$$t4(t2(x1, l1, x2), l2,$$
$$insert(k, t2(x3, l3, x4)),$$
$$l, x, m, y),$$
$$if(equ(i, 2),$$
$$t4(x, l, t2(x1, l1, x2), l2,$$
$$insert(k, t2(x3, l3, x4)), m, y),$$
$$t4(x, l, y, m, t2(x1, l1, x2), x2,$$
$$insert(k, t2(x3, l3, x4))))))));$$

: The equations for if, equ, less, and member are the same as in Example 16.3.2.

□

Computation using Example 16.3.4 proceeds as follows. Upon encountering a 2-node or a 3-node, the node is locked (with *chk*2 or *chk*3) and the proper subtree for insertion is located. That subtree becomes the second parameter of the function *chk*2 or *chk*3. If the root of that subtree is a 4-node, then the 4-node and the locked parent are restructured according to the transformations of Figure 16.3.3. After restructuring, the parent node is released. If the root of the subtree is a 3-node or a 2-node, then no restructuring is needed, and the parent node is released. If the subtree is empty, then the locked parent node is a leaf, and we insert the key. The equations also account for the possibility that the key to be inserted is in the tree already. Using these equations, we can only attempt inserting a key into a 2-node or a 3-node, thus no upward traversal is needed, and insertions can be done in parallel

One more variant of balanced search is programmed below, for comparison. The algorithm expressed by these equations comes from the section on "top-down algorithms" in [GS78]. The "black nodes" of [GS78] are represented by $node(s,i,t)$, and the "red nodes" are represented by $red(node(s,i,t))$. Some of the *where* clauses restricting substitutions for variables in the equations are semantically unnecessary, but are required to avoid illegal overlapping of left-hand sides (see restriction 4 in Section 5).

Example 16.3.5

Symbols

: Constructors for search trees
   tree: 1;
   node: 3;
   red: 1;
   nil: 0;

: Operations on search trees
   insert: 2;
   member: 2;

: Symbols used in the definition of insert
   inserti: 2;
   insertl, insertr: 2;

: Arithmetic and logical operators
   if: 3;
   less: 2;
   equ: 2;
   include integer_numerals, truth_values.

For all c, i, j, k, l, m, s, t, u, v, w, x, y, z:

: The symbol tree marks the root of a search tree.

   tree(red(s)) = tree(s);

: insert(i, t) inserts the integer i into the search tree t.

   insert(i, tree(s)) = tree(insert(i, s))
     where s is either node(t, j, u) or nil() end or end where;

   insert(i, nil()) = red(node(nil(), i, nil()));

   insert(i, red(s)) = red(insert(i, s))
     where s is either node(t, j, u) or nil() end or end where;

   insert(i, node(red(s), j, red(t))) =
     red(inserti(i, node(s, j, t)));

insert(i, node(s, j, t)) = inserti(i, node(s, j, t))
   where s, t are either node(u, k, v) or nil() end or end where;

insert(i, node(s, j, t)) = inserti(i, node(s, j, t))
   where s is red(w), t is either node(u, k, v) or nil() end or end where;

insert(i, node(s, j, t)) = inserti(i, node(s, j, t))
   where t is red(w), s is either node(u, k, v) or nil() end or end where;

: inserti(i, t) inserts the integer i into the search tree t, assuming that t is a
:   tree with at least two nodes, and the sons of the root are not both red.

inserti(i, node(s, j, t)) =
   if(equ(i, j), node(s, j, t),
   if(less(i, j), insertl(i, node(s, j, t)),
      insertr(i, node(s, j, t))));

: insertl(i, t) inserts the integer i into the left part of the tree t.

insertl(i, node(red(node(s, j, red(node(t, k, u)))), l, v)) =
   red(inserti(i, node(node(s, j, t), k, node(u, l, v))))
   where s is either node(w, m, x) or nil() end or end where;

insertl(i, node(s, j, t)) = node(insert(i, s), j, t)
   where s is either node(u, k, v) or nil() or red(node(w, l, x))
      where w, x are either node(y, m, z) or nil() end or end where
   end or end where;

: insertl(i, t) inserts the integer i into the right part of the tree t.

insertr(i, node(s, j, red(node(t, k, red(u))))) =
   red(inserti(i, node(node(s, j, t), k, u)))
   where t is either node(w, m, x) or nil() end or end where;

insertr(i, node(s, j, red(node(red(node(t, k, u)), l, v)))) =
   red(inserti(i, node(node(s, j, t), k, node(u, l, v))))
   where v is either node(w, m, x) or nil() end or end where;

insertr(i, node(s, j, t)) = node(s, j, insert(i, t))
   where t is either node(u, k, v) or nil() or red(node(w, l, x))
      where w, x are either node(y, m, z) or nil() end or end where
   end or end where;

: member(i, t) is true if and only if the integer i appears in the tree t.

member(i, nil()) = false;

member(i, tree(s)) = member(i, s)

where s is either node(t, j, u) or nil() end or end where;

member(i, red(s)) = member(i, s);

member(i, node(s, j, t)) = if(equ(i, j), true,
*   if(less(i, j), member(i, s),*
*   member(i, t)));*

if(true, s, t) = s;   if(false, s, t) = t;

include equint, lessint.

□

Notice that the membership test operator ignores balancing issues. Some schemes for maintaining balanced search trees attach explicit balancing behavior to the membership test. Such a technique is undesirable in the equational definitions of search trees, because the lack of side-effects during evaluation means that any balancing done explicitly by a membership test will not to benefit the execution of any other operations. The outermost evaluation strategy used by the interpreter has the effect of delaying execution of insertions until the resulting tree is used, so the actual computation is in fact driven by membership tests. It would be nice to take advantage of the observation in [GS78] that balancing may also be made independent of insertion, but that approach seems to lead into violations of the nonoverlapping and left-sequential requirements of Section 5.

17. Sequential and Parallel Equational Computations

This section develops a formal mechanism for distinguishing the sequentializable equational definitions supported by the current version of the equation interpreter, from inherently parallel definitions, such as the *parallel or*. Section 19 goes further, and shows that sequential systems, such as the Combinator Calculus, cannot stepwise simulate the parallel or.

17.1. Term Reduction Systems

Term reduction systems, also called *subtree replacement systems* [O'D77], and *term rewriting systems* [HL79], are a formal generalization of the sort of reduction system that can be defined by sets of equations.

Definition 17.1.1

Let Σ be a ranked alphabet, with $\rho(a)$ the rank of a for $a \in \Sigma$.

A $\Sigma-tree$ is a tree with nodes labelled from Σ.

$\Sigma_{\#} = \{\alpha |\ \alpha$ *is a* $\Sigma-tree$ & *every node in* α *labelled by* a *has exactly* $\rho(a)$ *sons*$\}$.

$\square$

If Σ is the set of symbols described in the *Symbols* section of an equational definition, then $\Sigma_{\#}$ is the set of well-formed expressions that may be built from those symbols.

The following definition is based on Rosen's notion of rule schemata [Ro73] (Def. 6.1, p.175).

Definition 17.1.2

Let Σ be ranked alphabet, and let V be an ordered set of nullary symbols not in Σ to be used as formal variables. A *rule schema* is a pair $<\alpha,\beta>$, written $\alpha \rightarrow \beta$, such that:

(1) $\alpha, \beta \in (\Sigma \cup V)_\#$

(2) $\alpha \notin V$

(3) Every variable in β is also in α.

A rule schema $\alpha \rightarrow \beta$ is *left linear* if, in addition, no variable occurs more than once in α.

Formal variables of rule schemata will be written as fat lower case letters, such as x, y, z.

Assume that that the variables in a left linear rule schema $\alpha \rightarrow \beta$ are always chosen so that $x_1, \cdots, x_m$ occur in α in order from left to right.

If $\alpha \rightarrow \beta$ is a rule schema over Σ, with variables $x_1, \cdots x_n \in V$, and $\gamma_1, \cdots, \gamma_n \in \Sigma_\#$, then $\alpha[\gamma_1/x_1, \cdots \gamma_n/x_n] \rightarrow \beta[\gamma_1/x_1, \cdots, \gamma_n/x_n]$ is an *instance* of $\alpha \rightarrow \beta$.

Let S be a finite set of rule schemata over Σ. The system $<\Sigma_\#, \rightarrow_S>$ is a *term reduction system,* where $\rightarrow_S$ is the least relation satisfying

$\alpha \rightarrow_S \beta$ if $\alpha \rightarrow \beta$ is an instance of a schema in S;

$\alpha \rightarrow_S \beta \implies \gamma[\alpha/x] \rightarrow_S \gamma[\beta/x]$ where $\gamma \in (\Sigma \cup V)_\#$ contains precisely one occurrence of the variable $x \in V$, and no other variables.

The subscript S is omitted whenever it is clear from context.

□

Every set of S equations following the context-free syntax of the equation interpreter defines a term reduction system, in which $\rightarrow_S$ represents one step of computation. The restrictions on equations from Section 5 induce a special subclass of term reduction systems.

Definition 17.1.3

Let S be a set of rule schemata.

S is *nonoverlapping* if for all pairs of (not necessarily different) schemata $\alpha_1 \to \beta_1$ and $\alpha_2 \to \beta_2$ the following holds (without loss of generality assuming that the variables are chosen in some standard order):

Let $\overline{\alpha_1} \to \overline{\beta_1}$ and $\overline{\alpha_2} \to \overline{\beta_2}$ be instances of the schemata above, with $\overline{\alpha_1} = \alpha_1[\gamma_{1,1}/x_1, \cdots, \gamma_{1,m}/x_m]$. Suppose that $\overline{\alpha_1} = \delta_1[\overline{\alpha_2}/x]$, where δ contains precisely one occurrence of x, $\delta \neq x$. Then there is an i, $1 \leqslant i \leqslant m$, such that $\overline{\alpha_2} = \gamma_{1,i}$. Intuitively, S is nonoverlapping if rule schemata may only be overlaid at variable occurrences, and at the root.

A set of rule schemata S is *consistent* if, for all pairs of schemata $\alpha_1 \to \beta_1$, $\alpha_2 \to \beta_2 \in S$, the following holds. If $\overline{\alpha} \to \overline{\beta_1}$, $\overline{\alpha} \to \overline{\beta_2}$ are instances of the schemata above, then $\overline{\beta_1} = \overline{\beta_2}$.

Intuitively, β_1 and β_2 are the same up to choice of variable names in the two schemata.

If S is a nonoverlapping, consistent set of left-linear rule schemata, then $\langle \Sigma_\#, \to_S \rangle$ is a *regular term reduction system*.

☐

This definition, adapted from [O'D77], is essentially the same as Huet and Lévy's [HL79] and Klop's [Kl80a] (Ch.II), but Klop allows bound variables in expressions, and instead of requiring consistency, Huet-Lévy and Klop outlaw overlap at the root entirely. The regular reduction systems are those defined by equations satisfying restrictions 1-4 from Section 5. Restriction 5 is a bit more subtle, and is treated in Sections 17.2 and 17.3.

17.2. Sequentiality

In discussion of procedural programming languages, "sequential" normally means *"constrained* to operate sequentially." Reduction systems are almost never constrained to operate sequentially, since any number of the redexes in an expression may be chosen for replacement. Rather, certain reduction systems are constrained to be interpreted in parallel. So, a *sequential reduction system* is one that is *allowed to* operate sequentially. For example, the equations for the *conditional*

$$if(true, x, y) = x; \quad if(false, x, y) = y$$

allow for parallel evaluation of all three arguments to an *if*, but they also allow sequential evaluation of the first argument first, then whichever of the other two arguments is selected by the first one. The sequential evaluation described above has the advantage of doing only work that is required for the final answer -- the parallel strategy is almost certain to perform wasted work on the unselected argument. By contrast, consider the *parallel or*, defined by

$$or(true, x) = true;$$
$$or(x, true) = true;$$
$$or(false, false) = false$$

The *or* operator seems to *require* parallel evaluation of its two arguments. If either one is selected as the first to be evaluated, it is possible that that evaluation will be infinite, and will prevent the unselected argument from evaluating to *true*. In the presence of the parallel *or*, there appears to be no way to avoid wasted evaluation work in all cases.

It is not obvious how to formally distinguish the sequential reduction systems from the parallel ones. Huet and Lévy [HL79] discovered a reasonable technical definition, based on a similar definition of sequential predicates by Kahn and Plotkin [KP78]. The key idea in Huet's and Lévy's definition is to regard a redex as a not-yet-known portion of an expression. Certain portions of an expression, e.g., γ in $if\,(true,\,\beta,\,\gamma)$, need not be known in order to determine a normal form. Others, e.g. α in $if\,(\alpha,\,\beta,\,\gamma)$, must be known. A *sequential term reduction system* is one in which we may always identify at least one unknown position (redex) that must be known to find a normal form.

In order to discuss unknown portions of an expression, Huet and Lévy use the nullary symbol ω to represent unknowns, $\geqslant$ for the relation "more defined than."

Definition 17.2.1 [HL79]

Let $\alpha,\beta \in (\Sigma \cup V \cup \{\omega\})_{\#}$.

$\alpha \geqslant \beta$ if β is obtained from α by replacing zero or more subexpressions in α with ω.

Let **S** be a set of rule schemata. $\alpha \in (\Sigma \cup \{\omega\})_{\#}$ is a *partial redex* if there is a rule schema $\alpha' \to \beta \in \Sigma$ such that $\alpha' \geqslant \alpha$.

α is a *definite potential redex* if there is a rule schema $\beta \to \gamma \in \Sigma$ and a term α', such that $\alpha' \geqslant \alpha$ and $\alpha' \to^* \beta$.

α is *root stable* if α is not a definite potential redex.

A *total normal form* for $(\Sigma \cup \{\omega\})_{\#}$ is a normal form in $\Sigma_{\#}$.

Let $\alpha \in (\Sigma \cup \{\omega\})_{\#}$, and let α have no total normal form.

An *index* of α is a term $\alpha' \in (\Sigma \cup \{\omega,x\})_{\#}$ with precisely one occurrence of x, such that $\alpha = \alpha'[\omega/x]$, and

$$\mathbf{V}\,\beta \geqslant \alpha \ (\beta \ has \ a \ total \ normal \ form) \implies \exists \gamma \neq \omega \ \beta = \alpha'[\gamma/x].$$

A regular reduction system is *sequential* if every term containing ω with no total normal form has at least one index.

□

Unfortunately, sequentiality is not a decidable predicate, and even indexes of sequential systems are not always computable [HL79]. So, Huet and Lévy define a stronger property called *strong sequentiality*. Essentially, a reduction system is *strongly sequential* if its sequentiality does not depend on the right-hand sides of rules.

Definition 17.2.2 [HL79]

$\alpha \to_\omega \beta$ if β is the result of replacing some redex in α with an arbitrarily chosen term in $\Sigma_\#$. Let $\alpha \in (\Sigma \cup \{\omega\})_\#$, and let there be no total normal form δ such that $\alpha \to_\omega^* \delta$. An index α' of α is a *strong index* of α if

$$\forall \beta \geqslant \alpha \ \beta \to_\omega^* \delta \ \& \ (\delta \text{ is a total normal form}) \implies \exists \gamma \neq \omega \ \beta \geqslant \alpha'[\gamma/x].$$

A set of rule schemata is *strongly sequential* if every term α containing ω such that α is in (nontotal) normal form, but for no δ in total normal form does $\alpha \to_\omega^* \delta$, contains at least one strong index.

α is a *potential redex* if there is a rule schema $\beta \to \gamma \in \Sigma$ and a term α', such that $\alpha' \geqslant \alpha$ and $\alpha' \to_\omega^* \beta$.

α is *strongly root stable* if α is not a potential redex.

□

Huet and Lévy give a decision procedure to detect strongly sequential systems, and an algorithm to find a strong index when one exists, or report strong stability when there is no index. These are precisely the sorts of algorithms needed by the equation interpreter. The sequentiality detection is used in a preprocessor to detect and reject nonsequential equations. The other algorithms are used to determine a traversal order of an input expression, detecting redexes when they are met. When an expression is found to be strongly root stable, the root may be output immediately, and the remaining subexpressions evaluated in any convenient order. Unfortunately, Huet's and Levy's algorithms are complex enough that it is not clear whether they have acceptable implementations for the equation interpreter. So, the current version of the equation interpreter applies the substantially stronger restriction of strong left-sequentiality to guarantee a particularly simple algorithm for choosing the sequential order of evaluation.

In Section 19, in trying to characterize the nondeterministic computational power of equationally defined languages, we treat another simplified notion of sequentiality. *Simple strong sequentiality* is defined to allow choice of a sequential order of evaluation by a process with no memory, simply on the basis of ordering the arguments to each function symbol independently.

Definition 17.2.3

Let **S** be a strongly sequential set of rule schemata. **S** is *simply strongly sequential* if there is a *sequencing function* $s:(\Sigma \cup \{\omega\})_{\#} \rightarrow (\Sigma \cup \{\omega,x\})_{\#}$ such that, for all partial redexes α and β, containing at least one ω each, $s(\alpha)$ is a strong index in α, and $s(\alpha)[s(\beta)/x]$ is a strong index in $s(\alpha)[\beta/x]$.

$\square$

A system with left-hand sides $f(a,a)$, $g(f(b,x))$, $h(f(x,b))$ is strongly sequential, but not simply strongly sequential, because the sequencing function cannot choose an index in $f(\omega,\omega)$ without knowing whether there might be a g or h above.

17.3. Left-Sequentiality

The *strongly left−sequential* systems of equations, defined in this section, were designed to support an especially simple pattern-matching and sequencing algorithm in the equation interpreter. Section 18.2.3 presents that algorithm, and shows that it succeeds on precisely the strongly left-sequential systems.

Definition 17.3.1

A $\Sigma-context$ is a term in $(\Sigma \cup \{\omega\})_\#$.

An *instance* of a context α is any term or context β resulting from the replacement of one or more occurrences of ω in α, i.e., $\beta \geqslant \alpha$.

A *left context* is a context α such that there is a path from the root of α to a leaf, with no occurrences of ω on or to the left of the path, and nothing but ωs to the right of the path.

A *left—traversal context* is a pair $<\alpha, l>$, where α is a left context, and l is a node on the path dividing ωs from other symbols in α.

An index α' of α is a *strong root index* of α if

$$\forall \beta \geqslant \alpha \ \beta \rightarrow_\omega^* \delta \ \& \ \delta \ is \ root \ stable \Rightarrow \exists \gamma \neq \omega \ \beta \geqslant \alpha'[\gamma/x]$$

A redex β in a term α is *essential* if $\alpha = \alpha'[\beta/x]$ where α' is a strong index of α.

A redex β in a term α is *root—essential* if $\alpha = \alpha'[\beta/x]$ where α' is a strong root index of α.

□

A context represents the information known about a term after a partial traversal. The symbol ω stands for an unknown portion. A left-traversal context contains exactly the part of a term that has been seen by a depth-first left traversal that has progressed to the specified node. $\rightarrow_\omega$ from Definitions 17.2.2 is the best approximation to reduction that may be derived without knowing the right-hand sides of equations. A strong root index is an unknown portion of a term that must be at least partially evaluated in order to produce a strongly root stable term. Since $\rightarrow_\omega$ allows a redex to reduce to anything, a strong root index must be partially evaluated to produce a redex, which may always be ω-reduced to a normal form.

In the process of reducing a term by outermost reductions, our short-term goal is to make the whole term into a redex. If that is impossible, then the term is root stable, and may be cut down into independent subproblems by removing the root.

Definition 17.3.2

A set of equations is *strongly left–sequential* if there is a set of left-traversal contexts **L** such that the following conditions hold:

1. For all $<\alpha,l>$ in **L**, the subtree of α rooted at l is a redex.

2. For all $<\alpha,l>$ in **L**, β an instance of α, l is essential to β.

3. For all left-traversal contexts $<\alpha,l>$ not in **L**, β an instance of α, a root-essential redex of β does not occur at l.

4. Every term is either root stable or an instance of a left context in **L**.

□

In a strongly left-sequential system, we may reduce a term by traversing it in preorder to the left. Whenever a redex is reached, the left-traversal context specifying that redex is checked for membership in **L**. If the left context is in **L**, the redex is reduced. Otherwise, the traversal continues. When no left context in **L** is found, the term must be root stable, so the root may be removed, and the resulting subterms processed independently. (1) and (2) guarantee that only essential redexes are reduced. (3) guarantees that no root-essential redex is skipped. (4) guarantees that the reduction never hits a dead end by failing to choose any redex. The analogous property to strong left-sequentiality, using reduction instead of ω-reduction, is undecidable. Notice that strong left-sequentiality, like strong sequentiality, depends only on the left-hand sides of equations, not on the right-hand sides.

Strongly left-sequential sets of equations are intended to include all of those systems that one might reasonably expect to process by scanning from left to right. Notice that Definition 17.3.2 does not explicitly require L to be decidable. Also, a strongly left-sequential system may not necessarily be processed by leftmost-outermost evaluation. Rather than requiring us to reduce a leftmost redex, Definition 17.3.2 merely requires us to *decide* whether or not to reduce a redex in the left part of a term, before looking to the right. Every redex that is reduced must be essential to finding a normal form. When the procedure decides not to reduce a particular redex, it is only allowed to reconsider that choice after producing a root-stable term and breaking the problem into smaller pieces. Section 18.2.3 shows a simple algorithm for detecting and processing strongly left-sequential systems. While strongly left-sequential systems are defined to allow a full depth-first traversal of the term being reduced, the algorithm of Section 18.2.3 avoids searching to the full depth of the term in many cases by recognizing that certain subterms are irrelevant to choosing the next step.

18. Crucial Algorithms and Data Structures for Processing Equations

Design of the implementation of the equation interpreter falls naturally into four algorithm and data structure problems.

1. Choose an efficient representation for expressions.

2. Invent a pattern-matching algorithm to detect redexes.

3. Invent an algorithm for selecting the next redex to reduce.

4. Choose an algorithm for performing the selected reduction.

The four subsections of this section correspond roughly to the four problems above. For sequential equations, the choice of the next redex to reduce is intimately tangled with pattern matching, so the sequencing problem is treated in Section 18.2, along with pattern matching. For inherently parallel equations, an additional mechanism is required to manage the interleaved sequence of reductions. This mechanism has not been worked out in detail, but what we know of it is described in Section 18.3. The current version of the equation interpreter does the most obvious procedure for performing reductions. Section 18.4 mentions some future optimizations to be tested for that problem.

18.1. Representing Expressions

Because reduction to normal form involves repeated structural changes to an expression, some sort of representation of tree structure by pointers seems inescapable. There are still a number of options to consider, and we are only beginning to get a feeling for which is best. The most obvious representation of expressions is similar to the one used in most implementations of LISP to represent S-expressions. Each function and constant symbol occupies one field of a storage record, and the other fields contain pointers to the representations of the arguments to that function. It is quite easy in this representation to avoid multiple copies of common subexpressions, by allowing several pointers to coalesce at a single node. Thus, although the abstract objects being represented are trees, the representations are really directed acyclic graphs. Figures 18.1.1 and 18.1.2 show the expression

$h(f(g(a,b), g(a,b)), g(a,b))$

with and without sharing of the subexpression $g(a,b)$.

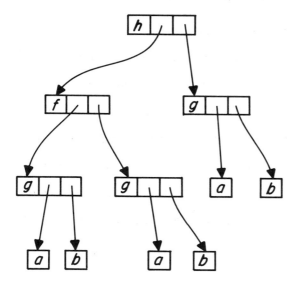

Figure 18.1.1

Unlike LISP, whose nodes are all either nullary or binary (0 or 2 pointers), the equation interpreter requires as many pointers in a node as the arity of the function symbol involved. The issue of how best to handle the variety of arities has not been addressed. Presumably, some small maximum number of pointers per physical node should be chosen, perhaps as small as 2, and virtual nodes of higher

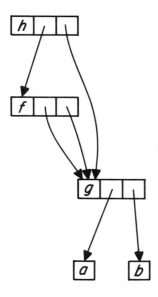

Figure 18.1.2

arities should be linked together from the smaller physical nodes, although varying-size physical nodes are conceivable as a solution. The best choice of physical node size, as well as the structure for linking them together (probably a linear list, but possibly a balanced tree) can best be chosen after experience with the interpreter yields some statistics on its use of storage. Currently, we simply allocate a node size sufficient to handle the highest arity occurring in a set of equations. This is certainly *not* the right solution in the long run, but since storage limits have not been a limiting factor in our experimental stage, it was a good way to get started.

Depending on the pattern-matching and sequencing algorithms chosen, it may be necessary to keep pointers from sons to fathers in the representation of an expression, as well as the usual father-son pointers. The most obvious solution --

one back pointer per node -- does not work, because the sharing of subexpressions allows a node to have arbitrarily many fathers. Some sort of linked list of fathers seems unavoidable. An elegant representation avoids the use of any extra nodes to link together the fathers. Both the son-father and father-son links are subsumed by a circular list of a son and all of its fathers. When a father appears on this list, it is linked to the next node through a son pointer, corresponding to the argument position held by the unique son on that list with respect to that particular father. The unique son on the list is linked through a single extra father pointer. Figure 18.1.3 shows the expression

$$h(f(g(a,b),g(a,b)),g(a,b))$$

again, with the $g(a,b)$ subexpressions shared, represented with circular father-son lists. Since each node may participate in a number of circular lists equal to its arity, the pointers must actually point to a component of a node, not to the node as a whole. Notice that, in order to get from a father to its ith son, it is necessary to follow the circular list going through the father's ith son pointer until that list hits the component corresponding to a father pointer. The node containing the unique father pointer in the circular list is the unique son on that list. The possibilities for breaking a virtual node of high arity into a linked structure of smaller physical nodes are essentially the same as with the LISP-style representation above, except that the linkage within a virtual node must also be two-way or circular. The pattern-matching algorithm used in the current version of the equation interpreter does not require back pointers, so the simpler representation is used. An earlier version used back pointers, and we have not had sufficient experience with the interpreter to rule out the possibility of returning to that representation in a later version.

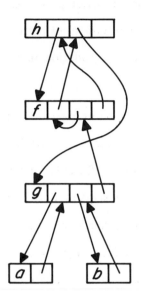

Figure 18.1.3

18.2. Pattern Matching and Sequencing

The design of the equation interpreter was based on the assumption that the time overhead of pattern matching would be critical in determining the usability of the interpreter. Each visit to a node in the equation interpreter corresponds roughly to one recursive call or return in LISP, so the pattern-matching cost per node visit must compete with manipulation of the recursion stack in LISP. So, we put a lot of effort into clever preprocessing that would allow a run-time pattern-matching cost of a few machine instructions per node visit. By contrast, most implementations of Prolog use a crude pattern-matching technique based on sequential search, and depend on the patterns involved being simple enough that this search will be acceptably quick. An indexing on the leftmost symbol of a Prolog clause limits the search to those clauses defining a single predicate, but even that set may in principle be quite large. Prolog implementations were designed on the assumption that unification [Ko79b] (instantiation of variables) is the critical determinant of performance. Only an utterly trivial sort of unification is used in the equation interpreter, so our success does not depend on that problem.

We do not have sufficient experience yet to be sure that the pains expended on pattern matching will pay off, but if equational programming succeeds in providing a substantially new intuitive flavor of programming, extremely efficient pattern matching is likely to be essential. Pattern matching based on sequential search allows the cost of running a single step of a program to grow proportionally to the number of equations and complexity of the left-hand sides. This growth discourages the use of many equations with substantial left-hand sides. Equational programs with only a few equations, with simple left-hand sides, tend to be merely syntactically sugared LISP programs, and therefore not worthy of a new implementation effort when so many good LISP processors are already available.

All of our pattern-matching algorithms are based on the elegant string-matching algorithm using finite automata by Knuth, Morris, and Pratt [KMP77], and its extension to multiple strings by Aho and Corasick [AC75]. The essential idea is that a set of pattern strings may be translated into a finite automaton, with certain states corresponding to each of the patterns. When that automaton is run on a subject string, it enters the accepting state corresponding to a given pattern exactly whenever it reaches the right end of an instance of that pattern in the subject. Furthermore, the number of states in the automaton is at most the sum of the lengths of the patterns, and the time required to build it is linear (with a very low practical overhead) in the lengths as well. In particular, the automaton always contains a tree structure, called a trie, in which each leaf corresponds to a pattern, and each internal node corresponds to a prefix of one or more patterns. As long as the subject is matching some pattern or patterns, the computation of the automaton goes from the root toward the leaves of that tree. The clever part of the algorithm involves the construction of backward, or failure, transitions for those cases where the next symbol in the subject fails to extend the pattern prefix matched so far. A finite automaton, represented by transition tables, is precisely the right sort of structure for fast pattern matching, since the processing of each symbol in the subject requires merely a memory access to that table, and a comparison to determine whether there is a match.

Tree pattern matching is different enough from the string case that exploration of several extensions of the Aho-Corasick technique to trees consumed substantial effort in the early stages of the interpreter project. Those efforts are described more fully in [HO82a, HO84], and are merely summarized here. In addition to the problems arising from working with trees instead of strings, we must face the problem of incremental execution of the pattern matcher after each reduction step. It is clearly unacceptable to reprocess the entire expression that is being reduced after each local reduction step, so our pattern-matching algorithm must be able to pick up some stored context and rescan only the portion affected by each change.

A decisive factor in the final choice of a pattern matcher turned out to be its integration with the sequencer. Although not so decisive in the design of the current implementation, the added complication of dealing with disjunctive *where* clauses restricting the substitutions for variables may ruin an algorithm that runs well on patterns with unrestricted variable substitutions.

18.2.1. Bottom-Up Pattern Matching

Three basic approaches were found, each allowing for several variations. The first, and perhaps most obvious is called the *bottom−up method*, because information flows only from the leaves of a tree toward the root. Each leaf is assigned a *matching state* corresponding to the constant symbol appearing there. Each function symbol has a table, whose dimension is equal to the arity of the symbol, and that table determines the matching state attached to each node bearing that function symbol, on the basis of the states attached to its sons. Every matching state may be conceived as representing a *matching set* of subtrees of the given patterns that can all match simultaneously at a single subtree of a subject. In particular, certain states represent matches of complete patterns. In the special case where every function symbol has arity 1, the bottom-up tables are just the state-transition tables for the Aho-Corasick string matching automaton [HO82a].

Example 18.2.1.1

Consider the pattern $f(g(h(x), h(a)), h(y))$, with variables x and y. The matching sets and states associated with this pattern are:

1: $\{x, y\}$

2: $\{x, y, a\}$

3: $\{x, y, h(x), h(y)\}$

4: $\{x, y, h(x), h(y), h(a)\}$

5: $\{x, y, g(h(x), h(y), h(a))\}$

6: $\{x, y, f(g(h(x), h(a)), h(y))\}$

Set 6 indicates a match of the entire pattern. Assuming that there is one more nullary symbol, b, the symbols correspond to tables as follows:

$a:$ 2

$b:$ 1

```
f:   1 2 3 4 5 6
    --------------------
  1 | 1 1 1 1 1 1
  2 | 1 1 1 1 1 1
  3 | 1 1 1 1 1 1
  4 | 1 1 1 1 1 1
  5 | 1 1 6 6 1 1
  6 | 1 1 1 1 1 1
```

```
g:   1 2 3 4 5 6
    --------------------
  1 | 1 1 1 1 1 1
  2 | 1 1 1 1 1 1
  3 | 1 1 1 5 1 1
  4 | 1 1 1 5 1 1
  5 | 1 1 1 1 1 1
  6 | 1 1 1 1 1 1
```

```
h:   1 2 3 4 5 6
    --------------------
     3 4 3 3 3 3
```

Figure 18.2.1.1 shows the matching states assigned to all nodes in the tree representing the expression

$$h\left(f\left(f\left(g\left(h\left(a\right),h\left(a\right)\right),h\left(b\right)\right),f\left(g\left(h\left(b\right),h\left(b\right)\right),h\left(a\right)\right)\right)\right).$$

☐

The bottom-up method is ideal at run time. An initial pass over the input expression sets all of the match states, which are stored at each node. After a reduction, the newly created right-hand side symbols must have their match states computed, plus a certain number of nodes above the point of the reduction may have their match states changed. The length of propagation of changes to states is at most the depth of the deepest left-hand side, and is usually shorter than that.

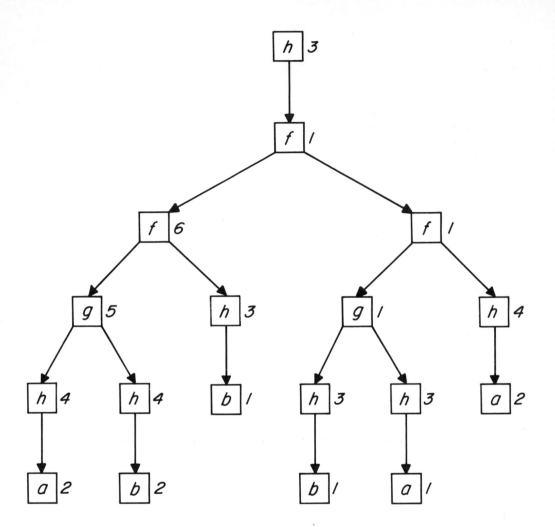

Figure 18.2.1.1

Because of sharing, there may be arbitrarily many paths toward the root along which changes must be propagated. The more complex representation of expressions allowing traversal from sons to fathers as well as fathers to sons must be used with the bottom-up method.

Unfortunately, the bottom-up method gets into severe trouble with the size of the tables, and therefore with the preprocessing time required to create those tables as well. There are two sources of explosion:

1. A symbol of arity n requires an n-dimensional table of state transitions. Thus, the size of one symbol's contribution to the tables is s^n, where s is the number of states.

2. In the worst case, the number of the states is nearly 2^p, where p is the sum of the sizes of all the patterns (left-hand sides of equations).

The exponential explosion in number of states dominates the theoretical worst case, but never occurred in the two years during which the bottom-up method was used. In [HO82a] there is an analysis of the particular properties of patterns that lead to the exponential blowup. Essentially, it requires subpatterns that are *incomparable* in their matching power -- subjects may match either one, both, or neither. For example, $f(x,a)$ and $f(a,x)$ are incomparable in this sense, because $f(b,a)$ matches the first, $f(a,b)$ matches the second, $f(a,a)$ matches both, and $f(b,b)$ matches neither. Such combinations of patterns are quite unusual in equational programs.

The theoretically more modest increase in table size due to the arity of symbols had a tremendous impact in practice. By suitable encodings, such as Currying (see Section 4.4), the maximum arity may be reduced to 2. In principle, reducing the arity could introduce an exponential explosion in the number of states, but this never happened in practice. Unfortunately, for moderate sized equational programs, such as those used in the syntactic front end of the equation interpreter itself, even quadratic size of tables is too much, leading to hour-long preprocessing. Tables may be compressed, by regarding them as trees with a level of branching for each dimension, and sharing equivalent subtrees. The resulting compression is quite substantial in practice, giving the appearance of a linear dependence with constant factor around five or ten. The time required to generate the large tables and then compress them is still unacceptable. For a short time, we used a program that produced the compressed tables directly, but it required a substantial amount of searching for identical subtrees, and the code was so complicated as to be untrustworthy. Cheng, Omdahl, and Strawn (Iowa State University) have made an extensive experimental study of several techniques for improving the bottom-up tables for a particular set of patterns arising from APL idioms. Their work suggests that a carefully hand-tuned bottom-up approach may be good for static sets of patterns, but substantial improvement in the algorithm is needed to make it a good choice when ever-changing pattern sets require completely automatic preprocessing.

The problems with table size alone may well have killed the bottom-up method, but more trouble arose when we considered the sequencing problem. The only bottom-up method for sequencing that we found was to keep track simultaneously of the set of subpatterns matched by a node (the *match set*), and the set of subpatterns that might come to match as a result of reductions at descendants of the node (the *possibility set*). The reduction strategy would be driven by an attempt to narrow the difference between the match set and the possibility set at a node. When no redex appears in the possibility set at a node, that node is stable, and may be output. A precise definition of possibility sets appears in the appendix to [HO79], and may also be derived from [HL79]. Possibility sets, just as match sets, may be enumerated once during preprocessing, then encoded into numerical state names. Possibility sets may explode exponentially, even in cases where the match sets do not. Possibility sets were never implemented for the equation interpreter, and the bottom-up versions actually performed a *complete reduction sequence*, by adding each redex to a queue as it was discovered, then reducing the one at the head of the queue - a very wasteful procedure. Bottom-up pattern matching in the equation interpreter will probably not be resurrected until a simpler sequencing technique is found for it.

A final good quality of the bottom-up method, although not good enough to save it, is its behavior with respect to *or*s in *where* clauses. A left-hand side of an equation in the form

$E = F$ *where x is either* G_1 *or* $\cdots$ *or* G_n *end or end where*

may be treated as a generalized pattern of the form $E[or(G_1, \cdots, G_n)/x]$ (the special expression $or(G_1, \cdots, G_n)$ is substituted for each occurrence of x). A pattern of the form $or(G_1, \cdots, G_n)$ matches an expression when any one of $G_1, \cdots, G_n$ matches. The subpatterns involved in these *or*s have no special impact on the number of states for bottom-up matching.

18.2.2. Top-Down Pattern Matching

The second approach to pattern-matching that was used in the equation interpreter is the *top−down* approach. Every path from root to leaf in a pattern is taken as a separate string. Numerical labels indicating which branch is taken at each node are included, as well as the symbols at the nodes. Variable symbols, and the branches leading to them, are omitted. If one string is a prefix of another one associated with the same pattern, it may be omitted.

Example 18.2.2.1

The expression $f(g(a, x), h(y, b))$, whose tree form is shown in Figure 18.2.2.1, produces the strings $f1g1a, f1g, f2h1a, f2h2b$. The string $f1g$ may be omitted, because it is a prefix of $f1g1a$.

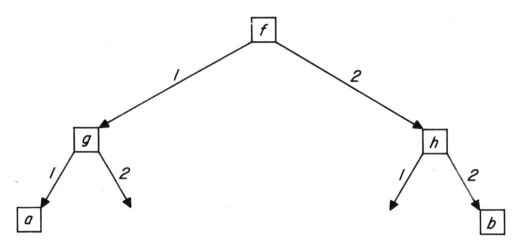

Figure 18.2.2.1

The Aho-Corasick algorithm may be applied directly to the set of strings derived in this way. Then, in a traversal of a subject tree, we may easily detect the leaf-ends of all subject paths that match a pattern path. By keeping states of the automaton on the traversal stack, we may avoid restarting the automaton from the root for each different path.

The hard part of the top-down method is correlating all the individual path matches to discover complete matches of patterns. We tried two ways of doing this. In the first, a counter for each pattern is associated with each node on the recursion stack. Each time a path is matched, the appropriate counter at the root end is incremented. If the traversal stack is stored as an array, rather than a linked list, the root end may be found in constant time by using a displacement in the stack. Whenever a counter gets up to the number of leaves in the appropriate pattern, a match is reported. In the worst case, every counter could go up nearly to the number of leaves in the pattern, leading to a quadratic running time. In a short experiment with this method, carried out by Christoph Hoffmann's advanced compiler class in 1982, such a case was not observed. [HO82a] analyzes the qualities of patterns that lead to good and bad behavior for the top-down method with counters, but two other problems led to its being abandoned.

After a change in the subject tree, resulting from a reduction step, the region above the change must be retraversed, and the counters corrected. This requires that the old states associated with the region be saved for comparison with the new ones, since only a change from acceptance to rejection, or *vice versa*, results in a change to a counter. This retraversal was found to be quite clumsy when it was tried. Also, no sequencing method for top-down pattern matching with counters was ever discovered.

Another variation on top-down pattern matching, using bit strings to correlate the path matches, led to much greater success. Each time a path matches, a bit string is created with one bit for each *level* of the pattern. All bits are set to 0, except for a 1 at the level of the leaf just matched. These bit strings are combined in a bottom-up fashion, shifting as they go up the tree, and intersecting all the bit strings at sons of a node to get the bit string for that node. When a 1 appears at the root level, a match is detected. The details are given in [HO82a].

Example 18.2.2.2

Consider again the pattern $f(g(h(x), h(a)), h(y))$ from Example 18.2.1.1, running on the expression

$$h(f(f(g(h(a), h(a)), h(b)), f(g(h(b), h(b)), h(a))).$$

Figure 18.2.2.2 shows the tree representation of this expression. A * is placed at the leaf end of each path matching a root-to-leaf path in the pattern. Each node is annotated with the bit string that would be computed for it in the bottom-up portion of the matching.

☐

Careful programming yields an algorithm in which the top-down and bottom-up activities are combined in a single traversal, and bit strings, as well as automaton states, are only stored on the traversal stack, not at all nodes of the tree. Multiple patterns are handled conceptually by multiple bit strings. It is easy, however, to pack all of the strings together, and perform one extra bitwise *and* with every shift to prevent bits shifting between the logical bit strings.

The top-down method with bit strings adapts well to incremental matching. After a change in the tree, merely reenter the changed portion from its father. The traversal stack still contains the state associated with the father, and the original processing of the changed portion has not affected anything above it, so there is no special retraversal comparable to the bottom-up method, or the top-down method with counters. Sequencing is handled by one more bit string, with one bit for each level of the pattern. In this string, a bit is 1 if there is a *possible* match at that level. The two bit strings used by the top-down method, in fact, correspond to the

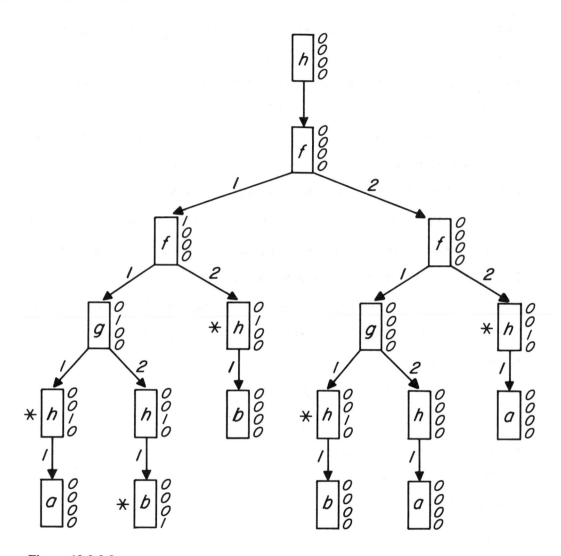

Figure 18.2.2.2

match sets and possibility sets of the bottom-up method. Since the top-down processing has already determined which root-to-leaf paths of a pattern are candidates for matching at a given point, the match and possibility sets need only deal with subpattern positions along a single path. Thus, instead of precomputing sets of subpatterns, then numbering them, we may store them explicitly as bit strings, using simple *shifts* and bitwise *and*s and *or*s to combine them. Such a technique did *not* work for the bottom-up method, because the *shifts* would become complicated *shuffle* operations, depending on the tree structure of the patterns.

The top-down pattern matching techniques do not perform as well as the bottom-up method with respect to disjunctions in *where* clauses restricting the substitutions for variables in equations. No better strategy has been found than to treat each disjunctive pattern as a notation for its several complete alternatives. For example,

f(x, y) = *g(x) where x is either h(u) or a end or,*
                            y is either h(v) or b end or
              end where

is equivalent to the four equations

f(h(u), h(v)) = *g(h(u))*;

f(h(u), b) = *g(h(u))*;

f(a, h(v)) = *g(a)*;

f(a, b) = *g(a)*

Notice that the effect is multiplicative, so a combinatorial explosion may result from several disjunctive *where* clauses in the same equation. Such an explosion only occurred once in our experience with the interpreter, but when it did, it was disastrous. At the end of Section 18.2.3 we discuss briefly the prospects for avoiding the disjunctive explosion without returning to bottom-up pattern matching, with its own explosive problems.

18.2.3. Flattened Pattern Matching

The final pattern-matching method, used in the current version of the interpreter, uses only one string per tree pattern. Tree patterns are flattened into preorder strings, omitting variables. The Aho-Corasick algorithm [AC75] is used to produce a finite automaton recognizing those strings. Each state in the automaton is annotated with a description of the tree moves needed to get to the next symbol in the string, or the pattern that is matched, if the end of the string has been reached. Such descriptions need only give the number of edges ($\geqslant 0$) to travel upwards toward the root, and the left-right number of the edge to follow downwards. For example, the patterns (equation left-hand sides) $f(f(a,x),g(a,y))$ and $g(x,b)$ generate the strings *ffaga* and *gb*, and the automaton given in Figure 18.2.3.1.

The automaton cannot be annotated consistently if conflicting moves are associated with the same state. Such conflicts occur precisely when there exist preorder flattened strings of the forms $\alpha\beta\gamma$ and $\beta\delta$, such that the annotations on the last symbol of β in the two strings are different. These differences are discovered directly by attempts to reassign state annotations in the automaton when α is the empty string, and by comparing states at opposite ends of failure edges when α is not empty. Fortunately, the cases in which the flattened pattern-matching automaton cannot be annotated properly are exactly the cases in which equations violate the restrictions of Section 5. When γ and δ are not empty, the conflicting annotations are both tree moves, and indicate a violation of the left-sequentiality restriction 5. When one of γ,δ is the empty string, the corresponding annotation reports a match, and there is a violation of restriction 3 or 4. In the example above, there is

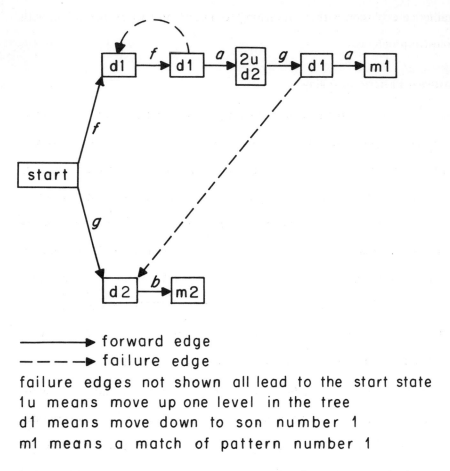

forward edge
---- failure edge
failure edges not shown all lead to the start state
1u means move up one level in the tree
d1 means move down to son number 1
m1 means a match of pattern number 1

Figure 18.2.3.1

a conflict with $\alpha = ffa$, $\beta = g$, $\gamma = a$, $\delta = b$. That is, after scanning $ffag$, the first pattern directs the traversal down edge number 1, and the second pattern directs the traversal down edge number 2. This conflict is discovered because there is a failure edge between states with those two annotations.

The restriction imposed on equations by the pattern-matching strategy above may be justified in a fashion similar to the justification of deterministic parsing strategies. That is, we show that the algorithm succeeds (generates no conflicts) on every set of equations that is strongly left-sequential according to the abstract definition of strong left-sequentiality in Section 17.3.

Theorem 18.2.3.1

The flattened pattern-matching algorithm succeeds (i.e., generates no conflicts) if and only if the input patterns are left-hand sides of a regular and strongly left-sequential set of equations.

Proof sketch:

($\Longrightarrow$) If the pattern matching-automaton is built with no conflicts, then **L** of Definition 17.3.2 may be defined to be the set of all left-traversal contexts $<\chi,l>$ such that l is the root of a redex in χ, and l is visited by the automaton, when started at the root of χ.

($\Longleftarrow$) If a conflict is found in the pattern-matching automaton, then there are two flattened preorder strings $\alpha\beta\gamma$ and $\beta\delta$ derived from the patterns, with conflicting tree moves from β to γ and from β to δ. Without loss of generality, assume that there are no such conflicts within the two occurrences of β. $\alpha\beta$, with its associated tree moves, defines a context χ, which is the smallest left context allowing the traversal specified by $\alpha\beta$. β defines a smaller left-traversal context ρ in the same way. ρ is contained as a subterm in χ, in such a way that the last nodes visited in the two traversals coincide. If one or both of γ, δ is empty, then χ demonstrates a violation of restriction (4) or (3), respectively. So, assume that γ, δ are not empty, and the annotations at the ends of the βs are both tree moves.

Consider the two positions to the right of χ specified by the two conflicting traversal directions for $\alpha\beta$ and β. Expand χ to ψ by filling in the leftmost of these two positions with an arbitrary redex, and let n be the root of this added redex. Let

equ_1 be the equation associated with whichever of $\alpha\beta\gamma$, $\beta\delta$ directed traversal toward this leftmost position, and let equ_2 be the equation associated with the remaining one of $\alpha\beta\gamma$, $\beta\delta$. $<\psi,n>$ cannot be chosen in **L**, because there is an instance ψ' of ψ in which a redex occurs above n matching the left-hand side of equ_2, and ψ' may be ω-reduced to normal form at this redex, without reducing the redex at n in ψ. $<\psi,n>$ cannot be omitted from **L**, because there is another instance ψ'' of ψ in which everything but n matches the redex associated with equ_1, and n is therefore root-essential to ψ''.

□

For example, the pair of equation left-hand sides $f(g(x,a),y)$ and $g(b,c)$ have the preorder strings fga and gbc. A conflict exists with $\alpha=f$, $\beta=g$, $\gamma=a$, $\delta=c$. The first equation directs the traversal down edge 2 after seeing fg, and the second equation directs it down edge 1. The conflicting prefixes fg and g produce the context $f(g(\omega,\omega),\omega)$. The context above is expanded to the left-traversal context consisting of $f(g(g(b,c),\omega),\omega)$ with the root of $g(b,c)$ specified. This left-traversal context cannot be chosen in **L** (i.e., it is not safe to reduce the redex $g(b,c)$ in this case), because the leftmost ω could be filled in with a to produce $f(g(g(b,c),a),\omega)$, which is a redex of the form $f(g(x,a),y)$, and can be ω-reduced to normal form in one step, ignoring the smaller redex $g(b,c)$. But, this left-traversal context may not be omitted from **L** (i.e., it is not safe to omit reducing $g(b,c)$), because the leftmost ω may also be filled in with c to produce $f(g(g(b,c),c),\omega)$, and reduction of $g(b,c)$ is essential to get a normal form or a root-stable term.

The flattened pattern-matching method is so simple, and so well suited to the precise restrictions imposed for other reasons, that it was chosen as the standard pattern matcher for the equation interpreter. In fact, this method developed from an easy way to check the restrictions on equations, which was originally intended to be added to the top-down method. As long as the interpreter runs on a conventional sequential computer, the flattened pattern-matching method will probably be used even when the interpreter is expanded to handle nonsequential sets of equations. In that case, conflicting annotations will translate into *fork* operations. By exploiting sequentiality insofar as it holds, the overhead of keeping track of multiple processes will be minimized. An interesting unsolved problem is to detect and exploit more general forms of sequentiality than left-sequentiality in an efficient manner. There are likely to be NP-hard problems involved.

The flattened method has the same shortcoming as the top-down method with respect to disjunctive *where* clauses. The current version merely treats a qualified pattern as if it were several simple patterns, causing an exponential explosion in the worst case. Brief reflection shows that the disjunctive patterns are, in effect, specifications of *nondeterministic* finite automata. The current version translates these into *deterministic* automata, preserving whatever portions are already deterministic in an obvious way. Usually the translated automaton is far from minimal. In most cases, there exists a deterministic automaton whose size is little or no greater than the nondeterministic one. A good heuristic for producing the minimal, or a nearly minimal, deterministic automaton *directly*, without explicitly creating the obvious larger version, would improve the practicality of the interpreter significantly. We emphasize the fact that this technique would probably only be *heuristic*, since the problem of minimizing an arbitrary nondeterministic finite automaton, or producing its minimal deterministic equivalent, provides a solution to the inequivalence problem for nondeterministic finite automata, which is

PSPACE-complete [GJ79].

We have discussed the incremental operation of each pattern matcher at matching time, as changes are made to the subject. As a user edits an equational program, particularly with the modular constructs of Section 14, it is desirable to perform incremental preprocessing as well, to avoid reprocessing large amounts of unchanged patterns because of small changes in their contexts. Robert Strandh is currently studying the use of suffix (or position) trees [St84] to allow efficient incremental preprocessing for the Aho-Corasick automaton, used in both the top-down and flattened pattern matchers. We have an incremental processor that allows insertion and deletion of single patterns for a cost linear in the size of the change, independent of the size of the automaton. We hope to develop a processor to combine two sets of patterns for a cost dependent only on their interactions through common substrings, and not on their total sizes.

18.3. Selecting Reductions in Nonsequential Systems of Equations

In principle, nonsequential equational programs, such as those including the parallel or, may be interpreted by forking off a new process each time the flattened pattern-matching automaton indicates more than one node to process next. The overhead of a general-purpose multiprocessing system is too great for this application. So, an implementation of an interpreter for nonsequential equations awaits a careful analysis of a highly efficient algorithm and data structure for managing these processes. Several interesting problems must be handled elegantly by this algorithm and data structure. First, whenever a redex α is found, all processes seeking redexes within α must be killed, since the work that they do may not make sense in the reduced expression. This problem requires some structure keeping track of all of the processes in certain subtrees. Substantial savings may be gained by having that structure ignore tree nodes where there is no branching of parallel processes.

Because of the sharing of identical subexpressions, two processes may wander into the same region, requiring some locking mechanism to avoid conflicts. It is not sufficient to have a process merely lock the nodes that it is actually working on, since the result would be that the locked out process would follow the working process around, duplicating a lot of traversal effort. On the other hand, it is too much to lock a process out of the entire path from the root followed by another process, since the new process might be able to do a reduction *above* the intersection of paths, as a result of information found *within* the intersection.

Example 18.3.1

Consider the equations

$$f(g(h(x, y))) = x;$$

$$or(true, x) = true; \quad or(x, true) = true$$

Suppose that we are reducing an intermediate expression of the form $or(f(g(h(true,\alpha))), g(h(true,\alpha)))$, with the common subexpression $g(h(true,\alpha))$ shared. At the *or* node, a process A will start evaluating the left-hand subexpression $f(g(h(true,\alpha)))$, and another process B will start evaluating the right-hand subexpression $g(h(true,\alpha))$. Perhaps process B reaches the common subexpression $g(h(true,\alpha))$ before A, and eventually transforms α into α'. If A waits at the f node, it will miss the fact that there is a redex to be reduced. A needs to go into the common subexpression just far enough to see the symbols g, h, and *true*. Then, $f(g(h(true,\alpha')))$ will be replaced by *true*, yielding $or(true, \alpha')$ which reduces to *true*. At this point, process B is killed. If A waits on B, it may wait arbitrarily long, or even forever. Figure 18.3.1 shows the expression discussed above in tree form, with the interesting positions of A and B.

☐

So, a process A wandering onto the path of process B must continue until it reaches the same state as B. At that point, A must go to sleep, until B returns to the node where A is. These considerations require a mechanism for determining what processes have visited a node, and in what states, and what processes are sleeping at a given node.

Of course, a low-overhead sequencer for any set of equations could be devised, by adding each newly discovered redex to a queue, and always reducing the head redex in that queue. The resulting *complete reduction sequence* [O'D77] is very wasteful of reduction effort, and probably would not be acceptable except as a temporary experimental tool.

18.4. Performing a Reduction Step

At first, the implementation of reduction steps themselves seems quite elementary. Simply copy the right-hand side of the appropriate equation, replacing variable instances by pointers to the corresponding subexpressions from the left-hand side. Right-hand side variables may easily be replaced during preprocessing by the addresses of their instances on the left-hand side, so that no search is required. For example, $f(g(a, x), y) = h(x, y)$ may be represented by $f(g(a, ?), ?) = h(<1,2>, <2>)$, indicating that the first argument to h is the 2nd son of the 1st son of the redex node, and the second argument is the 2nd son of the redex node. Given these addresses, we no longer need the names of the variables at all. The symbol h may be overwritten on the physical node that formerly contained the symbol f. One small, but crucial, problem arises even with this

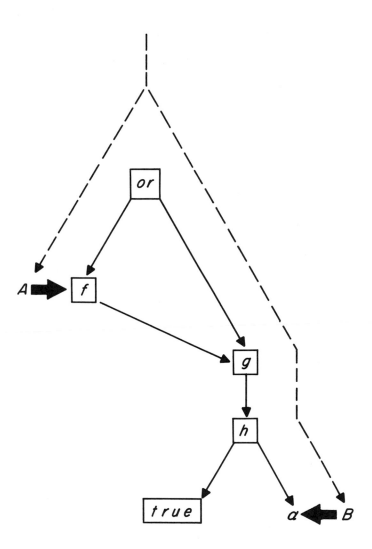

Figure 18.3.1

simple approach. If there is an equation whose right-hand side consists of a single variable, such as $car[(x \cdot y)] = x$, then there is no appropriate symbol to overwrite the root node of the redex (in this case containing the symbol car). Consider the expression $f[car[(\alpha \cdot \beta)]]$, for example, which reduces to $f[\alpha]$. We could modify the node associated with f, so that its son pointer goes directly to α, but then any other nodes sharing the subexpression $car[(\alpha \cdot \beta)]$ would not benefit by the reduction. Finding and modifying *all* of the fathers of $car[(\alpha \cdot \beta)]$, on the other hand, might be quite expensive. The solution chosen [O'D77] is to replace the *car* node by a special *dummy* node, with one son. Every time a pointer is followed to that dummy node, it may be redirected to the son of the dummy. Eventually, the dummy node may become disconnected and garbage collected for reuse. In effect, this solution requires a reduction-like step to be performed for every pointer to the redex $car[(\alpha \cdot \beta)]$, but that step is always a particularly simple one, independent of the complexity of the redex itself.

As the left-hand sides of equations become more substantial, the collecting of pointers to variable instances, by the simple technique above, might become non-trivially costly. It appears that there are some simple variations in which pointers to variables would be collected during the pattern-matching traversal. A careful analysis is needed to determine whether the savings in retraversal costs would pay for the extra cost of maintaining pointers to variable positions in partially matching subexpressions, when the matching fails later on. In any case, the retraversal for variables could certainly be improved to collect all variables in a single retraversal, rather than going after each variable individually. Somewhat more sophisticated optimizations would include performing some of the pattern-matching work for right-hand sides of equations during the preprocessing, and coalescing several reduction steps into one. Substantial savings might also be achieved by reusing some of the structure of a left-hand side in building the right. In particular the common form called *tail recursion*, in which a recursively defined function appears only outermost on a right-hand side, may be translated to an iteration by these means. For example, $f(x) = if(p(x), a, f(g(x)))$ may be implemented by coalescing the evaluation of an application of f with the subsequent evaluation of *if*, and reusing the f node by replacing its argument, instead of the f node itself. The OBJ project [FGJM85] has achieved substantial speedups with optimizations of this general sort, but their applicability to the equation interpreter has never been studied.

Another opportunity for improving performance arises when considering the strategy for sharing of subexpressions. The *minimal* sharing strategy should be to share all substitutions for a given variable x on the right-hand side of an equation. In fact, it is easier to program an interpreter with this form of sharing than one that copies out subterms for each instance of x. A natural improvement, not implemented yet, is to discover all shareable subterms of a right-hand side, during the preprocessing step. For example, in $f(x, y) = g(h(x, y), h(x, y))$, the entire subexpressions $h(x, y)$ may be shared, as well as the substitutions for x and y. Such an optimization could be rather cheap at preprocessing time, using a variation of the tree isomorphism algorithm [AHU74], and need not add any overhead at run time. More sophisticated strategies involve dynamic detection of opportunities for sharing at run time, trading off overhead against the number of evaluation steps required.

A simple sort of dynamic sharing is implemented in the current version of the interpreter. This technique is based on the *hashed cons* idea from LISP, and was proposed and implemented for the equation interpreter by Paul Golick. Whenever a new storage node is created during reduction, its value (including the symbol and all pointers) is hashed, and any identical node that already exists is discovered. Upon discovery of an identical node, the new one is abandoned in favor of another pointer to the old one. In order to maximize the benefit of this strategy, reductions are performed, not by immediate replacement of a left-hand side by a right, but by setting a pointer at the root of a redex to point to its reduced form. As discovered during the traversal of an expression, pointers to redexes are replaced by pointers to the most reduced version created so far. This use of reduction pointers subsumes the dummy nodes discussed at the beginning of this section

The hashed sharing strategy described above is rather cheap, and it allows programming techniques such as the automatic dynamic programming of Section 15.4. The results of this strategy are unsatisfyingly sensitive, however, to the physical structure of the reduction sequence, and the order of evaluation.

Example 18.4.1

Consider the equations

$f(a) = b;$

$c = a.$

In the expression $g(f(c), f(a))$, c reduces to a, yielding $g(f(a), f(a))$. We might expect the two instances of $f(a)$ to be shared, but the hashed sharing strategy will *not* accomplish this. Both nodes containing f existed in the original expression, and had different son pointers at that time, so that there could be no sharing. When c is replaced by a, the a occupies a new node, which is hashed, discovering the existing a node, and creating a sharing of that leaf. The change in the son pointer in the leftmost f node, however, does *not* cause that node to be hashed again, so the fact that it may now be shared with another f node is not discovered. Thus, two more reduction steps are required to reach the normal form $g(b, b)$, instead of the one that would suffice with sharing of $f(c)$.

□

Only one reduction step is wasted by the failure of sharing in Example 18.4.1, but arbitrarily many reduction steps might be involved from $f(a)$ to the normal form b in a more complex example, and all of those steps would be duplicated.

In order to achieve maximal sharing, we need to rehash a node each time any of its sons changes. This requires a more sophisticated use of hashing tables, allowing deletions as well as insertions, and the details have never been worked out. Perhaps some technique other than hashing should be applied in this case. Notice that, by allowing reduced terms to remain in memory, rather than actually replacing them, sharing may be accomplished between subexpressions that never exist simultaneously in any intermediate expression in a reduction sequence. Thus, no evaluation will ever be repeated. Such a complete sharing strategy would accomplish an even stronger form of automatic dynamic programming than that developed in Section 15.4, in which the most naive recursive equations would be applied efficiently, as long as they did not require many *different* expressions to be evaluated. Of course, there is a substantial space cost for such completeness. In practice, a certain amount of space could be allocated, and currently unused nodes could be reclaimed only when space was exhausted, providing a graceful degradation from complete sharing to limited amounts of reevaluation.

The sketch of a complete sharing strategy given above resembles, at least superficially, the *directed congruence closure* method of Chew [Ch80]. In *congruence closure* [NO80], equations are processed by producing a *congruence graph*, each node in the graph representing an expression or subexpression. As well as the father-son edges defining the tree structure of the expressions, the congruence graph contains undirected edges between expressions that are known to be equal. Initially, edges are placed between the left- and right-hand sides of equations, then additional edges are added as follows:

1.   (Transitivity) If there are edges from α to β and from β to γ, add an edge from α to γ.

2.   (Congruence) If there are edges from α_i to β_i for all i from 1 to n, add an edge from $f(\alpha_1, \cdots, n)$ to $f(\beta_1, \cdots, \beta_n)$.

A carefully designed algorithm for congruence closure [NO80, DST80] may be quite efficient for equations *without variables*, but must be modified for equations with variables, since there is no bound on the size of the graph that must be treated. The directed congruence closure method of Chew uses *directed* edges to indicate reductions, and adds nodes to the congruence graph only as they are needed to make progress toward a normal form. Every time a reduction edge is added, congruence closure is applied to the whole graph. Directed congruence closure was shown by Chew to avoid all reevaluation of the same expression. We conjecture that the rehashing strategy for dynamic sharing, sketched above, is essentially an optimization of the directed congruence closure method, in which closure is applied only to portions of the graph that turn out to be needed for progress toward a normal form. A careful implementation of some form of congruence closure would be an extremely valuable option in a future version of the equation interpreter. For cases where repeated evaluation is not expected to arise anyway, its overhead should be avoided by applying a less sophisticated sharing strategy.

Independently of the various issues discussed above, the equation interpreter needs a way to reclaim computer memory that was allocated to a subexpression that is no longer relevant. We tried the two well-known strategies for reclaiming memory: *garbage collection* and *reference counting*. The first implementations used a garbage collector. That is, whenever a new node must be allocated, and there is no free space available, the whole expression memory is traversed, detecting disconnected nodes. Garbage collection has the advantage of no significant space overhead, and no time wasted unless all storage is actually used. Unfortunately, as soon as we ran large inputs to the interpreter, garbage collection became unacceptably costly. Typical garbage collections would only free up a small number of nodes, leading to another garbage collection with rather little reduction in between. In fact, it was usually faster to kill a computation, recompile the interpreter with a larger memory allotment, and start the program over, than to wait for a space-bound program to finish. Based on this experience we chose the reference count strategy, in which each node contains a count of the pointers to it. When that count reaches zero, the node is instantly placed on a free list. Reference counting has a nontrivial space overhead, and adds a small time cost to each creation and deletion of a node. Unlike garbage collection, it does not cause all of the active nodes to be inspected in order to reclaim inactive ones.

19. Toward a Universal Equational Machine Language

While the equation interpreter project has attempted to provide an efficient implementation for the widest possible class of equational programs, other researchers have sought a fixed set of primitive functions defined by equations as a universal programming language. Pure LISP [McC60] may be viewed as a particular equational program, defining a general purpose programming language interpreter. More recently, Backus [Ba78] has defined a Functional Programming language by a fixed set of equations. Turner [Tu79] suggests the Combinator Calculus as a universal language, into which all others may be compiled. There are a number of attractions to a fixed, universal, equationally defined programming language:

1. The designer of such a language may choose primitives that encourage a particular programming style.

2. A well-chosen set of equations might be implemented by special-purpose techniques more efficient than the more general techniques used in the equation interpreter.

3. A particular equationally defined programming language might provide the machine language for a highly parallel computer.

While agreeing with the motivation for choosing a fixed set of equations, we believe that the criteria for such a choice are not well enough understood to allow it to be made on rational grounds. Aside from the subjective issues of convenience, and the technology-dependent issues of efficiency, there is no known method for establishing the theoretical sufficiency of a particular equational language to simulate all others. In this section, we investigate the theoretical foundations for universal equational programs, and produce evidence that the Combinator Calculus is *not* an appropriate choice. Since FP, SASL, and many similar proposed languages compile into combinators, they are also insufficient. Unfortunately, we have not found an acceptable candidate to propose in its place, but we can characterize some of the missing qualities that must be added.

First, consider the more usual procedural languages and their sequential machines. Accept for the moment the architectural schema of a Random Access Machine, with an unbounded memory accessed by a central processor capable of performing some finite set of primitive operations between finite sequences of stored values. Each choice of primitive-operation set determines a programming language and a machine capable of executing it directly. In order to build a general-purpose machine, we usually choose a set of primitive operations that is *universal* in the sense that every other finite set of computable operations may be compiled into the universal one. In theory textbooks, we often state only the result that some universal set of operations is sufficient to compute all of the computable functions. In fact, we usually expect, in addition, that compiling one operation set into another has low complexity, and that the compiled program not only produces the same result as the source program, but does so by an analogous computation. The low complexity of the compilation is not usually stated formally, but the analogousness of the computation is often formalized as *stepwise simulation*.

A reasonable-seeming candidate for a universal reduction language is the *S−K Combinator Calculus*, a language with the two nullary symbols *S* and *K*, plus the binary symbol *AP* for application. For brevity, $AP(\alpha,\beta)$ is written $\alpha\beta$ and parentheses are to the left unless explicitly given. Reduction in the combinator calculus is defined by

$$K\alpha\beta \rightarrow \alpha$$
$$S\alpha\beta\gamma \rightarrow \alpha\gamma(\beta\gamma)$$

The Combinator Calculus is well-known to be capable of defining all of the computable functions [Ch41, CF58, St72], and has been proposed as a machine language [Tu79, CG80]. Certain *computations*, however, apparently cannot be simulated by this calculus.

Consider a language containing the Boolean symbols T and F, and the *parallel or* combinator D, with the rules

$$DT\alpha \rightarrow T$$
$$D\alpha T \rightarrow T$$
$$DFF \rightarrow F$$

Intuitively, in order to evaluate $D\alpha\beta$ we *must* evaluate α and β in parallel, in case one of them comes out T while the other is undefined. On the other hand, it is possible to evaluate combinatory $S-K$ expressions in a purely sequential fashion, by leftmost-outermost evaluation [CF58]. Thus, the only way to simulate the D combinator in the $S-K$ calculus seems to be to program what is essentially an operating system, simulating parallelism by time-sliced multiprogramming. Such a simulation appears to destroy the possibility of exploiting the parallelism in D, and can hardly be said to produce an analogous computation to the original.

This section formalizes the concept of simulation of one reduction system by another, and studies the powers of the $S-K$ combinator calculus and its extensions by the *parallel or* (D) and *arbitrary choice* (A) operators. Section 19.1 defines *reduction systems* in a natural and very general way, and defines the *confluence (Church-Rosser) property* that holds for certain reduction systems. Section 19.2 develops useful properties of the combinator calculi. Section 19.3 defines *simulation* of one reduction system by another, gives examples of plausible simulations, and shows that a weaker definition allows intuitively unacceptable "simulations." Section 19.4 shows that the $S-K$ calculus does not simulate the $S-K-D$ calculus, and that the $S-K-A$ calculus is universal. Section 19.5 shows that the $S-K$ calculus simulates all simply strongly sequential systems. Section 19.6 shows that the $S-K-D$ calculus simulates all regular systems.

19.1. Reduction Systems

The equational programs discussed in this book are viewed through the formalism of *term reduction systems,* presented in Section 17.1. The theoretical foundations for studying simulations of reduction systems seem to require a more general framework, where the states of a computation do not necessarily take the form of terms. *Reduction systems* are a more general class of formal computational structures. The essence of a reduction system is a set of possible states of computation, and a relation that determines the possible transitions from one state to the next. States with no possible transitions are called *normal forms,* and represent situations in which the computation halts. There is no loss of generality in assuming that, in any state with a possible transition, some transition is taken.

Definition 19.1.1

A *reduction system* is a pair $<\mathbf{S}, \ \rightarrow>$, where

$\mathbf{S}$ is a set of *states*

$\rightarrow \subseteq \mathbf{S} \times \mathbf{S}$ is a binary relation on $\mathbf{S}$, called *reduction.*

In most cases, we refer to the system $<\mathbf{S}, \ \rightarrow>$ as $\mathbf{S}$, and use the same $\rightarrow$ symbol in different contexts to indicate the reduction relation of different systems.

Such a reduction system is *effective* if

1. $\mathbf{S}$ is decidable (without loss of generality, $\mathbf{S}$ may be the nonnegative integers),

2. $\{\beta|\ \alpha \rightarrow \beta\}$ is finite for all α, and the *branching function* $n(\alpha) = |\{\beta|\ \alpha \rightarrow \beta\}|$ is

total computable,

3. the *transition function* $t: S \rightarrow P(S)$ defined by $t(\alpha) = \{\beta | \alpha \rightarrow \beta\}$ is total computable.

Intuitively, $\alpha \rightarrow \beta$ means that a computation may go from α to β in one step.

Definition 19.1.2

Let $<S, \rightarrow>$ be a reduction system.

$\eta \in S$ is a *normal form* if there is no ν such that $\eta \rightarrow \nu$.

$N_S = \{\eta \in S | \eta$ *is a normal form*$\}$

Definition 19.1.3

A reduction system $<S, \rightarrow>$ is *confluent* if

$\forall \alpha, \beta, \gamma \in S \ (\alpha \rightarrow^* \beta \ \& \ \alpha \rightarrow^* \gamma) \Rightarrow \exists \delta \in S \ (\beta \rightarrow^* \delta \ \& \ \gamma \rightarrow^* \delta)$

(See Figure 19.1.1)

The confluence property is often called the *Church—Rosser* property, since Church and Rosser established a similar property in the λ calculus. The confluence property is important because it guarantees that normal forms are unique, and that normal forms may be found by following the $\rightarrow$ relation in the forward direction only. For example, consider a reduction system with states α, β, γ, δ_1, $\delta_2 \cdots$, and reduction relation defined by $\alpha \rightarrow \beta$, $\alpha \rightarrow \gamma$, $\alpha \rightarrow \delta_1$, $\delta_i \rightarrow \delta_{i+1}$. β and γ are the only normal forms. See Figure 19.1.2 for a picture of this reduction system. Because of the failure of the confluence property in this reduction system, α has two different normal forms, β and γ. Furthermore, δ_1 cannot be reduced to normal form, even though it is equivalent to the normal forms β and γ according to the natural

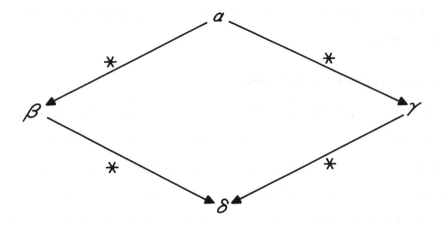

Figure 19.1.1

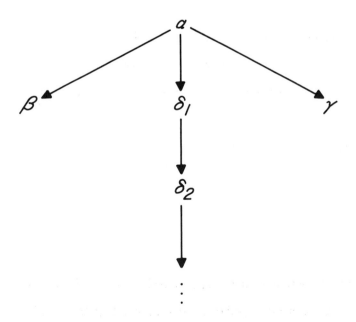

Figure 19.1.2

equivalence relation generated by $\rightarrow$. In order to find β or γ from δ_1, we must take a *reverse* reduction to α.

19.2. The Combinator Calculus, With Variants

The $S-K$ *combinator calculus* [Sc24, CF58, St72] was developed by logicians to demonstrate that the concept of a variable in mathematics may be eliminated in favor of more primitive concepts. More recently, Turner [Tu79, CG80] has proposed this calculus as a machine language, into which higher level languages may be compiled. Viewed as a reduction system, the combinator calculus is defined as follows. The particular reduction relation defined below is sometimes called *weak reduction* [St72]. *Strong reduction* mimics the λ-calculus more closely, but requires an extended set of terms.

Definition 19.2.1

The $S-K$ *calculus* is the reduction system $<C[S,K],\ \rightarrow>$, where

$C[S,K] = \{S,K,AP\}_\#$ is the set of all terms built from the constants S and K, and the binary operation AP (as mentioned before, the AP operation is abbreviated by juxtaposition);

$\rightarrow$ is the least relation satisfying

$K\alpha\beta \rightarrow \alpha$

$S\alpha\beta\gamma \rightarrow \alpha\gamma(\beta\gamma)$

$\alpha \rightarrow \beta \Rightarrow \alpha\gamma \rightarrow \beta\gamma \ \& \ \gamma\alpha \rightarrow \gamma\beta$

for all $\alpha,\beta,\gamma \in C$.

The $S-K-D$ *calculus* is the reduction system $<C[S,K,D],\ \rightarrow>$ obtained from the $S-K$ calculus by adding the constant symbol D and augmenting the relation $\rightarrow$ with the rules

$DK\alpha \rightarrow K$

$D \alpha K \rightarrow K$

$D (K (SKK)) (K (SKK)) \rightarrow K (SKK)$

(K represents *truth* and $K (SKK)$ represents *falsehood*)

The $S-K-A$ *calculus* is the reduction system $<C[S,K,A], \rightarrow>$ obtained from the $S-K$ calculus by adding the constant symbol A and augmenting the relation $\rightarrow$ with the rules

$A \alpha \beta \rightarrow \alpha$

$A \alpha \beta \rightarrow \beta$

□

The $S-K$ calculus is definable in the current version of the equation interpreter (see Section 9.9), and the $S-K-D$ calculus will be handled by a future version. The $S-K-A$ calculus is unlikely to be supported, because of its inherent indeterminacy. See Section 15.2 for a discussion of the difficulties in dealing with indeterminate constructs.

Conventional presentations of combinators usually include the additional symbol I, with the rule $I \alpha \rightarrow \alpha$. For symbolic parsimony, we omit the I, since its effect may be achieved by SKK, as $SKK \alpha \rightarrow K \alpha (K \alpha) \rightarrow \alpha$. The following properties of the $S-K$ calculus are well-known [St72], and clearly hold for S-K-D and S-K-A as well.

Lemma 19.2.1

Let $I \equiv SKK$.

Let α be a term built from S,K,D,A, the variables $x,y,z, \cdots$, and the binary operation AP (variables are not allowed in $C[S,K]$, $C[S,K,D]$, $C[S,K,A]$ as defined above).

Let $\alpha[\beta/x]$ be the result of replacing each occurrence of the variable x in α by β.

Let $\lambda x.\alpha$ be defined by

$\lambda x.x \equiv I$

$\lambda x.y \equiv Ky$ for $x \not\equiv y$

$\lambda x.S \equiv KS$

$\lambda x.K \equiv KK$

$\lambda x.D \equiv KD$

$\lambda x.A \equiv KA$

$\lambda x.(\alpha\beta) \equiv S(\lambda x.\alpha)(\lambda x.\beta)$

Then, $(\lambda x.\alpha)\beta \rightarrow^* \alpha[\beta/x]$ for all $\alpha \in C[S,K,D] \cup C[S,K,A]$.

□

Notice that the definitions above translate all λ terms into combinatory terms with variables, and all λ terms with no free variables into $C[S,K]$.

Lemma 19.2.2 [Ch41, St72]

Let ϕ be any acceptable indexing of the partial recursive functions.

There is a total computable function $^-$ from the nonnegative integers (N) to the normal forms of $C[S,K]$ ($N_{C[S,K]}$) and a term $v \in N_{C[S.K]}$, such that

$v \bar{\imath} \bar{\jmath} \rightarrow^* \overline{\phi_i(j)}$ for all $i,j \in N$.

In particular, the function $^-$ may always be defined by

$\bar{\imath} \equiv \lambda x.\lambda y.x(x(\cdots(xy)\cdots))$, where the number of occurrences of the variable x applied to y is i [Ch41].

□

Lemma 19.2.3 [CF58, Kl80a]

There is a term $\mu \in C[S,K]$ that implements the *least fixpoint function*. That is,

$\mu\alpha \rightarrow^* \alpha(\mu\alpha)$ for all $\alpha \in C[S,K]$.

μ may be used to construct $\alpha_1,\cdots,\alpha_m \in C[S,K]$ solving any simultaneous recursive definitions of the form

$$\alpha_1 x_{1,1} \cdots x_{1,i_1} \to^* \beta_1$$

$$\cdots$$

$$\alpha_m x_{m,1} \cdots x_{m,i_m} \to^* \beta_m$$

where each β_j is a term built from $\alpha_1, \cdots, \alpha_m, x_{j,1}, \cdots x_{j,i_j}, S, K, D, A$ and AP.

Specifically, $\mu \equiv (\lambda x. \lambda f. f(xxf))(\lambda x. \lambda f. f(xxf))$

□

Lemma 19.2.1 allows us to define procedures that substitute parameters into terms with variables. Lemma 19.2.2 guarantees the existence of terms to compute arbitrary computable functions on integers, saving us the trouble of constructing them explicitly. Lemma 19.2.3 lets us construct terms that perform arbitrary rearrangements of their arguments and themselves, even though those arguments may not be integers. That is, we may write explicitly recursive programs.

Although arbitrary data structures, such as lists, may in principle be encoded as integers, and all computable operations may be carried out on such encodings, the *computation steps* involved in manipulations of encoded data structures may not correspond correctly to the intended ones. So, we define structuring operations in a new, but straightforward, way.

Definition 19.2.2

$T \equiv K$

$F \equiv KI$

$P \equiv \lambda x. \lambda y. \lambda z. zxy$

$L \equiv \lambda x. xT$

$R \equiv \lambda x. xF$

$C \equiv \lambda x. \lambda y. \lambda z. x(yz)$

$M \equiv \lambda x.PxT$

$<\alpha,\beta> \equiv \lambda z.z\alpha\beta$

$if\ \alpha\ then\ \beta\ else\ \gamma \equiv \alpha\beta\gamma$

□

T and F represent the usual truth values. $P\alpha\beta$, or $<\alpha,\beta>$, represents the ordered pair of α and β. L and R are the left- and right-projection operations, respectively. $P\alpha\beta\gamma$ represents the conditional term that gives α when γ is T, and β when γ is F. These observations are formalized by the following straightforward lemma.

Lemma 19.2.4

For all $\alpha,\beta,\gamma \in C[S,K,D] \cup C[S,K,A]$:

$P\alpha\beta \rightarrow^* <\alpha,\beta>$

$L<\alpha,\beta> \rightarrow^* \alpha$

$R<\alpha,\beta> \rightarrow^* \beta$

$P\alpha\beta\gamma \rightarrow^* if\ \gamma\ then\ \alpha\ else\ \beta$

$if\ T\ then\ \alpha\ else\ \beta \rightarrow^* \alpha$

$if\ F\ then\ \alpha\ else\ \beta \rightarrow^* \beta$

$C\alpha\beta\gamma \rightarrow^* \alpha(\beta\gamma)$

$M\alpha \rightarrow^* <\alpha,T>$

□

The more conventional pairing and projection operators defined on numerical encodings satisfy similar properties for those α,β,γ that actually represent integers. This restriction is particularly troublesome, since all integer representations are in normal form. Thus, integer-encoded operators are strict, while $L(P\alpha\beta)$ as defined above reduces to α even if β has no normal form.

Pairing functions may be used to define lists. In order to be able to test a list for emptiness, we pair up every element with a Boolean value indicating whether the end of list has been reached. This is necessary because the property of being an ordered pair, in the sense of $<\ >$, is not testable within the calculus.

Definition 19.2.3

$[\ \ ]$ abbreviates $<F,F>$

$[\alpha_1, \alpha_2, \cdots, \alpha_n]$

abbreviates $<T,<\alpha_1,<T,<\alpha_2, \cdots <T,<\alpha_n,<F,F>>> \cdots >>>>$, for $n \geqslant 1$.

☐

All of the usual list operators may be defined by terms in $C[S,K]$ in such a way that reduction to normal form produces the same result as a "lazy" or outermost LISP program [FW76, HM76, O'D77].

Lemma 19.2.5

The $S-K$ and $S-K-D$ combinator calculi are confluent, but the $S-K-A$ calculus is not.

Proof sketch:

See [CF41, St72] for the $S-K$ calculus. The general results of [O'D77, Kl80a] cover $S-K-D$. $ATF \rightarrow T$ and $ATF \rightarrow F$, disproving confluence for $S-K-A$.

☐

Reduction systems, in general, may have no meaningful ways of identifying different reduction steps, other than by the states that they connect. When the states are terms, as in the three combinatory calculi, and when the definition of the arrow relation is given by rules allowing the replacement of certain subterms, it is natural and useful to identify reduction steps with the occurrences of subterms that they replace.

Definition 19.2.4

In any of the three reduction systems defined in this section, a *redex* is an occurrence of a subterm that may be replaced by the $\rightarrow$ relation.

When $\alpha \rightarrow \beta$, a *residual* of a redex r in α is a redex in β directly resulting from r.

☐

For example, in the $S-K$ calculus, a *redex* is an occurrence of a subterm in one of the forms $K\alpha\beta$, $S\alpha\beta\gamma$. In a reduction of the form $\alpha[S\beta\gamma\delta] \rightarrow \alpha[\beta\delta(\gamma\delta)]$, the only residual of a redex within α in the leftmost expression, is the redex in exactly the same position in the rightmost expression. The only residual of a redex within β or γ is the redex in the corresponding position in the explicit copy of β or γ, and the two residuals of a redex within δ are the two redexes in corresponding positions in the two explicit copies of δ. The redex $S\beta\gamma\delta$ has no residual in this case, because it is destroyed by the reduction. Residuals generalize naturally to arbitrarily long sequences of reductions. When it is necessary to trace residuals through reduction sequences, we will write $\alpha \xrightarrow{r} \beta$ to indicate that α reduces to β by replacing r or one of its residuals in α. For a more precise treatment of residuals, see [HL79, O'D77]. For the purposes of this section, the intuitive treatment above should suffice.

Huet and Lévy also define *sequentiality* for reduction systems such as $S-K$ and $S-K-D$, but their definition depends on the term structure of the states in these systems. See Section 16 for a discussion of sequentiality in term rewriting systems. We will isolate one consequence of the sequentiality of $S-K$, and nonsequentiality of $S-K-D$, that may be expressed purely in terms of the reduction graphs.

Definition 19.2.5

A reduction system $<S, \rightarrow>$ has *property A* if there is a function $f: N \rightarrow N$ such that the following holds for all $\alpha, \beta, \gamma, \delta \in S$:

if α is a (not necessarily unique) least common ancestor of β, γ in the graph of $\rightarrow$, and $\beta \rightarrow^m \delta$, $\gamma \rightarrow^n \delta$, then there is a reduction sequence $\alpha \rightarrow^k \delta$ with $k \leqslant f(m,n)$.

$\square$

Intuitively, property A says that the upper reductions shown in Figure 19.2.1 cannot be too much longer than the lower ones.

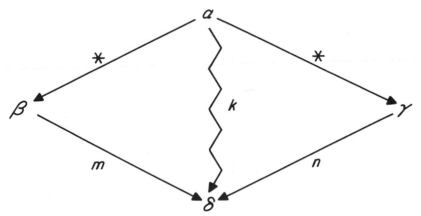

Figure 19.2.1

   In order to establish property A for the S-K calculus, we need a way of choosing a standard reduction sequence for a particular pair of terms.

Definition 19.2.6 [CF58]

The reduction sequence $\alpha_0 \xrightarrow{r_0} \alpha_1 \xrightarrow{r_1} \cdots \xrightarrow{r_{m-1}} \alpha_m$ is *standard* if, whenever r_{i+j} is a residual of a redex s in α_i, r_i either contains s as a subterm, or is disjoint from s and to the left of it. In other words, redexes are reduced starting with the leftmost-outermost one, and any left-outer redex that is skipped in favor of a right or inner one will never be reduced.

☐

The following lemma is from Curry and Feys [CF58].

Lemma 19.2.8

In the $S-K$ calculus, if $\alpha \rightarrow^i \beta$, then there is a standard reduction of α to β with at most 2^i steps.

☐

Lemma 19.2.9

The $S-K-D$ calculus does not have property A.

The $S-K$ calculus has property A, with the function $f(i,j)=2^i+2^j$.

Proof sketch:

The $S-K-D$ calculus contains subgraphs of the form described in Definition 19.2.5, with $m=n=1$, but k arbitrarily large. Let $I_0 \equiv I$, $I_{i+1} \equiv I_i I$. Notice that $I_{i+1} \rightarrow^2 I_i$, and there are no other reductions possible on I_{i+1}. Let $\alpha = D(I_i T)(I_i T)$, $\beta = DT(I_i T)$, $\gamma = D(I_i T)T$, $\delta = T$. $\beta \rightarrow^1 \delta$, and $\gamma \rightarrow^1 \delta$, but $\alpha \rightarrow^{i+2} \delta$ is the shortest reduction sequence from α to δ.

For the $S-K$ calculus, let $\alpha,\beta,\gamma,\delta \in C[S,K]$, $m,n \in N$ be as in the statement of Definition 19.2.5. Since α is a *least* common ancestor of β,γ, the two reduction sequences $\alpha \rightarrow^* \beta$ and $\alpha \rightarrow^* \gamma$ have no steps in common (i.e., reducing residuals of the same redex). Let $\alpha \rightarrow^* \beta$, $\alpha \rightarrow^* \gamma$, $\alpha \rightarrow^k \delta$, $\beta \rightarrow^{m'} \delta$, $\gamma \rightarrow^{n'} \delta$ be the standard reductions. By Lemma 19.2.8, $m' \leqslant 2^m$, and $n' \leqslant 2^n$.

Consider a redex r that is reduced in $\alpha \rightarrow^* \beta$, but not in $\gamma \rightarrow^{n'} \delta$. Since r is not reduced in $\alpha \rightarrow^* \gamma$, it must be eliminated in $\alpha \rightarrow^* \gamma \rightarrow^{n'} \delta$ by an application of the rule $K\iota\kappa \rightarrow \iota$, with r in κ. In the standard reduction $\alpha \rightarrow^k \delta$, the K-reduction above comes before the reduction of r, so r is not reduced in $\alpha \rightarrow^k \delta$. Thus, every redex that is reduced in $\alpha \rightarrow^* \beta$, and in $\alpha \rightarrow^k \delta$ must also be reduced in $\gamma \rightarrow^{n'} \delta$. A symmetric argument covers $\alpha \rightarrow^* \gamma$ and $\beta \rightarrow^{m'} \delta$. Every redex reduced in $\alpha \rightarrow^k \delta$ comes from either $\alpha \rightarrow^* \beta$ or $\alpha \rightarrow^* \gamma$, so $k \leqslant m' + n' \leqslant 2^m + 2^n$.

□

19.3. Simulation of One Reduction System by Another

In the introduction to Section 19 we argued that, although every function computed in the $S-K-D$ calculus may be computed in the $S-K$ calculus, there are certain computations, with a parallel flavor, that can be produced by $S-K-D$ but not by $S-K$. In this subsection, we propose a definition of simulation for reduction systems, that seems to capture the essential elements of simulations that preserve the general structure of a computation. As in the definition of stepwise simulation for conventional random access machines, we associate with each state in a *guest* system one or more states in a *host* system, which will represent the guest state. The association of guest computation steps with host computation steps is trickier. It is not appropriate to insist that every guest computation step be associated with a single contiguous path in the host system, since potentially parallel guest steps, when interpreted as multistep paths in the host, could well have their individual steps interleaved. On the other hand, it is not enough merely to require that $\alpha \rightarrow \beta$ in the guest if, and only if, $\alpha' \rightarrow^* \beta'$ for associated states in the host, since that requirement still allows pathological behaviors in the host that do not correspond to any such behavior in the guest. For example, if there is a large, simple cycle $\alpha_1 \rightarrow \alpha_2 \rightarrow \cdots \rightarrow \alpha_n \rightarrow \alpha_1$ in the guest, the host would be allowed to have spurious reduction paths directly between α_i' and α_j', without involving the appropriate intermediate steps. The host could even have infinite reductions within equivalence classes of states representing a single host state.

The following definition of simulation is not clearly the right one, but it is at least a very plausible one, and addresses the concerns described above. The positive and negative results about simulations in Sections 19.4, 19.5 and 19.6 provide evidence that the definition is reasonable, since they agree with a programming intuition about what attempts at simulation are and are not acceptable. The intent of the definition is to capture the idea that the set of possible choices in the host system must be *exactly* the same as the set of possible choices in the guest system, when the differences between different host representations of the same guest state are ignored. We do *not* require, however, that decisions in the host be made in the same order that they are made in the guest. Choices of different host representations for the same guest state may predetermine future choices between different guest states. Roughly speaking, the host may be allowed to, but must not be required to, plan ahead in a computation sequence. Invisible book-keeping steps in the host are allowed, which do not change the represented guest state, but such steps are not allowed to grow without bound, else they could surreptitiously simulate potential guest computation steps that have not been officially chosen for execution in the host computation.

Definition 19.3.1

Let $<S_g, \rightarrow_g>$ (the *guest*) and $<S_h, \rightarrow_h>$ (the *host*) be reduction systems. S_h *weakly simulates* S_g if there exist

an *encoding set* $E \subseteq S_h$,

a *decoding function* $d:S_h \rightarrow S_g \cup \{nil\}$ $(nil \notin S_g)$

a *computation relation* $\rightarrow_c \subseteq \rightarrow_h$

such that

1. $d[E] = S_g$ & $d^{-1}[N_{S_g}] \cap E \subseteq N_{S_h}$

2. $\forall \alpha, \beta \in S_h \ \alpha \rightarrow_c \beta \Rightarrow d(\alpha) \rightarrow_g d(\beta)$

3. $\forall \alpha, \beta \in S_h \ \alpha(\rightarrow_h - \rightarrow_c)\beta \Rightarrow d(\alpha) = d(\beta)$

4.

$\forall \alpha \in E, \beta \in S_g \ d(\alpha) \rightarrow_g \beta \Rightarrow \exists \delta \in E \ \alpha(\rightarrow_h - \rightarrow_c)^* \rightarrow_c (\rightarrow_h - \rightarrow_c)^* \delta$ & $d(\delta) = \beta$

5. $\forall \alpha \in N_{S_h} \ d(\alpha) \in N_{S_g} \cup \{nil\}$

6. There is no infinite $\rightarrow_h - \rightarrow_c$ path

$\langle S_h, \rightarrow_h \rangle$ *simulates* $\langle S_g, \rightarrow_g \rangle$ if, in addition, there exists a *bound function* $b : S_g \rightarrow N$ such that

6'. $\forall \alpha, \beta \in E \ \alpha(\rightarrow_h - \rightarrow_c)^m \rightarrow_c (\rightarrow_h - \rightarrow_c)^n \beta \Rightarrow m < b(d(\alpha))$ & $n < b(d(\beta))$

A (weak) simulation is *effective* if the appropriate E, d, $\rightarrow_c$, and b are all total computable.

□

Intuitively, (1) requires that d maps E onto S_g, respecting normal forms. $d(\alpha) \in S_g$ is the unique expression encoded by $\alpha \in S_h$, but each $\beta \in S_g$ may have infinitely many encodings. The allowance for multiple encodings corresponds with common practice, where, for example, a stack is encoded by any one of many arrays containing the contents of the stack, plus extra meaningless values in unused components of the array. (2), (3) and (4) require that each $\rightarrow_g$ reduction is simulated by any number of $\rightarrow_h - \rightarrow_c$ reductions, which do not change the encoded expression, followed by exactly one $\rightarrow_h$ reduction to effect the change in the encoded expression. (5) prevents dead ends in the simulation.

Notice that the effect of (1)-(4) is to select a subset E of S_h to represent S_g, and divide it into equivalence classes in a one-one correspondence to S_g. A state

$\alpha \in S_h$ − E that is accessible by reductions from a state in E must also be associated with a unique $d(\alpha) \in S_g$. Each one-step reduction on S_g is simulated by one or more reduction sequences between the equivalence classes in E. There may be $\rightarrow_h$ reduction sequences that slip between the various classes $d^{-1}[\beta] \cap E$, but they still mimic $\rightarrow_g$ reductions by their behavior on the classes $d^{-1}[\beta]$. Alternatively, think of $d^{-1}[\beta] \cap E$ as the set of *canonical* encodings of β *from which any* $\rightarrow_g$ *reduction may yet be chosen.* Members of $d^{-1}[\beta]$ − E still represent β, but may require some additional reductions to display β canonically, or may predetermine some restrictions on the $\rightarrow_g$ reductions of β.

The relation $\rightarrow_c$ could be always taken as the restriction of $\rightarrow_h$ to $\bigcup_{\alpha \neq \beta} d^{-1}[\alpha] \times d^{-1}[\beta]$, except for the necessity of representing self-loops of the form $\alpha \rightarrow_g \alpha$. (6) prevents infinite reductions in $\rightarrow_h$ that do not accomplish anything with respect to $\rightarrow_g$. (1)-(6) together allow us to find a normal form for $\alpha \in S_g$ by encoding it in a $\beta \in E \cap d^{-1}[\alpha]$, reducing β to a normal form γ, then taking $d(\gamma)$ for the normal form of α. (6') strengthens (6) to require that the maximum length of possible $\rightarrow_h$ − $\rightarrow_c$ reductions to $\alpha \in S_h$ is a function only of the encoded expression $d(\alpha)$, not of the particular encoding α. Restriction 6' enforces the intuitive rule that invisible book-keeping steps in the host computation must not be so complex that they actually simulate potential guest computation steps that the host chose not to perform.

Notice that Definition 19.3.1 really has to do with simulating a certain degree of *nondeterminism*, rather than parallelism. Simulating all possible degrees of nondeterminism appears to be *necessary* for simulating all degrees of parallelism, but is certainly *not* sufficient. It is not clear to us how to capture degree of parallelism precisely at an appropriate level of abstraction.

The following lemma is straightforward, but tedious, to prove.

Lemma 19.3.1

(Effective) weak simulation and simulation are reflexive and transitive relations on reduction systems.

☐

While the bounding restriction (6′) might seem excessive, there are certain weak simulations that are intuitively unacceptable.

Theorem 19.3.1

The $S-K$ calculus effectively weakly simulates the $S-K-D$ calculus.

Proof sketch:

The basic idea is to encode a term $D\alpha\beta$ by an $S-K$ term of the form $\rho<\iota,\kappa>$. ι and κ are programs producing possibly infinite lists of static data structures representing the possible reductions of α and β respectively. ρ is a program using "lazy" evaluation to alternately probe one step farther in ι and κ respectively, until a T is found in one or the other, or an F is found in each. When such Boolean values are found, ρ throws away the lists ι and κ, and produces the appropriate Boolean value. The decoding function maps $\rho<\iota,\kappa>$ to $D\alpha\beta$, where α and β are the last items actually appearing on the lists ι and κ respectively, as long as no T appears. As soon as a T appears, followed by *nil* (encoded as $<F,F>$) to mark the end of list, the decoding function maps to T, even though the program ρ has not yet discovered the T.

☐

The weak simulation outlined above is intuitively unsatisfying, because it really simulates the parallel *or* behavior of $D\alpha\beta$ by an explicit and rigid alternation of steps on α and β. Although at first the programs ι and κ may proceed completely independently, the behavior of ρ forces the first one of them to reach T to wait for the other one to make at least as many steps before the normal form can be reached. All of this catching up is hidden within the equivalence class encoding T. In consequence, arbitrarily long sequences of reductions may go on entirely within this equivalence class. It is precisely such arbitrarily long reductions within an equivalence class that are ruled out by (6′) in Definition 19.3.1.

It is useful to apply a geometric intuition to reduction systems by treating them as (usually infinite) directed graphs whose nodes are the states, and whose edges show the reduction relation. In the weak simulation of Theorem 19.3.1, consider a term $D\alpha\beta$, where α and β each reduce by a unique path to T. The graph representing the part of the $S-K-D$ calculus below $D\alpha\beta$ is suggested in Figure 19.3.1. Reductions down and to the left indicate those applying to α, and those down and to the right apply to β. The terms along the lower left edge are all of the form $DT\gamma$, where $\beta \rightarrow^* \gamma$, and those on the lower right are of the form $D\delta T$, where $\alpha \rightarrow^* \delta$.

Figure 19.3.2 shows the part of the $S-K$ graph below the encoding $\rho<\iota,\kappa>$ of $D\alpha\beta$. In this case, terms that show the same reductions to ι,κ, but different amounts of reductions involving ρ, are gathered into one blob. Reductions to the left indicate reductions to ι, those to the right to κ. Reductions involving ρ are hidden in the blobs. The lower left edge contains terms of the form $\rho<(\,\cdots\,T),\gamma>$, where $\kappa \rightarrow^* \gamma$, the lower right contains terms of the form $\rho<\gamma,(\,\cdots\,T)>$, where $\iota \rightarrow^* \gamma$. The dotted lines surround blobs representing T. Notice how arbitrarily long paths arise along the lower edges within the region representing T. These long paths violate (6′).

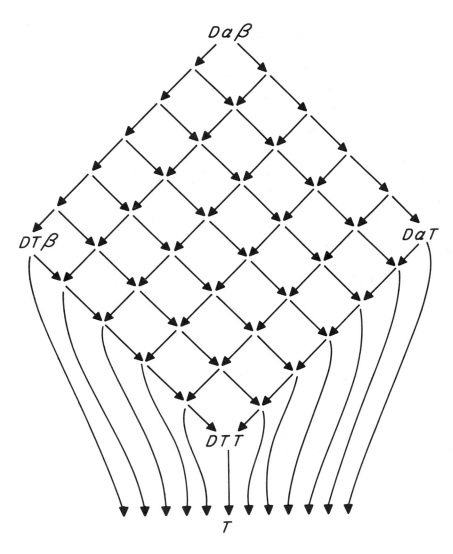

Figure 19.3.1

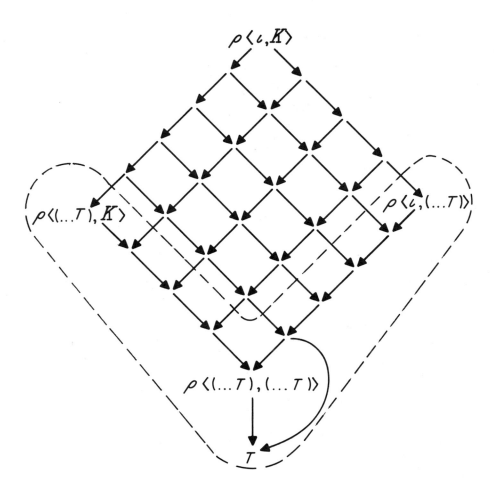

Figure 19.3.2

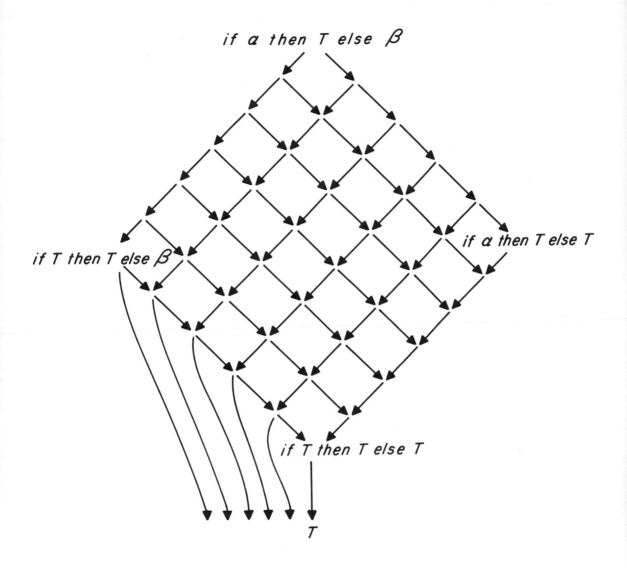

Figure 19.3.3

For comparison purposes, Figure 19.3.3 shows the part of the $S-K$ graph below a term of the form *if* α *then* T *else* β, where α,β each reduce to T. This form is often called the *conditional or* of α and β. The lower left edge contains terms of the form *if* T *then* T *else* γ, and the lower right edge contains terms of the form *if* γ *then* T *else* T.

Definition 19.3.2

An effective reduction system is *universal* if it effectively simulates all effective reduction systems.

□

19.4. The Relative Powers of $S-K$, $S-K-D$, and $S-K-A$

Theorem 19.4.1

The $S-K$ calculus does not simulate the $S-K-D$ calculus.

Proof sketch:

Suppose the contrary, and let b be the bound function in the simulation. Consider the $S-K-D$ terms $\alpha=D(I_{2^{b(T)}}T)(I_{2^{b(T)}}T)$, $\beta=DT(I_{2^{b(T)}}T)$, $\gamma=D(I_{2^{b(T)}}T)T$, $\delta=T$. Notice that α is a least common ancestor of β and γ, and the shortest reduction of α to δ is of length $2^{b(T)+1}+1$. Choose $S-K$ terms $\alpha'\in d^{-1}[\alpha]$, $\beta'\in d^{-1}[\beta]\cap E$, $\beta''\in d^{-1}[\beta]$, $\gamma'\in d^{-1}[\gamma]\cap E$, $\gamma''\in d^{-1}[\gamma]$, $\delta'\in d^{-1}[\delta]\cap E$, such that $\alpha'\rightarrow^*\beta'\rightarrow^*\beta''$, $\alpha'\rightarrow^*\gamma'\rightarrow^*\gamma''$, α' is a least common ancestor of β'',γ'', and β'',γ'' cannot be reduced further within $d^{-1}[\beta]$, $d^{-1}[\gamma]$ (see Figure 19.4.1). The existence of such terms is guaranteed by 3 and 4 of Definition 19.3.1, and by the confluence property. The shortest reduction of α' to δ' must be of length at least $2^{b(T)+1}+1$. So, by Lemma 19.2.9, $\beta''\rightarrow^m\delta'$, $\gamma''\rightarrow^n\delta'$, with $2^{b(T)+1}+1\leqslant2^m+2^n$. At least one of m,n must be $>b(T)$, contradicting restriction $6'$ of Definition 19.3.1

□

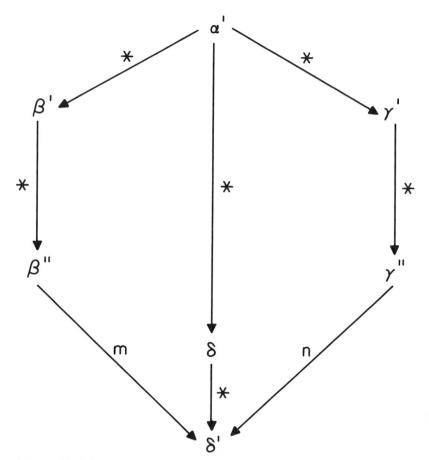

Figure 19.4.1

Theorem 19.4.2

The $S-K-D$ calculus does not simulate the $S-K-A$ calculus.

Proof sketch:

The proof is elementary, since no confluent system may simulate a system that is not confluent.

☐

Theorem 19.4.3

The $S-K-A$ calculus is universal.

Proof sketch:

Let $<N, \rightarrow>$ be an arbitrary effective reduction system, with nonnegative integers for states (no loss of generality comes from the use of nonnegative integers). The function $^-:N \rightarrow C[S,K]$ is the encoding of integers into combinatory terms from Lemma 19.2.2. Let $\xi \in C[S.K]$ be an equality test for encoded integers. Let $\eta \in C[S,K]$ be a combinatory term for a program that takes an argument $\bar{\alpha}$, representing $\alpha \in N$, and computes the encoded integer $\overline{n(\alpha)}$, where $n(\alpha) = |\{\beta \in N \mid \alpha \rightarrow \beta\}|$. Let $\rho \in C[S,K]$ be a combinatory term for a program that takes an argument $\bar{\alpha}$, and an encoded integer $\bar{\imath}$, and computes the encoded state $\bar{\beta}$, $\beta \in N$ that results from performing the ith possible reduction to α. That is,

$$\forall i,j \in N \quad i = j \Rightarrow \xi \bar{\imath} \, \bar{\jmath} \rightarrow^* T \ \& \ i \neq j \Rightarrow \xi \bar{\imath} \, \bar{\jmath} \rightarrow^* F,$$

$$\forall \alpha \in S \quad \eta \bar{\alpha} \rightarrow^* \overline{n(\alpha)},$$

and

$$\forall \alpha \in S, i \in N \quad \rho \bar{\alpha} \, \bar{\imath} \rightarrow^* \overline{\beta_{\alpha,i}},$$

where $\alpha \rightarrow \beta_{\alpha,i}$ is the ith reduction from α. Such η, ρ exist by Lemma 19.2.2. Let $K^0 \equiv I$, $K^{i+1} \equiv \lambda x.K(K^i x)$, $A^0 \equiv I$, $A^{i+1} \equiv \lambda x.A(K^i x)A^i$. By Lemmas 19.2.2, 19.2.3, there is an $\iota \in C[S,K,A]$ such that

$$\iota \bar{\alpha} \rightarrow^* if \ \xi(\eta \bar{\alpha})\bar{0} \ then \ \bar{\alpha} \ else \ \iota(\rho \bar{\alpha}(A^{n(\alpha)} \bar{0} \, \bar{1} \cdots \overline{n(\alpha)}))$$

Now, we may encode each $\alpha \in N$ as $\iota \bar{\alpha} \in E$ if α is not in normal form, as $\bar{\alpha} \in E$ if α is in normal form. Let the non*nil* values of d be determined by the following rule: if $\iota \bar{\alpha} \rightarrow^* \beta$ by a reduction sequence involving only A redexes and redexes in

$\iota\bar{\alpha} \rightarrow^* if\ \xi(\eta\bar{\alpha})\bar{0}\ then\ \bar{\alpha}\ else\ \iota(\rho\bar{\alpha}(A^{n\,(\alpha)}\ \bar{0}\ \bar{1}\ \cdots\ \overline{n\,(\alpha)})) \rightarrow^*$

$\quad if\ T\ then\ \bar{\alpha}\ else\ \iota(\rho\bar{\alpha}(A^{n\,(\alpha)}\ \bar{0}\ \bar{1}\ \cdots\ \overline{n\,(\alpha)})) \rightarrow^*\bar{\alpha}$

(when α is in normal form), or

$\iota\bar{\alpha} \rightarrow^* if\ \xi(\eta\bar{\alpha})\bar{0}\ then\ \bar{\alpha}\ else\ \iota(\rho\bar{\alpha}(A^{n\,(\alpha)}\ \bar{0}\ \bar{1}\ \cdots\ \overline{n\,(\alpha)})) \rightarrow^*$

$\quad if\ F\ then\ \bar{\alpha}\ else\ \iota(\rho\bar{\alpha}(A^{n\,(\alpha)}\ \bar{0}\ \bar{1}\ \cdots\ \overline{n\,(\alpha)}))$

(when α is not in normal form), then $d\,(\beta)=\alpha$.

□

Although the $S-K-A$ calculus is technically universal, it is *not* a good foundation for equational computing. In fact, the universality of $S-K-A$ illustrates that our definition of simulation captures degree of *nondeterminism*, rather than degree of parallelism, since the arbitrary choice operator is intuitively a sequential but nondeterministic construct. Many, if not most, parallel computations that a programmer wants to define have uniquely determined final results, in spite of nondeterminism in the computation. The inherently indeterminate behavior of the A combinator makes it dangerous as a fundamental constructor for determinate computations. The best foundation for equational computing is probably a layered language, containing a subset of symbols that produce all of the desired determinate computations, and something like the A combinator, to be used in the infrequent cases where truly indeterminate behavior is required. There may be other layers of disciplined behavior that should also be covered by simple sublanguages. In the next two subsections, we illuminate the behaviors that may be simulated by the $S-K$ and $S-K-D$ calculi. Section 19.7 develops other systems to simulate the behavior of the lambda calculus, which apparently cannot be simulated by any of the combinatory calculi discussed so far.

19.5. The $S-K$ Combinator Calculus Simulates All Simply Strongly Sequential Term Reduction Systems

In order to simulate an arbitrary simply strongly sequential term reduction system (see Definition 17.2.3) **S** over Σ in the $S-K$ calculus, the basic idea is to let contiguous portions of an $S-K$ term represent terms in $(\Sigma \cup \{\omega\})_\#$. Initially, each such term is of the form $f(\omega, \cdots, \omega)$, with exactly one symbol in Σ and the rest ωs. Whenever one of the represented $(\Sigma \cup \{\omega\})_\#$ terms becomes stable, it produces a direct syntactic representation of itself, that is accessible to operations from above. As long as a represented $(\Sigma \cup \{\omega\})_\#$ term is a strictly partial redex, it absorbs the topmost symbol from an index position below it (which can only be done after that index position becomes stable). When a represented $(\Sigma \cup \{\omega\})_\#$ term becomes a complete redex, it produces the associated right hand side of a rule in **S**, in the initial form of $f(\omega, \cdots, \omega)$ representations.

First, we define the direct syntactic representation of terms in $(\Sigma \cup \{\omega\})_\#$. This representation is essentially the representation of terms by nested lists in LISP [McC60], composed with the encoding of lists in $S-K$ of Definition 19.2.3.

Definition 19.5.1

The *syntactic encoder* **syn**$:(\Sigma \cup \{\omega\})_\# \to \mathbf{C}[S,K]$ is defined as follows.

Let $\alpha' \in (\Sigma \cup V)_\#$ be the result of replacing the occurrences of ω in α by $x_1, x_2, \cdots$ in order from left to right.

closure$_m(\beta) = \lambda x_1. \cdots \lambda x_m. \beta$

syn$(\alpha) = $ **closure**$_n($**syn**$'(\alpha'))$, where n is the number of ωs in α, and

syn$':(\Sigma \cup V)_\# \to (\{S,K,AP\} \cup V)_\#$ is defined inductively by the following equations:

syn$'(x) = x$ for $x \in V$

syn$'(a_i) = [\,\bar{\imath}\,]$ if $\rho(a_i) = 0$

$$\mathbf{syn}'(a_i(\alpha_1, \cdots, \alpha_{\rho(a_i)})) = [\ \bar{i}, \mathbf{syn}'(\alpha_1), \cdots, \mathbf{syn}'(\alpha_{\rho(a_i)})]$$

In the lines above, the expressions $[\ \bar{i}\ ]$ and $[\ \bar{i}, \mathbf{syn}'(\alpha_1), \cdots]$ indicate the list encodings of Definition 19.2.3.

☐

Notice that $\mathbf{syn}(\alpha)$ contains no variables, and is in normal form.

Now, we define the active semantic representation of a term in $(\Sigma \cup \{\omega\})_{\#}$. We depend on Lemma 19.2.3, which guarantees the ability to solve multiple simultaneous recursive definitions in $S-K$. Only a finite number of $(\Sigma \cup \{\omega\})_{\#}$ terms need be represented, so we do not need an infinitary mutual recursion.

Definition 19.5.2

Let $\mathbf{P} = \{\alpha \in (\Sigma \cup \{\omega\})_{\#} |\ \alpha$ *is a partial redex*,

　　or α is stable and $\mathbf{V} \beta \leqslant \alpha\ \beta$ *is a partial redex*}

$\mathbf{P}$ is a finite set.

Let $\psi \in C[S, K]$ implement the selector function for lists, with

$$\mathbf{V}\ \alpha_1, \cdots, \alpha_m \in C[S, K], 1 \leqslant i \leqslant m\ \ \psi \bar{i} [\alpha_1, \cdots, \alpha_m] \rightarrow^* \alpha_i.$$

Let $\sigma_{m,i} \in C[S, K]$ implement a spreading function, such that $\mathbf{V}\ \alpha, \beta_1, \cdots, \beta_m \in C[S, K], j \in N$

$$\sigma_{m,i}\ \bar{j}\ \alpha\beta_1 \cdots \beta_m \rightarrow^* \alpha\beta_1 \cdots \beta_{i-1}(\psi\ \bar{2}\ \beta_i) \cdots (\psi\ \overline{\rho(a_j)+1}\ \beta_i)$$
$$\cdots \beta_{i+1} \cdots \beta_m.$$

The *semantic encoders* $\mathbf{sem}{:}\Sigma_{\#} \rightarrow C[S, K]$ and $\mathbf{sem}'{:}\mathbf{P} \rightarrow C[S, K]$ are defined by simultaneous recursion as follows:

$\mathbf{sem}'(\alpha) \rightarrow^* \mathbf{syn}(\alpha)$ if α is stable

$\mathbf{sem}'(\alpha) \rightarrow^* \mathbf{closure}_m(\mathbf{sem}(\beta))$ if $\alpha \equiv \alpha'[\omega/x_1, \cdots, \omega/x_m]$ and $\alpha' \rightarrow \beta \in \mathbf{S}$.

$$\mathbf{sem'}(\alpha)x_1 \cdots x_m \to^* \sigma_{m,i}(\psi\,\overline{1}\,x_i)(\psi(\psi\,\overline{1}\,x_i)(\mathbf{sem'}(\alpha_1)\ \cdots\ \mathbf{sem'}(\alpha_k)))x_1 \cdots x_m$$

where α is a partial redex but not a redex, the sequencing function for $\mathbf{S}$ chooses the index α' for α, there are $i-1$ ωs to the left of the variable in α', and $\alpha_j \equiv \alpha'[a_j(\omega, \cdots, \omega)/x_i]$.

$\mathbf{sem}(x) \equiv x$ where $x \in V$

$\mathbf{sem}(a_i) \equiv \mathbf{sem'}(a_i)$ if $\rho(a_i)=0$

$\mathbf{sem}(a_i(\alpha_1, \cdots, \alpha_{\rho(a_i)})) \equiv \mathbf{sem'}(a_i(\omega, \cdots, \omega))\mathbf{sem}(\alpha_1) \cdots \mathbf{sem}(\alpha_{\rho(a_i)})$

Lemma 19.2.3 guarantees a solution for each $\mathbf{sem}(\alpha)$.

□

The definitions of **sem** and **sem'** above may be understood as producing a set of communicating sequential processes, which partition among themselves the nodes of a term $\alpha \in \Sigma_\#$, and whose communication network represents the tree structure of the term. Initially, each node of α is in a separate process, that knows only the symbol at that node. Each process simultaneously tries to gather up enough nodes to form a redex, or to learn that its nodes are stable. As long as a process possesses a strictly partial redex, it requests the head node of the unique son process specified by the sequencing function given in the definition of simply strongly sequential. When a process possesses a whole redex, it performs the reduction associated with that redex. When a process discovers that its nodes are stable, it halts and produces messages that can be read by its father when the father process wishes to gather up more nodes.

It is convenient to use a more reduced form of $\mathbf{sem}(\alpha)$ as the canonical representative of a term. The *encoding function* **e** gives the canonical representative.

Definition 19.5.3

The *encoding function* $e:\Sigma_\# \to C[S.K]$ is defined by:

$e(\alpha[\beta_1/x_1, \cdots ,\beta_m/x_m]) \equiv sem'(\alpha[\omega/x_1, \cdots ,\omega/x_m])e(\beta_1) \cdots e(\beta_m)$ where α is a left hand side of a rule, or $\alpha[\omega/x_1, \cdots ,\omega/x_m]$ is a partial redex and $\beta_1, \cdots ,\beta_m$ are not strongly stable.

$e(\alpha[\beta_1/x_1, \cdots ,\beta_m/x_m]) \equiv syn(\alpha)[e(\beta_1)/x_1, \cdots ,e(\beta_m)/x_m]$ where every node in α is strongly stable, and $\beta_1, \cdots ,\beta_m$ are not strongly stable.

□

e partitions a term (considered in graphical form) into contiguous regions that form maximal partial redexes, and the intervening stable regions. Each partial redex is represented by the semantic encoding, and each stable region is represented by the syntactic encoding. The nonoverlapping property of regular reduction systems (Definition 17.1.3) guarantees that the partition, hence e, is well-defined.

Lemma 19.5.1

1) **syn, sem,** and **e** are one-to-one.

2) $sem(\alpha) \to^* e(\alpha)$

3) If $\alpha \to \beta \in S$, and $\bar{\alpha} \to \bar{\beta}$ is an instance of $\alpha \to \beta$ with $\bar{\alpha} = \alpha[\gamma_1/x_1, \cdots ,\gamma_m/x_m]$, then

$e(\bar{\alpha}) \equiv sem'(\alpha)e(\gamma_1) \cdots e(\gamma_m) \to^* sem(\beta)[e(\gamma_1)/x_1, \cdots e(\gamma_m)/x_m] \to^* e(\bar{\beta})$

4) If α is in normal form, then $e(\alpha) \equiv syn(\alpha)$ is also in normal form.

Proof sketch:

All is straightforward except 2. The key fact in showing 2 is that the nonoverlapping property of Definition 17.1.3 guarantees that when α is a left hand side of a rule schema, then every proper subterm of $\alpha[\omega/x_1, \cdots, \omega/x_m]$, other than ω, is strongly stable. Thus, the nonroot nodes of a redex convert to the syntactic encoding, and may be gathered into the appropriate semantic encoding form at the root of the partial redex.

□

Theorem 19.5.1

The $S-K$ calculus effectively simulates every simply strongly sequential term reduction system.

Proof:

Let the encoding set **E** be the range of **e**. The non*nil* values of the decoder d are defined by the following condition: if $\alpha \to \beta_1, \cdots, \alpha \to \beta_k$ are all of the possible one-step reductions of α, and $\mathbf{sem}(\alpha) \to^* \gamma$ by reducing a subset of the redexes in the shortest reductions

$$\mathbf{sem}(\alpha) \to^* \mathbf{e}(\alpha) \to^* \mathbf{sem}(\beta_1), \quad \cdots \quad \mathbf{sem}(\alpha) \to^* \mathbf{e}(\alpha) \to^* \mathbf{sem}(\beta_k),$$

not containing all of the redexes in any one of the preceding reductions, then $d(\gamma) = \alpha$.

$$\to_c \ = \ \to \cap (\mathbf{C}[S,K] \times \mathbf{E}).$$

□

19.6. The $S-K-D$ Combinator Calculus Simulates All Regular Term Reduction Systems

The basic idea of the simulation of an arbitrary regular term reduction system by $S-K-D$ is similar to the simulation of simply strongly sequential systems by $S-K$ in Section 19.5. Instead of choosing a unique index position to absorb into a partial redex, the simulation tries in parallel to match every redex at every node in the term. The parallelism between different nodes is treated by similar parallelism in the $S-K-D$ calculus; parallelism at a single node uses the D combinator. The problem is that D merely gives the *or* of its arguments, it does not tell us which one came out T. In some cases, where the left hand sides of rules are unifiable, the right hand sides must be the same, so it is not important to know which of the unifiable left hand sides applied. In other cases, where right hand sides are different, it is crucial to determine which one to use. The solution is to first discover that *some* rule applies at a particular node, then test, in sequence, each left hand side of a rule. In testing a given rule schema, check every node in the left hand side of that rule schema in parallel (using the obvious simulation of a parallel *and* by a parallel *or*). The regularity of the system guarantees that, given that some rule applies, the parallel test whether a particular rule applies must halt. The following simple example illustrates this idea. The left hand sides in this example come from [HL79].

Example 19.6.1

Consider the rule schemata $f(x,a,b) \rightarrow 1$, $f(b,x,a) \rightarrow 2$, $f(a,b,x) \rightarrow 3$. The system defined by these rules is not strongly sequential, because there is no way to choose which son of an f to work on first. In a simulation of a computation in this system, suppose the test "does the current node match rule 1 *or* rule 2 *or* rule 3?", carried out with the parallel *or*, answers T. In order to find out which of the three rules applies, try the three tests: "is the 2nd son a *and* the 3rd son b?", "is the 1st son b *and* the 3rd son a?", "is the 1st son a *and* the 2nd son b?", sequentially, using a parallel *and* in each one. (equivalently, test "is *not* the 2nd son *not a or* the 3rd son *not b*?", etc.). Since the nonoverlapping property holds, the tests that do not correspond to the applicable rule must differ from the correct one in some position, so the parallel *and* will produce an F response, rather than nontermina-tion.

□

The simulation of regular systems by $S-K-D$ uses the same syntactic encoder **syn** of Definition 19.5.1, but a new semantic encoder.

Definition 19.6.1

Let the regular set **S** of rule schemata be partitioned into equivalence classes $S_1, \cdots, S_k$, where $\alpha_1 \to \beta_1$ is equivalent to $\alpha_2 \to \beta_2$ if α_1 and α_2 are unifiable.   By the definition of regularity, β_1 and β_2 must be the same.

Let **P** and ψ be as in Definition 19.5.2.

In addition, let $K^0 \equiv I$, $K^{i+1} \equiv \lambda x.K(K^i x)$, $D^0 \equiv I$, $D^{i+1} \equiv \lambda x.D(K^i x)D^i$.

Let $N \equiv \lambda x.xFT$ implement logical negation, and let $\chi_1 \in C[S,K]$ be a program to check one symbol in a syntactic encoding against the corresponding position in a rule schema. That is,

$$\mathbf{V}_{\alpha \in (\Sigma \cup \{\omega\})_\#}, i, j \in \mathbf{N}$$

α *agrees with the jth symbol in rule schema i* $\Rightarrow \chi_1 \bar{i} \bar{j} \mathbf{syn}(\alpha) \to^* T$ &

α *does not agree with the jth symbol in rule schema i* $\Rightarrow \chi_1 \bar{i} \bar{j} \mathbf{syn}(\alpha) \to^* F$

χ_2 checks a rule schema in parallel, that is,

$$\mathbf{V}_{\alpha \in C[S.K], i \in \mathbf{N}} \; \chi_2 \bar{i} \alpha \to^* N(D^{s_i}(N(\chi_1 \bar{i} \bar{1} \alpha)) \cdots (N(\chi_1 \bar{i} \bar{s_i} \alpha))),$$

where s_i is the size of the ith left hand side.

χ checks an entire equivalence class of rule schemata in parallel, that is,

$$\mathbf{V}_{\alpha \in C[S,K], j \in \mathbf{N}} \; \chi \bar{j} \alpha \to^* D^{t_j}(\chi_2 \bar{i_1} \alpha) \cdots (\chi_2 \bar{i_{t_j}} \alpha)$$

where $i_1, \cdots, i_{t_j}$ are the numbers of the rule schemata in the jth equivalence class.

Let $\mathbf{a}: C[S,K] \times (\Sigma \cup V)_\# \to (\{S,K,AP\} \cup V)_\#$ be a function that builds a syntactic encoding of a term, applying a given combinator to every node. That is,

$\mathbf{a}(\alpha,\mathbf{x}) \equiv \mathbf{x}$ for $\mathbf{x} \in V$

$\mathbf{a}(\alpha,a_i(\beta_1, \cdots ,\beta_m)) \equiv \alpha[\ \overline{i},\mathbf{a}(\alpha,\beta_1), \cdots ,\mathbf{a}(\alpha,\beta_m)]$

Let σ_j be a program that constructs a right hand side instance of the *jth* equivalence class of rule schema from a left hand side instance, with a specified operator applied to each node in the right hand side. That is,

$\mathbf{V}\ \gamma_1, \cdots ,\gamma_m,\delta \in \Sigma_{\#}\ \ \sigma_j\delta\ \mathbf{syn}(\alpha)[\gamma_1/\mathbf{x}_1, \cdots ,\gamma_m/\mathbf{x}_m] \rightarrow^* \mathbf{a}(\delta,\beta)[\gamma_1/\mathbf{x}_1, \cdots ,\gamma_m/\mathbf{x}_m]$

where $\alpha \rightarrow \beta$ is in the jth equivalence class.

The *parallel semantic encoders* $\mathbf{psem'} \in C[S,K]$ and $\mathbf{psem}:\Sigma_{\#} \rightarrow C[S,k]$ are defined by recursion as follows:

$\mathbf{psem'}\ \mathbf{x} \rightarrow^* if\ D^k(\chi\ \overline{1}\ \mathbf{x}) \cdots (\chi\ \overline{k}\ \mathbf{x})\ then$

$\qquad\qquad (if\ \chi\ \overline{1}\ \mathbf{x}\ then\ \sigma_1\ \mathbf{psem'}$

$\qquad\qquad else\ if\ \chi\ \overline{2}\ \mathbf{x}\ then\ \sigma_2\ \mathbf{psem'}$

$\qquad\qquad \cdots$

$\qquad\qquad else\ if\ \chi\ \overline{k}\ \mathbf{x}\ then\ \sigma_k\ \mathbf{psem'})\mathbf{x}$

$\qquad\qquad else\ \mathbf{x}$

where k is the number of equivalence classes of rule schemata in **S**.

$\mathbf{psem}(\alpha) \equiv \mathbf{a}(\mathbf{psem'},\alpha)$

☐

As before, we define a more reduced encoding than that given by **psem**.

Definition 19.6.2

The *parallel encoder* $\mathbf{pe}:\Sigma_{\#} \rightarrow C[S,K]$ is defined by:

$\mathbf{pe}(a_i(\alpha_1, \cdots ,\alpha_m)) \equiv$

$\qquad\qquad \mathbf{psem'}[\ \overline{i},\mathbf{pe}(\alpha_1), \cdots ,\mathbf{pe}(\alpha_m)]$ if $a_i(\alpha_1, \cdots ,\alpha_m)$ is an ω-potential redex

$[\bar{i}, \mathbf{pe}(\alpha_1), \cdots, \mathbf{pe}(\alpha_m)]$ if $a_i(\alpha_1, \cdots, \alpha_m)$ is strongly stable

Lemma 19.6.1

1) **psem** and **pe** are one-to-one.

2) $\mathbf{psem}(\alpha) \to^* \mathbf{pe}(\alpha)$

3) If $\alpha \to \beta \in \mathbf{S}$, and $\bar{\alpha} \to \bar{\beta}$ is an instance of $\alpha \to \beta$ with $\bar{\alpha} = \alpha[\gamma_1/x_1, \cdots, \gamma_m/x_m]$,

then $\mathbf{pe}(\bar{\alpha}) \to^* \mathbf{psem}(\beta)[\mathbf{pe}(\gamma_1)/x_1, \cdots \mathbf{pe}(\gamma_m)/x_m] \to^* \mathbf{pe}(\bar{\beta})$

4) If α is in normal form, then $\mathbf{pe}(\alpha) \equiv \mathbf{syn}(\alpha)$ is also in normal form.

Proof sketch: analogous to Lemma 19.5.1.

☐

Theorem 19.6.1

The $S-K-D$ combinator calculus effectively simulates every regular term reduction system.

Proof sketch: analogous to Theorem 19.5.1.

☐

19.7. The Power of the Lambda Calculus

Another mathematically natural candidate for a universal equational language is the *Lambda Calculus* [Ch41].

Definition 19.7.1

Given an infinite set of nullary symbols **V**, called *variables*, $\lambda[\mathbf{V}] = \{\lambda x \mid x \in \mathbf{V}\}$. Each λx is intended as a one-argument function symbol.

The *Lambda Calculus* is the reduction system $<\Lambda|\equiv, \to>$ where $\Lambda = (\{AP\} \cup \mathbf{V} \cup \lambda[\mathbf{V}])_\#$ is the conventional set of *lambda terms*. As in the combinator calculus, AP is abbreviated by juxtaposition, and associates to the left. $\lambda x(\alpha)$ is written $\lambda x.\alpha$. An occurrence of a variable x in $\lambda x.\alpha$ is a *bound* occurrence,

all other occurrences of variables are *free*.

$\alpha \equiv \beta$ if α may be transformed to β by systematic renaming of bound variables (e.g., $\lambda x.x \equiv \lambda y.y$). In the sequel, a lambda term α denotes the equivalence class $\{\beta \mid \alpha \equiv \beta\}$.

$\rightarrow$ is defined by

$$(\lambda x.\alpha)\beta \rightarrow \alpha[\beta/x]$$

$$\alpha \rightarrow \beta \Rightarrow \alpha\gamma \rightarrow \beta\gamma \,\&\, \gamma\alpha \rightarrow \gamma\beta$$

where $\alpha[\beta/x]$ denotes the result of substituting β for each free occurrence of x in α, renaming bound variables as necessary so that free variables remain free.

□

The Lambda Calculus is, *a priori*, a weaker candidate for a universal equational machine language than the $S-K$ Combinator Calculus, because a single reduction step appears to require an unbounded amount of work, depending on the number of occurrences of the variable being substituted for.

The Lambda Calculus may be compiled into the $S-K$ Combinator Calculus by the translation $^-$ defined as follows.

Definition 19.7.2

$$\bar{x} = x$$

$$\overline{\lambda x.x} = I$$

$$\overline{\lambda x.y} = Ky, \text{ where } x \neq y$$

$$\overline{\lambda x.\alpha\beta} = S\overline{\lambda x.\bar{\alpha}}\overline{\lambda x.\bar{\beta}}$$

$$\overline{\alpha\beta} = \bar{\alpha}\bar{\beta} \quad □$$

The translation of Definition 19.7.2 has been proposed as a method for compiling the Lambda Calculus into the more primitive Combinator Calculus, because it satisfies the desirable property of the well-known Theorem 19.7.1 [St72].

Theorem 19.7.1

$\overline{(\lambda x.\alpha)\beta} \to \overline{\alpha[\beta/x]}$, for all $x \in V$, $\alpha, \beta \in \Lambda$.

☐

Unfortunately, the translation does *not* satisfy the stronger property $\alpha \to \beta \Rightarrow \overline{\alpha} \to \overline{\beta}$.

Example 19.7.1 [St72]

$\lambda x.((\lambda y.y)z) \to \lambda x.z$, yet $\overline{\lambda x.((\lambda y.y)z)} = S(KI)(Kz)$, which is in normal form. Consider the translation of $\lambda x.((\lambda y.y)z)$ into combinators, step by step:

$\overline{\lambda x.((\lambda y.y)z)} = S\overline{\lambda x.(\lambda y.y)}\overline{\lambda x.z} = S\overline{\lambda x.I}\overline{\lambda x.z} = S(KI)\overline{\lambda x.z} = S(KI)\overline{\lambda x.z} =$
$S(KI)(Kz)$

Compare the derivation of $\overline{\lambda x.((\lambda y.y)z)}$ to the following one of the subexpression $\overline{(\lambda y.y)z}$:

$\overline{(\lambda y.y)z} = \overline{(\lambda y.y)}\overline{z} = I\overline{z} = Iz$

Notice that, by itself, the subexpression $(\lambda y.y)z$ translated to Iz, which reduces to z. But, inside the binding λx, the I and the z are separated into $S(KI)(Kz)$. Once the latter expression is *applied to an argument*, the redex corresponding to the Iz is created, as in

$S(KI)(Kz)w \to KIw(Kzw) \to I(Kzw) \to Kzw \to z$.

☐

Example 19.7.1 shows that the translation into combinators enforces outermost evaluation in some cases, eliminating the possibility of taking an innermost step. Since, in principle, the two redexes in $\lambda x.((\lambda y.y)z)$ might be reduced concurrently, the translation into combinators does not provide a simulation of the *Lambda Calculus* according to Definition 19.3.1. Intuitively, the standard translation into combinators seems to be deficient if the translated program is to be executed on parallel hardware. There are a number of improvements to the simple translation of Definition 19.7.2, which solve the problem of Example 19.7.1 and similar small examples. None of the known improvements realizes the full parallelism of the Lambda Calculus, however. The equational program for the Lambda Calculus presented in Section 9.10 suffers from a similar loss of parallelism.

We have not been able to prove that the Combinator Calculus *cannot* simulate the Lambda Calculus, but we conjecture that it cannot. Klop [Kl80b] has demonstrated some interesting graph-theoretic differences between the λ-calculus and the $S-K$ calculus, but they do not rule out the possibility of a simulation. It is well-known in combinatory logic that no finite set of equations between combinators can provide a full simulation of the Lambda Calculus under the standard translation (or any of the known variants). Furthermore, informal reflection on Example 19.7.1, and similar examples, shows that, in the Lambda Calculus, reduction of an outer redex may leapfrog an inner redex to substitute for a variable inside it. Neither the Combinator Calculus, nor any other regular term reduction system, may display such behavior. The translations allowed by Definition 19.3.1, however, include ones that completely change the term structure, so this observation does not lead to a proof.

There is a variation on the Lambda Calculus, similar to that in Section 9.6, that preserves all of the apparent parallelism while doing only a small, bounded amount of work in each reduction step [OS84]. The essence of the variation is given by the first set of equations in that section, before removing overlap. The difficult part of the variation is the efficient renaming of bound variables to avoid capture. This variation cannot be programmed in the equation interpreter, because it involves an inherent violation of the nonoverlapping restriction. The Lambda Calculus has Property A of Definition 19.2.5, so it cannot simulate the parallel *or*. The apparent deficiency of combinators resulting in the inability to simulate the *Lambda Calculus* is separate, then, from the deficiency with respect to the parallel *or*. Having found these two deficiencies, we should be very careful about accepting any reduction system, even the Lambda Calculus plus the parallel *or*, as sufficient for parallel computation, without a solid proof.

19.8. Unsolved Problems

The definition of simulation in this section is plausible, but is not precisely the right one. The results of this section should be taken as a critique of the definition of simulation, as much as statements about the particular reduction systems studied. Besides the essential problem of characterizing parallelism, instead of just non-determinism, the definition of simulation may not be exactly right even for capturing the degree of nondeterminism.

It is disturbing that, although the intuitive difference between the $S-K$ and $S-K-D$ calculi has to do with optional sequential or parallel computation versus required parallelism, the proof that $S-K$ cannot simulate $S-K-D$ hinges on simple abstract graph-theoretic properties of the two calculi. We had expected the proof that $S-K$ does not simulate $S-K-D$ to use recursion theory, since the critical difference between $S-K$ and $S-K-D$ has to do with the existence of a computable function to pick the next *required* computation step in $S-K$, and the lack of any such computable function in $S-K-D$. In particular, it appears that effective simulation of $S-K-D$ by $S-K$ should contradict standard recursion-theoretic results by providing a recursive separation of $\{i \mid \phi_i(0)=0\}$ and $\{i \mid \phi_i(0)=1\}$. We could construct an $S-K-D$ term of the form $D\alpha\beta$, where α

tests $\phi_i(0)=0$, and β tests $\phi_i(0)=1$, simulate it with an $S-K$ term γ, and if the leftmost-outermost reduction of γ simulated reductions to α but not β, we should be able to conclude that $\phi_i(0)\neq1$, and vice versa. We have not succeeded in proving that the leftmost-outermost reductions of γ cannot simulate interleaved reductions to α and β in such a case, although such a simulation looks impossible.

Whether or not the definition of simulation is exactly right, the simulations of simply strongly sequential systems by $S-K$, and regular systems by $S-K-D$ are intuitively satisfying, and should be allowed by any reasonable definition. It would be useful to know other simple reduction systems that simulate all systems in some natural restricted classes. In particular, the existence of a confluent effective reduction system that effectively simulates all other confluent effective reduction systems is an important open question. Also, a strongly sequential reduction system that simulates all others of its class would be useful. We conjecture that $S-K$ does not simulate all strongly sequential systems.

An interesting hierarchy could develop around a natural sequence of more and more powerful combinators. We conjecture that the $S-K-P$ calculus, using the *positive parallel or* with the rules $PT\alpha \rightarrow T$, $P\alpha T \rightarrow T$, does *not* simulate the $S-K-D$ calculus, nor does the $S-K-D$ simulate the $S-K-E$ calculus with the *equality test* defined by $E\alpha\alpha \rightarrow T$, and that the $S-K-E$ calculus does not simulate the $S-K-F$ calculus with the rule $F\alpha\alpha \rightarrow \alpha$. All of these systems are confluent [Kl80a, Ch81]. A classification of the power of combinatory systems should include the λ-calculus and the $S-K-C$ (*parallel if*) calculus with the rules $CT\alpha\beta \rightarrow \alpha$, $CF\alpha\beta \rightarrow \beta$, and $C\alpha\beta\beta \rightarrow \beta$, which may be even more powerful than $S-K-F$.

20. Implementation of the Equation Interpreter

Implementation of the algorithms, discussed in Section 18, for pattern matching, sequencing, and reduction, is a rather well-defined programming task. The design and coordination of the algorithmically conventional syntactic processors involved in the interpreter constitute the more interesting implementation problems, so that aspect is discussed in this section.

20.1. Basic Structure of the Implementation

The goals of the interpreter implementation were to determine the practicality of the novel aspects of an equational interpreter as a computing engine, and provide the facility for preliminary experiments in the usefulness of the equational programming language as a programming language. These two goals are in some ways contrary to one another. Preliminary experiments in equational programming could be performed well on a very naive interpreter that would execute small programs with a combined preprocessing and running time of a few seconds. In order to test the practicality of evaluation strategies as sources of computing power, we needed to provide better run-time performance than was needed for the programming experiments, even at the cost of substantial preprocessing work. We decided to emphasize the first goal, as long as the preprocessing time could be kept tolerable for small programs. This decision led to a two-dimensional structure for the interpreter, as shown in Figure 20.1.1. The vertical dimension shows the processing of an equational program into tables suitable to drive a fast interpreter. The horizontal dimension shows an input term being reduced to an output normal form by the resulting interpreter.

Very early experience convinced us that even simple programming experiments

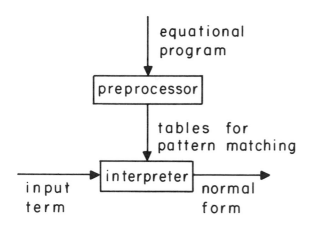

Figure 20.1.1

would be prohibitively difficult without a good syntax for terms. In particular, we started out naively with the standard mathematical notation for terms (*Standmath* of Section 4.1). Although this is fine for metanotation, when we used it to write equations for a pure LISP interpreter, writing *cons*(*A*, *cons*(*B*, *nil*)) instead of the special LISP notation (*A B*), the result was very difficult to manage. Since pure LISP is defined by a reasonably small and simple equational program, we decided that the fault was in the notation. At the same time we realized that LISP notation is unacceptably clumsy for other problems, such as the lambda calculus. So, we decided to separate parsing and other syntactic manipulations *completely* from the semantic essentials of the interpreter, allowing for a library of different syntaxes to be chosen for different problems.

In this section the semantic essentials of the interpreter and preprocessor are called the *core* programs, and the parsers and other syntactic transformers that analyze the input and pretty-print the output are called *syntactic shells*. We concentrated the implementation effort on the performance of the core programs, since syntactic problems are already rather well understood. Design effort connected with the shells went mostly toward flexibility of their interfaces, rather than the internals of the parsers, etc.

We decided that it was important to be able to vary, not only the syntactic forms seen by a user, but also the way in which terms are presented to the core programs. The issue first arose regarding the efficiency of the pattern matcher -- in some cases pattern-matching tables could be much smaller if each term of the form $f(A, B, C)$ were *Curried* into *apply* (*apply* (*apply* (f, A), B), C), reducing the arity of symbols to a maximum of 2. In other cases, Currying could be wasteful, and there are many other variations in the presentation of terms. In order to allow flexibility in choosing an efficient internal form (the *inner syntax* of Section 4.4), while guaranteeing functional equivalence at the user's level, we separated the syntactic shell into two levels, shown in Figure 20.1.2

We use the terminology of *transformational grammars* [Ch65] to discuss the levels of syntactic processing, even though we do not use the transformational formalism to define that processing. The source text produced by a user as input, or provided to a user as output, is called *concrete syntax*. The parsed form of *concrete syntax*, showing the tree structure inherent in its text, is called *surface abstract syntax* -- from the *surface structures* of transformational grammars. Essentially, the translations between concrete syntax and surface abstract syntax are context-free, so a list of variables in the concrete syntax is still a list of variables, in the same order, in the surface abstract syntax. Surface abstract syntax is transformed in non-context-free ways into *deep abstract syntax*. In particular, declarations of symbols and variables are processed, and each occurrence of a sym-

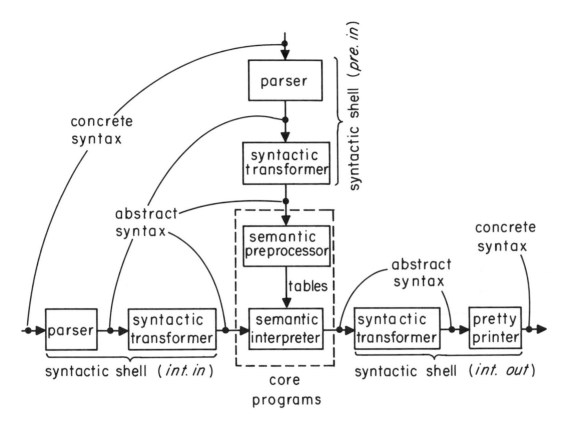

Figure 20.1.2

bol is marked with the information in its declaration. This sort of processing is called "semantic analysis" in much of the literature on compiling, but we believe it is more illuminating to think of it as another component of syntactic analysis. Structural transformations, such as Currying, are also performed in the translation from surface to deep structure. Future versions of the interpreter may use transformations on abstract syntax to implement modular program constructors of the sort discussed in Section 14. The uniformity of the representation of abstract syntax at different levels allows both sorts of transformations, as well as the non-context-free syntactic processing, to be implemented by equational programs.

Communication between different portions of the equation interpreter system is always done by files of characters. These files are implemented as pipelines whenever possible. Except for the input produced by, and the output seen by, a user, and the Pascal code produced by the preprocessor for inclusion in the interpreter, all communication follows a standard format for abstract symbolic information, in which an abstract symbol is given by its length, type, and a descriptive string of characters. Section 20.1 describes this abstract symbolic format. A thorough understanding of symbol format is crucial to the sophisticated user who wishes to produce his own syntactic processors.

20.2. A Format for Abstract Symbolic Information

Input to, and output from, the cores of the preprocessor and interpreter are always presented in a versatile and abstract syntactic form, which is computationally trivial to parse. Use of this special form is intended to remove all questions of syntactic processing from the core programs, both in order to simplify and clarify these programs, and to allow great flexibility in manipulating their syntactic shells. Because the equation interpreter is used as part of its own syntactic processing, it is easy to lose orientation when thinking about symbolic files. The key idea is that the format of a symbolic file must always be appropriate to the equational program for which it is the immediate input or output.

The details of the representation of abstract syntax described below, were designed for ease of experimentation. Although intended for internal use in computations, they are readable enough to be useful for debugging. As a result, the representations are highly inefficient, taking more space in most cases than the concrete syntax. A more mature version of the equation interpreter will compress the internal representations of abstract syntax, sacrificing readability for debugging purposes in favor of efficiency.

A file of abstract symbols contains a contiguous sequence of abstract symbols, with no separators and no terminator. Each abstract symbol is of the form

> *length type content*

presented contiguously with no separators. *length* is given as a nonnegative integer in normal base-10 notation, with no leading zeroes (except that zero itself is presented as "0"). *type* is a single character, with a meaning described later. *content* is a sequence of characters, the number of characters being exactly the given length. The idea for this representation was taken from FORTRAN's FORMAT statements.

There are 5 types of abstract symbol that are important to the equation interpreter system. The motivation for each of these types refers to the preprocessor or interpreter core program for which the symbol is an immediate input or output. A symbol that is presented to an interpreter has the same meaning as if it were presented to the preprocessor that produced that interpreter.

M Metasymbol: a symbol with a special predetermined meaning to the system.

L Literal symbol: a symbol whose meaning is given by the user in his definitions.

A Atomic symbol: a symbol with no discernible structure or special meaning.

C Character string: a symbol intended to denote the very sequence of characters that is its content.

I Integer symbol: a symbol intended to denote an integer number.

T Truth symbol: a symbol denoting a truth value.

Examples of abstract symbols are "*1M(*", "*5Aabcde*", "*10Cdefinition*", "*1TT*", "*1TF*", "*4I1111*", "*4I-124*". Informally, we will refer to abstract symbols by their contents when the type and length are clear from context.

Metasymbols include left and right parentheses, "(" and ")", and codes for the predefined classes of symbols, equations, and operations. Integer symbols are presented in normal base-10 notation, with a single preceding minus sign, "-", for negative integers. Truth symbols include "*T*" for truth and "*F*" for falsehood. The other three types of symbol are very easily confused, and require some initial study. Character strings are taken by the equation interpreter to which they are present- ed, and by the equation interpreter produced by the preprocessor to which they are presented, as textual data to be manipulated by concatenation, extraction of sub- strings, etc. The lexical relationships between different character strings may be important to the interpreter program that manipulates them. Literal symbols, presented to a preprocessor, are intended to be given meanings by the equations that the preprocessor is reading; presented to an interpreter, they are intended to have the meanings given by the equations from which that interpreter was pro- duced. The lexical structure of literal symbols is irrelevant. Atomic symbols are opaque symbols with no meanings beyond their identities. The lexical structure of atomic symbols is irrelevant to an equational program that is processing them, but may become relevant in a later step if some nonequational syntactic transforma- tion, such as the *content* operation of Section 13.2, maps atomic symbols to some other types of symbols.

Either an atomic symbol, or a character string, may have a content with a spe- cial meaning to an earlier or later step in a sequence of programs. Thus, "*4Acons*" is an atomic symbol, whose content is "*cons*". That content could be accessed by a nonequational program at some point to produce the literal symbol "4*Lcons*". This near-brush with confusion is necessary in order for an equational program to be part of the syntactic processor for the equation preprocessor. Thus, equations defining a syntactic processor may use literal symbols, such as "4*Lcons*", in order to perform syntactic transformations on expressions containing the atomic symbol "4*Acons*", which will later become the literal symbol "4*Lcons*" when presented to the core of the preprocessor.

The metasymbols that are meaningful to the equation interpreter system are:

"(", ")"   used to present the tree-structure of a term as input to or output from the preprocessor or the interpreter

The remaining metasymbols are used only in input to the preprocessor

"*V*"   marks an address of a formal variable

"*U*"   union of syntactic classes in variable qualification

"?"   the universal syntactic class

"#"   the empty syntactic class

"*A*"   the class of atomic_symbols

"*I*"   the class of integer_numerals

"*C*"   the class of character_strings

"*T*"   the class of truth_values

"+", "-", "*", "/", "m", "=", "<" the predefined functions, used on right-hand sides

Text containing the metasymbols "(" and ")" is intended to represent a term in the natural way. Such text will often be displayed for informal discussion with commas, spaces, and indentation to improve readability, although no such notation appears inside the machine.

20.3. Syntactic Processors and Their Input/Output Forms

The main goal in the organization of the syntactic processors is versatility. In addition to the variations in the external concrete syntax typed and seen by the user, described in Section 4, there are variations in the form in which material is presented to the core programs. These variations in internal syntax are provided because different encodings of terms may have radically different effects on the efficiency of the pattern-matching algorithms in the interpreter. The reasons for these effects are explained in Section 18.2, and the details of the different internal syntaxes are given in Section 4.

Figure 20.3.1 refines Figure 20.1.2 to show all of the levels of syntactic analysis. The configurations for the preprocessor input analyzer, *pre.in*, the interpreter input analyzer, *int.in*, and the interpreter output pretty-printer, *int.out*, are essentially the same, except that *pre.in* has one more step than the others, and *int.out* transforms from inner form into outer form -- the opposite direction from *pre.in* and *int.in*. In describing the different levels of syntactic processing, we will always refer to *pre.in*, which has the most complex forms. The forms for *int.in* and *int.out* are merely the term portions of *pre.in* syntaxes.

Concrete syntax is defined in Sections 3, 4 and 8. Surface abstract syntax is intended to represent the concrete syntax directly, with purely typographical considerations removed. Surface abstract syntax is in the form:

sspec(ssymspec(list_of_symspecs), sequspec(list_of_variables, list_of_equations))

"sspec", *"ssymspec"*, *"sequspec"*, and all other explicitly-given symbols, are literal symbols. The lists are represented in the usual way by the literal symbols *"cons"*

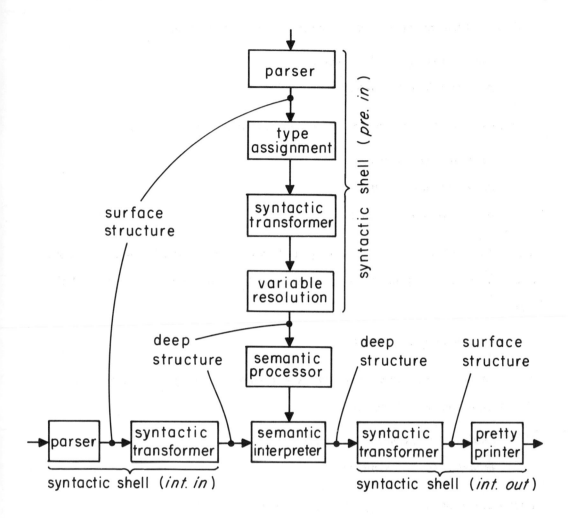

Figure 20.3.1

and *"nil"*. Elements of the *list_of_symspecs* are of the two forms:

>   *usersym(list_of_symbols, arity)*
>
>   *predefsym(list_of_symbols)*

Elements of the *list_of_symbols* and *list_of_variables* are of the forms:

>   *litsym(atomic_symbol)*
>
>   *atomsym(atomic_symbol)*
>
>   *metasym(atomic_symbol)*

The contents of these *atomic_symbol*s will become literal symbols, atomic symbols, and metasymbols respectively when they reach the core program. Arity is of the form

>   *intnum (atomic_symbol)*

The contents of this *atomic_symbol* will become an integer. Elements of the *list_of_equations* are of the two forms:

>   *qualequ(term,term,list_of_quals)*
>
>   *predefequ(list_of_symbols)*

Each element of the *list_of_quals* is of the form:

>   *qualify (list_of_variables,list_of_terms)*

Terms within qualifiers may include the binary literal operator *"qualterm"* to introduce nested qualifications in the form:

>   *qualterm (term ,list_of_quals)*

Qualifiers may be nested.

Because the syntactic processors will perform syntactic, rather than semantic, manipulations on terms, each term is represented somewhat indirectly by an abstract syntax showing its applicative structure, as described in Section 13.2. Thus,

$$f(a,b,c,d)$$

is represented by

$$multiap[litsym[f]; (a\ b\ c\ d)]$$

In general, the structure of a specification given by the keywords in concrete syntax is translated directly into the structure of the surface abstract syntax term, shown by its literal symbols. Tokens other than keywords in the surface concrete syntax, including user-defined symbols, symbols intended to indicate predefined classes of symbols or equations, integers, character strings, and atomic symbols, are all translated into atomic symbols in the surface abstract syntax. All instances of integers, character strings, truth values, literals, and metasymbols are marked by the literal operators *"intnum"*, *"charstr"*, *"truthval"*, *"litsym"*, and *"metasym"* as shown above. Atomic symbols are not yet marked with *"atomsym"* because they have not yet been distinguished from variables.

Deep abstract syntax is similar to surface abstract syntax, but information has been organized in a form more convenient to the core program than is the surface form. In particular, user-defined and predefined symbol declarations are separated, arities and similar tags are distributed over lists of symbols, symbols are marked appropriately as variables, atomic symbols, integer numerals, character strings, and literals. Finally, all qualifications on variables replace the left-hand-side occurrences of variables that they qualify, and right-hand-side occurrences of variables are shown as

   varaddr (*list_of_integers*)

where the *list_of_integers* gives the sequence of tree branches to be followed to find the corresponding left-hand-side occurrence of the variable, and equation schemata are substituted for invocations of predefined classes of equations.

A specification in deep abstract syntax is of the form:

   dspec(dsymspec(list_of_user_syms,
                  list_of_predef_syms
          ),
      dequspec(list_of_equations
)
)

Elements of the *list_of_user_syms* are of the form:

   usersym (*symbol ,arity*)

Elements of the *list_of_predef_syms* are of the form:

   predefsym (*symbol*)

Elements of the *list_of_equations* are of the form:

   equate (*term ,term*)

As in the surface abstract syntax, symbols given explicitly above are literal symbols, symbols taken from the surface concrete syntax are atomic symbols, and terms are represented in syntactic form with the operator "*multiap*". Every atomic symbol is now marked in one of the following forms to show its intended type:

   metasym(symbol)

   litsym(symbol)

atomsym(symbol)

charstr(symbol)

truthval(symbol)

intnum(symbol)

In order to accommodate inner syntactic translations, such as Currying, the transformation of surface abstract syntax to deep abstract syntax goes in three steps.

1. Declarations of literal symbols and variables are processed, and each occurrence of a symbol is marked by the appropriate tag. A variable x is given as *qualvar*[x; *qualifications*] if it is on the left-hand side of an equation, and simply *variable*[x] if it is on the right-hand side.

2. Any inner syntactic transformations, such as Currying, are performed.

3. Right-hand-side variables are replaced by the corresponding left-hand-side addresses, and all variable names are eliminated.

Notice that this order of work is critical -- syntactic transformations may depend on the types of symbols encountered, and variable addresses must be assigned based on the *transformed* versions of the left-hand sides. Immediately before it is presented to a core program, each term in deep abstract syntax is transformed by the *content* operation of Section 13.2, to produce the semantically appropriate terms without mediation by the *multiap* symbol.

Bibliography

AC75   Aho, A. V. and Corasick, M. J. Efficient String Matching: An Aid to Bibliographic Search, *Communications of the ACM* 18:6 (1975) pp. 333-340.

AHU74   Aho, A. V., Hopcroft, J. E., Ullman, J. D. *The Design and Analysis of Computer Algorithms,* Addison-Wesley (1974).

AHU83   Aho, A. V., Hopcroft, J. E., Ullman, J. D. *Data Structures and Algorithms,* Addison-Wesley (1983).

AU72   Aho, A. V. and Ullman, J. D. *The Theory of Parsing, Translation, and Compiling,* Prentice-Hall (1972).

AW76   Ashcroft, E. and Wadge, W. Lucid – A Formal System for Writing and Proving Programs. *SIAM Journal on Computing* 5:3 (1976) pp.336-354.

AW77   Ashcroft, E. and Wadge, W. Lucid, a Nonprocedural Language with Iteration, *Communications of the ACM* 20:7 (1977) pp. 519-526.

At75   Atkins, D. E. Introduction to the Role of Redundancy in Computer Arithmetic, *IEEE Computer* 8:6 (1975) pp. 74-76.

Av61   Avizienis, A. Signed-Digit Number Representations for Fast Parallel Arithmetic, *Institute of Radio Engineers Transactions on Electronic Computers* (1961) p. 389.

Ba74   Backus, J. Programming Language Semantics and Closed Applicative Languages. *ACM Symposium on Principles of Programming Languages* (1974) pp. 71-86.

Ba78   Backus, J. Can Programming Be Liberated from the von Neumann Style? A Functional Style and its Algebra of Programs, *Communications of the ACM* 21:8 (1978) pp. 613-641.

BB79   Bauer, F. L., Broy, M., Gnatz, R., Hesse, W., Krieg-Bruckner, B., Partsch, H., Pepper, P., Wossner, H. Towards a Wide Spectrum Language to Support Program Development by Transformations. *Program Construction: International Summer School, Lecture Notes in Computer Science* v. 69, Springer-Verlag (1979) pp. 543-552; *SIGPLAN Notices* 17:12 (1978) pp. 15-24.

BS76   Belnap, N. D. and Steel, T. B. *The Logic of Questions and Answers,* Yale University Press (1976).

BL77   Berry, G. and Lévy, J.-J. Minimal and Optimal Computations of Recursive Programs. *4th ACM Symposium on Principles of Programming Languages* (1977) pp. 215-226.

BL79   Berry, G. and Lévy, J.-J. Letter to the Editor, *SIGACT News* v. 11, no. 1 (1979) pp. 3-4.

Bi67   Bishop, E. *Foundations of Constructive Analysis,* McGraw-Hill, New York (1967).

Bj72   Bjorner, D. Finite State Tree Computations (Part I). IBM Research Technical Report RJ 1053 (#17598) (1972).

Br69   Brainerd, W. S. Tree generating regular systems. *Information and Control* 14 (1969) pp. 217-231.

Br79   Bridges, D. S. *Constructive Functional Analysis,* Pitman, London (1979).

Br76   Bruynooghe, M., An Interpreter for Predicate Logic Programs Part I, Report CW10, Applied Mathematics and Programming Division, Katholieke Universiteit, Leuven, Belgium (1976).

BG77   Burstall, R. M. and Goguen, J. A. Putting Theories Together to Make Specifications. *5th International Joint Conference on Artificial Intelligence,* Cambridge, Massachusetts (1977) pp. 1045-1058.

CaJ72   Cadiou, J., Recursive Definitions of Partial Functions and Their Computations, Ph.D. Dissertation, Computer Science Dept., Stanford University (1972).

Ca76   Cargill, T., Deterministic Operational Semantics for Lucid, Research Report CS-76-19, University of Waterloo (1976).

Ch80   Chew, L. P. An Improved Algorithm for Computing With Equations. *21st Annual Symposium on Foundations of Computer Science* (1980) pp. 108-117.

Ch81   Chew, L. P. Unique Normal Forms In Term Rewriting Systems With Repeated Variables. *13th Annual ACM Symposium on Theory of Computing,* (1981) pp. 7-18.

Ch65   Chomsky, N. *Aspects of the Theory of Syntax,* MIT Press, Cambridge MA (1965).

Ch41   Church, A. *The Calculi of Lambda-Conversion.* Princeton University Press, Princeton, New Jersey, 1941.

deB72   de Bruijn, N. G. Lambda Calculus Notation with Nameless Dummies, Nederl. Akad. Wetensch. Proc. Series A 75 (1972) pp. 381-392.

CG80   Clarke, T. J. W., Gladstone, P. J. S., MacLean, C. D., and Norman, A. C. SKIM - The S, K, I Reduction Machine. *1980 LISP Conference,* Stanford University (1980) pp. 128-135.

CF58   Curry, H. B., and Feys, R., *Combinatory Logic* v. I. North-Holland, Amsterdam, (1958).

DS76   Downey, P. J. and R. Sethi, Correct Computation Rules for Recursive Languages. *SIAM Journal on Computing* 5:3 (1976) pp. 378-401.

DST80   Downey, P. J., Sethi, R., and Tarjan, R. E. Variations on the Common Subexpression Problem. *Journal of the ACM* 27:4 (1980) pp. 758-771.

Di76   Dijkstra, E. W. *A Discipline of Programming* Prentice-Hall, Englewood Cliffs, NJ (1976).

Fa77   Farah, M., Correct Compilation of a Useful Subset of Lucid, Ph.D. Dissertation, Department of Computer Science, University of Waterloo (1977).

FW76   Friedman, D., and Wise, D. Cons should not evaluate its arguments, *3rd International Colloquium on Automata, Languages and Programming,* Edinburgh University Press (1976) pp. 257-284.

FGJM85 Futatsugi, K., Goguen, J. A., Jouannaud, J.-P., Meseguer, J. Principles of OBJ2, *12th Annual Symposium on Principles of Programming Languages,* New Orleans LA (1985).

GJ79   Garey, M. R. and Johnson, D. S. *Computers and Intractability -- a Guide to the Theory of NP-Completeness* W. H. Freeman, New York (1979).

GS78   Guibas, L. and R. Sedgewick, A Dichromatic Framework for Balanced Trees, *19th Symposium on Foundations of Computer Science* (1978) pp. 8-21.

GH78   Guttag, J. V. and Horning, J. J. The Algebraic Specification of Abstract Data Types, *Acta Informatica* 10:1 (1978) pp. 1-26.

GHM76 Guttag, J., Horowitz, E., and Musser, D.   Abstract Data Types and Software Validation, Information Science Research Report ISI/RR-76-48, University of Southern California, (1976).

Go77   Goguen, J. A. Abstract Errors for Abstract Data Types, *IFIP Working Conference on Formal Description of Programming Concepts,* E. J. Neuhold, ed., North-Holland (1977).

Go84   Goguen, J. A. Parameterized Programming, *IEEE Transactions on Software Engineering* 10:5 (1984) pp. 528-544.

HM76   Henderson, P., and Morris, J. H. A Lazy Evaluator, *3rd ACM Symposium on Principles of Programming Languages* (1976) pp. 95-103.

Ho62   Hoare, C. A. R. Quicksort, *Computer Journal* 5:1 (1962) pp. 10-15.

Ho78   Hoffmann, C., Design and Correctness of a Compiler for a Nonprocedural Language, *Acta Informatica* 9 (1978) pp. 217-241.

HO79   Hoffmann, C. and O'Donnell, M. Interpreter Generation Using Tree Pattern Matching, *6th Annual Symposium on Principles of Programming Languages* (1979) pp. 169-179.

HO82a Hoffmann, C. and O'Donnell, M. Pattern Matching in Trees, *Journal of the ACM* (1982) pp. 68-95.

HO82b Hoffmann, C. and O'Donnell, M. Programming With Equations, *ACM Transactions on Programming Languages and Systems (1982) pp. 83-112.*

HO83   Hoffmann, C. and O'Donnell, M. Implementation of an Interpreter for Abstract Equations, *10th Annual ACM Symposium on Principles of Programming Languages* (1984) pp. 111-120.

HD83   Hsiang, J. and Dershowitz, N. Rewrite Methods for Clausal and Non-Clausal Theorem Proving, *10th EATCS International Colloquium on Automata, Languages, and Programming,* Spain (1983).

HL79   Huet, G. and Lévy, J.-J. Computations in Non-ambiguous Linear Term Rewriting Systems, IRIA Technical Report #359 (1979).

HO80   Huet, G. and Oppen, D. Equations and Rewrite Rules: a Survey, *Formal Languages: Perspectives and Open Problems,* R. Book, ed., Academic Press (1980).

Hu52   Huffman, D. A. A Method for the Construction of Minimum-Redundancy Codes, *Proceedings of the Institute of Radio Engineers* 40 (1952) pp. 1098-1101.

Ir61   Irons, E. T. A Syntax Directed Compiler for ALGOL 60, *Communications of the ACM* 4:1 (1961) pp. 51-55.

Jo78   Johnson, S. C. Yacc: Yet Another Compiler Compiler, In *UNIX Time-Sharing System: UNIX Programmer's Manual, Volume 2A* Bell Telephone Laboratories.

Jo77   Johnson, S. D. An Interpretive Model for a Language Based on Suspended Construction, Technical Report #68, Dept. of Computer Science, Indiana University (1977).

KM77   Kahn, G. and MacQueen, D. B. Coroutines and Networks of Parallel Processes, *Information Processing 77,* B. Gilchrist ed., North-Holland (1977) pp. 993-998.

KP78   Kahn, G. and Plotkin, G. Domaines Concrets, Tech. Rep. 336, IRIA Laboria, LeChesnay, France (1978).

KM66   Karp, R. M. and Miller, R. E. Properties of a Model for Parallel Computations: Determinacy, Termination, Queueing, *SIAM Journal on Applied Mathematics* 14:6 (1966) pp. 1390-1141.

Kl80a   Klop, J. W. Combinatory Reduction Systems, Ph. D. dissertation, Mathematisch Centrum, Amsterdam (1980).

Kl80b   Klop, J. W. Reduction Cycles in Combinatory Logic. *To H. B. Curry,* Seldin and Hindley, eds., Academic Press (1980) pp. 193-214.

Kn68   Knuth, D. E. Semantics of Context-Free Languages, *Mathematical Systems Theory* 2:2 (1968) pp. 127-146.

KMP77   Knuth, D. E., Morris, J., Pratt, V. Fast Pattern Matching in Strings, *SIAM Journal on Computing* 6:2 (1977) pp. 323-350.

KB70   Knuth, D. E. and Bendix, P. Simple Word Problems in Universal Algebras. *Computational Problems in Abstract Algebra,* J. Leech, ed., Pergammon Press, Oxford (1970) pp. 263-297.

Ko79a   Kowalski, R. Algorithm = Logic + Control. *Communications of the ACM* 22:7 (1979) pp. 424-436.

Ko79b   Kowalski, R. *Logic for Problem Solving,* Elsevier North-Holland, New York (1979).

La65   Landin, P. J. A Correspondence Between ALGOL 60 and Church's Lambda-Notation: Part I. *Communications of the ACM* 8:2 (1965) pp. 89-101.

Le83   Lescanne, P. Computer Experiments with the REVE Term Rewriting System Generator, *10th Annual Symposium on Principles of Programming Languages,* Austin TX (1983).

Le68   Lewis, P. M. II and Stearns, R. E. Syntax-Directed Transduction. *Journal of the ACM* 15:3 (1968) pp. 465-488.

McC60   McCarthy, J., Recursive Functions of Symbolic Expressions and Their Computation by Machine, *Communications of the ACM* 3:4 (1960) pp. 184-195.

McC62   McCarthy, J. Towards a Mathematical Science of Computation. *IFIP Munich Conference 1962,* North-Holland, Amsterdam (1963).

McI68   McIlroy, M. D., Coroutines, Internal report, Bell Telephone Laboratories, Murray Hill, New Jersey (1968).

MvD82   Meyerowitz, N. and van Dam, A. Interactive Editing Systems: part II, *ACM Computing Surveys* 14:3 (1982) pp. 353-415.

My72   Myhill, J. What is a Real Number? *American Mathematical Monthly* 79:7 (1972) pp. 748-754.

NO78   Nelson, G. and Oppen, D. C. A Simplifier Based on Efficient Decision Algorithms, *5th Annual ACM Symposium on Principles of Programming Languages* (1978) pp. 141-150.

NO80   Nelson, G. and Oppen, D. C. Fast Decision Algorithms Based on Congruence Closure, *Journal of the ACM* 27:2 (1980) pp. 356-364.

O'D77   O'Donnell, M., *Computing in systems Described by Equations, Lecture Notes in Computer Science* v. 58, Springer-Verlag (1977).

O'D79   O'Donnell, M. J. Letter to the Editor, *SIGACT News,* 11:2 (1979) p. 2.

OS84   O'Donnell, M. J. and Strandh, R. I. Toward a Fully Parallel Implementation of the Lambda Calculus, Technical Report JHU/EECS-84/13, The Johns Hopkins University (1984).

OI79   Owens, R. M. and Irwin, M. F. On-Line Algorithms for the Design of Pipeline Architectures, *Annual Symposium on Computer Architecture* Philadelphia (1979) pp. 12-19.

RoG77   Roberts, G., An Implementation of Prolog, M.S. Thesis, Dept. of Computer Science, University of Waterloo (1977).

Ro65   Robinson, J. A. A Machine-Oriented Logic Based on the Resolution Principle, *Journal of the ACM* 12:1 (1965) pp. 23-41.

Ro79   Robinson, J. A. *Logic, Form and Function: the Mechanization of Deductive Reasoning.* Elsevier North-Holland, New York (1979).

Re84   Reps, T. *Generating Language-Based Environments,* MIT Press, Cambridge, MA (1984).

RTD83   Reps, T., Teitelbaum, T., and Demers, A. Incremental Context-Dependent Analysis for Language-Based Editors, *ACM Transactions on Programming Languages and Systems* 5:3 (1983) pp. 449-477.

Ro73   Rosen, B. K. Tree Manipulation Systems and Church-Rosser Theorems, *Journal of the ACM* 20:1 (1973) pp. 160-187.

Sc24   Schönfinkel, M. Uber die Bausteine der Mathematischen Logik, *Math. Ann.* 92 (1924) pp. 305-316.

St77   Staples, J. A Class of Replacement Systems with Simple Optimality Theory, *Bulletin of the Australian Mathematical Society,* 17:3 (1977) pp. 335-350.

St79   Staples, J. A Graph-Like Lambda Calculus For Which Leftmost-Outermost Reduction Is Optimal. *Graph Grammars and Their Application to Computer Science and Biology, Lecture Notes in Computer Science,* v. 73, V. Claus, H. Ehrig, G. Rosenberg eds., Springer-Verlag (1979).

St72   Stenlund, S. *Combinators, Lambda-Terms, and Proof Theory.* D. Reidel Publishing Company, Dordrecht, Holland (1972).

ST84   Strandh, R. I. Incremental Suffix Trees with Multiple Subject Strings, Technical Report JHU/EECS-84/18, the Johns Hopkins University (1984).

Th73   Thatcher, J. W. Tree Automata: An Informal Survey. Chapter 4 of *Currents in the Theory of Computing,* A. V. Aho, editor, Prentice-Hall, Englewood Cliffs NJ (1973) pp. 143-172.

Th85   Thatte, S. On the Correspondence Between Two Classes of Reduction Systems, to appear in *Information Processing Letters* (1985).

Tu79   Turner, D. A. A New Implementation Technique For Applicative Languages, *Software - Practice and Experience,* v. 9 (1979) pp. 31-49.

Vu74   Vuillemin, J. Correct and Optimal Implementations of Recursion in a Simple Programming Language, *Journal of Computing and Systems Science,* 9:3 (1974) pp. 332-354.

WA85   Wadge, W. W. and Ashcroft, E. A. *Lucid, the Dataflow Programming Language* Academic Press, London (1985).

Wa76   Wand, M. First Order Identities as a Defining Language, *Acta Informatica* v. 14 (1976) pp. 337-357.

Wa77   Warren, D., Implementing Prolog, Research Reports #39, 40, Dept. of Artificial Intelligence, University of Edinburgh (1977).

Wi83   Winograd, T. Language as a Cognitive Process, Addison-Wesley, Reading, MA (1983).

Index

The MIT Press, with Peter Denning as consulting editor, publishes computer science books in the following series:

ACM Doctoral Dissertation Award and Distinguished Dissertation Series

Artificial Intelligence, Patrick Winston and Michael Brady, editors

Charles Babbage Institute Reprint Series for the History of Computing, Martin Campbell-Kelly, editor

Computer Systems, Herb Schwetman, editor

Foundations of Computing, Michael Garey, editor

History of Computing, I. Bernard Cohen and William Aspray, editors

Information Systems, Michael Lesk, editor

The MIT Electrical Engineering and Computer Science Series

Scientific Computation, Dennis Gannon, editor

For information on submission of manuscripts for publication, please call or write to:

Frank P. Satlow
Executive Editor
The MIT Press
28 Carleton Street
Cambridge, MA 02142

617/253-1623